ROUTLEDGE LIBRARY EDITIONS: THE LABOUR MOVEMENT

Volume 38

THE LABOUR PARTY AND WHITEHALL

THE LABOUR PARTY
AND WHITEHALL

KEVIN THEAKSTON

R Routledge
Taylor & Francis Group

LONDON AND NEW YORK

First published in 1992 by Routledge

This edition first published in 2019
by Routledge
2 Park Square, Milton Park, Abingdon, Oxon OX14 4RN

and by Routledge
711 Third Avenue, New York, NY 10017

Routledge is an imprint of the Taylor & Francis Group, an informa business

© 1992 Kevin Theakston

British Library Cataloguing in Publication Data
A catalogue record for this book is available from the British Library

ISBN: 978-1-138-32435-0 (Set)
ISBN: 978-0-429-43443-3 (Set) (ebk)
ISBN: 978-1-138-32583-8 (Volume 38) (hbk)
ISBN: 978-1-138-32585-2 (Volume 38) (pbk)
ISBN: 978-0-429-45021-1 (Volume 38) (ebk)

Publisher's Note
The publisher has gone to great lengths to ensure the quality of this reprint but points out that some imperfections in the original copies may be apparent.

Disclaimer
The publisher has made every effort to trace copyright holders and would welcome correspondence from those they have been unable to trace.

The Labour Party and Whitehall

Kevin Theakston

ROUTLEDGE

London and New York

First published 1992
by Routledge
11 New Fetter Lane, London EC4P 4EE
Simultaneously published in the USA and Canada
by Routledge
a division of Routledge, Chapman and Hall, Inc.
29 West 35th Street, New York, NY 10001

© 1992 Kevin Theakston

Typeset in Times by
Input Typesetting Ltd, London
Printed and bound in Great Britain by
Mackays of Chatham PLC, Chatham, Kent

British Library Cataloguing in Publication Data
Theakston, Kevin *1958–*
    The Labour Party and Whitehall. – (Public sector
management series).
    1. Great Britain. Civil service, related to political
parties
    I. Title II. Series
    324.24107
ISBN 0–415–06701–4

Library of Congress Cataloging in Publication Data
Theakston, Kevin. 1958–
    The Labour Party and Whitehall / Kevin Theakston.
        p. cm.
    Includes bibliographical references and index.
    ISBN 0–415–06701–4
    1. Labour Party (Great Britain) 2. Civil service—Great Britain.
3. Socialism—Great Britain. 4. Great Britain—Politics and
government—20th century. I. Title.
JN1129.L32T46 1991
354.41006—dc20   91–8389
                                                              CIP

Contents

General Editor's preface   vii
Preface   ix
1 Introduction   1
2 Labour governments and the mandarins   15
3 The Attlee government and the reform of the civil service   73
4 Labour and the Fulton Report   113
5 Efficiency or democracy? Labour and civil service
    recruitment   141
6 Labour, parliamentary accountability and open government   158
7 Labour, Thatcher and the future of the civil service   187
Notes   207
Index   229

General Editor's preface

The Routledge Public Sector Management series is designed to contain a mixture of academic monographs and other volumes intended to have a wider readership, either because they are textbooks or because they will appeal to practitioners.

The Labour Party and Whitehall is the second monograph to be published in the series. It is an original contribution to the literature of administrative history because no other book has traced the administrative reform proposals of one political party, examined in depth how they emerged from within the party, and then considered how the proposals were adopted and put into practice. Its special perspective helps cast new light on important episodes in the development of the Whitehall machine in the twentieth century, and it shows the value of an historical approach to aid the understanding of contemporary government. This achievement is the result of an impressive mastery of both manuscript sources and party records and of an enormous amount of biographical and autobiographical material. Whilst the Labour Party, and the Fabian Society in particular, is certainly not the only source of ideas that have been adopted for administrative reform, it emerges as the most clearly definable provenance of such reforms in the twentieth century. The party had the benefit during this period of some remarkable individuals including Sidney and Beatrice Webb, Harold Laski, G. D. H. Cole, Sir Stafford Cripps, Richard Crossman and Tony Benn, to mention just a few. It also provided a forum through which ideas could be discussed and developed so that policies could emerge which were not only implementable in practice (in whole or in part) but contributions to the evolution of a philosophy about the role of the civil service in the British system of government.

However, this book is not only an historical narrative. It is also a study of a particular aspect of public sector management. It raises important questions about contemporary institutions and policies and debates about reform. These include questions about the criteria for recruiting and promoting officials, how the work of government departments should be controlled and made accountable to elected representatives in Parliament, the extent to which government should be more open in a liberal democracy, and how government can best ensure that its policies are carried out with minimum cost but also according to criteria which encompass policy decisions and respect for individual citizens. These and similar questions, of as much relevance to the 1990s as they were in earlier decades of this century, emerge clearly from various aspects of this study.

Dr Theakston's book is an important addition to the Public Sector Management series. It is a book founded on a deep understanding of British government, and especially of the civil service. The author demonstrates a masterly control of his material and his book is written in a style and with an enthusiasm that makes reading it a pleasure. It is an historical study with contemporary relevance, which focuses on issues that will continue to attract the attention of politicians and citizens in the last decade of the twentieth century. Moreover, these issues are not narrowly relevant to the United Kingdom; they are issues that are of increasing concern to everyone involved in the practice and study of public sector management in many countries at the present time.

Richard A. Chapman
Series Editor

Preface

I have had two main aims in writing this book. First, I have been concerned to examine the Labour Party's experience in office and to try to assess the validity of the claims frequently made in Labour circles that socialist ministers are obstructed or sabotaged by the civil servants who are supposed to help them to carry out their policies. Tony Benn, Richard Crossman and many others have popularized a left-wing version of *Yes, Minister*, in which a devious and conspiratorial Whitehall bureaucracy represents a formidable obstacle to the achievement of Labour's socialist programme. Such views are not new – as I attempt to show – for suspicion and mistrust of the actions and motives of the mandarins have been present in the party ever since its debut in office in the 1920s. My argument is, however, that Labour's problems, frustrations and 'failures' in office are political in origin rather than due to civil service sabotage and obstruction.

My second aim has been to explore the development of Labour and socialist thinking about the civil service and to analyse the party's ideas about the reform of the Whitehall machine; I have also tried to audit the record of Labour governments in terms of actually putting into effect schemes of administrative reform. Many different topics come up here: civil service recruitment, training and management; the debate about secrecy and 'open government'; ways of strengthening the position of ministers in their departments; and so on. The continual recycling over the years of very similar ideas and proposals for reform stands out in this analysis, as does the limited and halting progress made towards their implementation when Labour governments have been in office. I try to explain the reasons for this. And looking at both the main themes of the book – the experience of office and ideas about reform – it will become apparent that there are many different strands of Labour thinking.

There is and has been, in fact, no single, coherent 'Labour Party view' about the nature and problems of the civil service or its reform.

My focus throughout has been on the Labour Party, and on the individual socialist intellectuals and the Fabian Society groups which have fed in ideas and proposals to the party and its leaders. I have not analyzed the experience in office of Conservative governments and ministers (save for some brief remarks about the Thatcher government) or the administrative reform ideas of other parties or groupings; to have done so would have required a different approach and would have resulted in a different book. I am, of course, very well aware that the Labour Party, the Fabian Society and assorted left-wing intellectuals have not had a monopoly on ideas about the role and reform of the civil service in the twentieth century. At appropriate places throughout the book I note ideas and proposals issuing from other sources and point out that, often, Labour's own schemes have been derivative, with the party simply latching on to fashionable thinking and wider currents of opinion. That said, it still seems to me a useful exercise to try to trace and make sense of the thinking and the experiences of one of the main British political parties in relation to Whitehall and the civil service.

I am grateful to the Labour Party and to the Fabian Society for permission to quote from documents and papers lodged in their archives. Crown-copyright material in the Public Record Office is reproduced by permission of the Controller of Her Majesty's Stationery Office. The editors of *Contemporary Record* and of *Public Policy and Administration* have very kindly allowed me to reproduce material previously published in articles which I wrote for those journals. Sabbatical leave for the summer term of 1990 enabled me to finish writing this book, and for that I am indebted to Leeds University and its Department of Politics. I am grateful for the advice, comments and encouragement I have received from academic colleagues at Leeds University and elsewhere, but of course I alone am responsible for the contents of this book. My greatest debt, for support and forbearance during this whole project, and for much else besides, is to Breda Theakston.

Kevin Theakston

1 Introduction

When Attlee succeeded Churchill as Prime Minister in 1945, and returned to the Potsdam peace conference, he was accompanied by the same team of civil servants (including the same principal private secretary) that had made up his predecessor's delegation. This continuity surprised the Americans and the Russians, but the officials concerned made the transition without apparent difficulty and the Labour leader himself had no doubts about the impartiality or loyalty of his staff. Out of office in the 1950s, Attlee would boast to international socialist conferences that the British career civil service was unequalled in the world, one of the strongest bulwarks of democracy, and that the same officials who had worked out the details of Labour's programme were now busy pulling it to pieces for their Conservative masters. Other leading members of the 1945–51 Labour government also praised the Whitehall machine – Herbert Morrison, for instance, who penned an uncritical account of the working of the British system of government which ended with a 'Tribute to the British Civil Service'.[1]

Morrison's biographers have rightly described him as 'a fervent champion of the British administrative class.' His view was that 'The relationship between the Minister and the civil servants should be – and usually is – that of colleagues working together in a team, co-operative partners seeking to advance the public interest and the efficiency of the Department'. He insisted, 'The belief among some of the public and even some Members of Parliament that civil servants do not work in harmony with Ministers I have hardly ever found to be justified'.[2] The contrast with the critical comments on Whitehall personalities, civil service obstruction and the negative power of the Treasury found in the diaries written by ministers serving in the 1964–70 and 1974–9 governments is marked. Searching for 'what went wrong' after the 'failures' of the Wilson and

Callaghan governments, many on the Labour left seized on the higher bureaucracy as a scapegoat. Without major reform of Whitehall, the mandarins could not be relied upon to assist in Labour's socialist project; rather they would systematically sabotage it.

Richard Crossman apparently thought that *Government and Parliament* was an 'odious book' and intended his diaries to provide the raw material for a work debunking Morrison and establishing himself as a modern-day Bagehot. In the event, Crossman's own strongly expressed views, on how Whitehall functions and how the mandarins relate to their political masters, themselves require debunking (see chapter 2). But however unreliable a source he may be, views like Crossman's have nevertheless become widespread in left-wing circles.

Tony Benn is also at the opposite pole to Herbert Morrison and Attlee. As he sees it,

> It is one of the great myths of British parliamentary democracy that the British civil service is politically neutral, ready, anxious and willing to work with equal enthusiasm for any political party that may form a majority. This is a complete illusion largely spread by those who know perfectly well that the civil service is neither ready, anxious nor willing to work for socialist policies but has to be presented in that way so that it can perform its task of obstruction without being accused of partiality.

'Life is so much easier for a minister who goes along with what his officials want and it is very difficult indeed to defeat them', Benn says on the basis of what is, after all, a considerable ministerial experience, one only a little shorter than Morrison's – eleven years as a minister, compared to Morrison's thirteen. On the other hand, Denis Healey, another veteran Labour minister and a Cabinet colleague of Crossman and Benn, has stated his view that it is the 'sheer intractability of the process of Government in Britain as it is now conducted' that is the problem rather than 'bureaucratic sabotage or political prejudice' on the part of the civil service. 'Whitehall's obsession with procedure rather than policy has left it poorly equipped to handle change', he believes, finding fault with the system's 'tendency to produce a soggy compromise', with the Treasury's stifling of the initiative of others, and with management and administrative training that does not match that provided by the famous French *ENA*. But from the outside, looking in, so to speak, the left-wing activist Hilary Wainwright does not share these technocratic views. Seeing the power of the higher civil service built up from the nineteenth century onwards as 'a protection against the political consequences of the working-class franchise', she believes 'the rapid dismantling [*sic*] of the entrenched mandarin Civil Service' to be a precondition of any sort of meaningful socialist and democratic advance. And, writing seventy years before Wainwright, Arthur Henderson – a key figure in the early decades of the party – expressed his view that 'the great administrative services, swathed in red tape, hampered by tradition, conservative by instinct, saturated with class prejudice, are a more effective check upon the reforming impulse than even a Parliament dominated by aristocratic and capitalist influences'.[3]

It is clear that there are major disagreements within the Labour Party, and among both participants in and observers of Labour governments, about the role, power and nature of the civil service. Is it a party-politically neutral and efficient administrative instrument at the disposal of a Labour (or any other) Cabinet? Or is it a brake on radical ministers, a conservative – if not actually a Conservative – force? Is the civil service properly equipped to deal with the problems of modern government and to run the interventionist economic and social programmes to which Labour is committed? Is Whitehall sufficiently accountable to Parliament and the public? Is government too secretive? Labour's experience in office and the work of socialist writers and academics over the years has yielded no single, coherent theory of bureaucracy, no answers to questions like these, that would be accepted throughout the Labour Party and the Labour movement. Labour in fact has often not paid much serious attention to these issues. This is rather curious, it is often observed, given that the party's success or failure in office depends to a crucial extent on its relations with the civil service, on the efficient use of the government machine and on the quality of the administrative apparatus and personnel available to it in Whitehall.[4]

On a wider front, Jones and Keating have spelt out at length how Labour 'has rarely given any sustained attention to the form of the state whose power and role it is pledged to extend'. It has spent little time thinking about the ground rules of the constitution: parliamentary sovereignty, Cabinet government, ministerial responsibility, and so on. The frequent lack of clarity, the confusion, the tensions and ambiguities that mark Labour's thinking about the civil service also characterize its approach to the British state and the constitution in general. Jones and Keating's historical review makes plain Labour's 'relatively uncritical acceptance of existing constitutional norms' and its 'uncritical inheritance of a British pre-democratic state form' in the course of the party's emergence and development and its integration into the British political system. Its attitudes and (in office) its actions towards reform of the institutions and practices of the state – including the civil service – have not been based on clear reasoning about constitutional first principles or about the institutional requirements of socialism, but have instead been piecemeal and pragmatic, and sometimes inconsistent and incoherent. To a great extent, when it has thought about constitutional matters at all Labour has simply taken over nineteenth-century Radical views. It is an interesting comment on the nature of the British Labour Party that some of its leading left-wing figures, such as Aneurin Bevan, Michael Foot and Tony Benn, should be the strongest defenders of parliamentarism and of what is essentially a pre-socialist view of the constitution.[5]

In the 1930s some on the Labour left, such as Harold Laski and Sir Stafford Cripps, took up what amounted to a Marxist position on the nature of the state and its relations with the dominant economic class, arguing that the existing constitutional arrangements were in fact a formidable barrier to the success of a Labour government's socialist programme. Despite all their excitable talk about 'executive dictatorship', emergency powers and so on, however, they did not in practice seem to envisage sweeping away the existing institutional landscape of British government (save for abolition of the House of Lords) so much as adapting it to serve socialist purposes more efficiently: streamlining parliamentary procedure, reorganizing the departmental structure of Whitehall and getting a stronger political grip on the civil service.[6] Even then, it must be said, their ideas failed to find much support in the party outside a fringe of left-wing intellectuals. The party leadership continued to hold strongly to the Fabian belief in the essential neutrality of the state. On this view, the state had no inherent class nature – Labour could win control of it through the normal channels of electoral and parliamentary politics and without needing to go outside the accepted conventions of the constitution. Indeed, Ramsay MacDonald regarded questions of political and constitutional reform as red herrings, diversions away from the real tasks facing socialists. Hugh Dalton pooh-poohed the Laski–Cripps type of 'panic talk' and 'theatrical nightmares of violent head-on collisions', and Attlee, the party leader, was confident that with some fairly modest reforms the existing government machinery could be used to bring about socialism. Labour, he declared, was 'resolved to preserve the essential fabric of the British system of government'.[7]

The fact that the Labour government elected in 1945 was able to successfully implement its far-reaching programme through Parliament and the civil service without major institutional reconstruction (see chapters 2, 3 and 6) appeared to vindicate the approach of the parliamentary leadership, as Laski himself seemed to acknowledge in his last work on British government.[8] Eleven continuous years in office (first in the wartime coalition and then in the first majority Labour government) served to cement the identification of the party's leadership with the existing machinery of the state and with the constitutional status quo. It was hardly surprising that in retirement Attlee and Morrison were to celebrate – even venerate – the system that had worked so well for them.

In the 1960s the reform debate reopened. Parliament, the civil service and local government all came on to the agenda, but in an uncoordinated and opportunistic way, and with Labour's unwillingness to rethink basic constitutional questions and make connections between the different issues predictably leading to only limited change in practice (see chapters 4 and 6). The focus on administrative modernization and efficiency, reflecting the running together of long-standing Fabian concerns with the then fashionable managerialist thinking, also rather glossed over important questions of elitism and power. In the late 1970s (and continuing after 1979), as it tried to work out the lessons of the Labour governments of 1964–70 and 1974–9 and debated the institutional reforms it deemed necessary to implement a left-wing programme, there was something of a throwback on the Labour left to the ideas of the 1930s about the existing state set-up being an 'obstacle' to socialism. The left's sights were on government secrecy, civil service and prime-ministerial power, reform of the Commons, and abolition of the Lords, but once again fundamental constitutional issues tended to be overlooked or disposed of too glibly. The tensions involved in simultaneously wanting strong programmatic government, strengthened parliamentary accountability and stronger party controls over the party leadership were also never properly resolved (see chapters 6 and 7). For their part, most Labour ministers in the 1970s were strong defenders of the traditional institutions and practices of government, a stance symbolized by the non-reform of the Official Secrets Act, despite a manifesto pledge to the contrary (see chapter 6).

Many important, first-order constitutional issues arose during the

1974–9 Labour government: devolution and the future of the United Kingdom, the implications of EEC membership, collective Cabinet responsibility (abandoned during the EEC referendum), the implications of the referendum device itself for parliamentary sovereignty, and the issues of electoral reform and a bill of rights also came on to the public agenda. Significantly, the latter two items were absent from the left's reform schemes. But neither the Labour government nor the party as a whole had an overall and coherent view on these issues, reacting instead in an *ad hoc* fashion and giving priority to tactical and partisan considerations. Only after the third successive Thatcher electoral victory in 1987 was there evidence that Labour was even starting to come round from its constitutional somnolence, but the leadership's relatively cautious and piecemeal approach, and doubts about the priority given to the issue, disappointed its critics in the party and in outside groups such as 'Charter 88'. A long tradition of constitutional conservatism and a pragmatic approach to institutional reform was not something that could be easily or quickly shrugged off, however.

'The gentleman in Whitehall really does know better what is good for people than the people know themselves', Douglas Jay famously (notoriously?) wrote in his book *The Socialist Case* in 1937. To be fair to him, Jay was apparently 'only' referring to the cases of nutrition, health and education policy, but his remark really has a wider relevance and reveals much about the dominant tradition of socialism in Britain. The dominance of a centralist and statist approach in Labour's political thinking and practice obviously gives a vital role to the civil service and the Whitehall machine in the achievement of socialism. The alternative tradition of decentralization and 'municipal socialism' was rapidly downgraded as Labour became a major parliamentary party and the actual or alternative government in the 1920s and 1930s. The 1945–51 period saw 'a relentless drive towards centralisation and bureaucracy sweeping everything else out of the way', in W. A. Robson's words. The revival of interest in the potential for 'local socialism' in the 1980s (reflecting Labour's exit from power at the national level) and the party's emerging plans for a system of regional assemblies represent something of a challenge to the 'Whitehall knows best' philosophy, but it is not clear that the full implications of these developments have been thought through either in constitutional terms or in terms of the potential impact on the pursuit of Labour's nation-wide economic and welfare policy goals and its redistributive aims.[9]

'Socialists – at any rate the type represented by the present

Government – idealise the salaried public servant: they look to him to save the world', Beatrice Webb wrote in her diary in February 1924 as ministers in the first (minority) Labour government were settling into their new jobs. The Webbs and the Fabian socialist tradition have had a crucially important influence on Labour thinking about the civil service (see chapters 3 and 4). Although they were early champions of 'municipal socialism' and decentralization (with Beatrice still dreaming up schemes for devolved assemblies when she was in her seventies), the Webbs' socialism had an unmistakable centralist and bureaucratic flavour. A major role in bringing about and then governing a socialist society would be played by a selfless, dedicated, unassuming and public-spirited elite of expert bureaucrats. The Webbs wanted 'to make the Civil Service something very like the Fabian Society in power', as Rodney Barker has wryly observed. Competitive examinations and expert training (the Webbs founded the London School of Economics) would provide a new meritocratic elite to man the state machine and push forward with the social research and government action central to Fabian socialism. A 'bureaucratic nightmare' was how Margaret Cole described their blueprint for the future socialist state, *A Constitution for the Socialist Commonwealth of Great Britain* (1920); the Webbs' critics seized on their talk about a new body of 'Samurai' and their later admiration for Stalin's Russia to point out the authoritarian, illiberal and anti-democratic tendencies in their thought. The Webbs' insistence that their key 'disinterested professional expert' would have 'no power of command and no right to insist on his suggestions being adopted' does seem rather optimistic, if not actually naive. As Sidney Webb once admitted, 'Experts are the danger of democracy. They are absolutely necessary, but they must be controlled by the electors, that is, by amateurs, and this is by no means an easy matter.' And Beatrice Webb was acutely aware of the problem of 'combining bureaucratic efficiency with democratic control' when she served on the Haldane Committee. The Webb's constitution-mongering did include elaborate arrangements for remodelling Parliament to try to improve accountability together with an early commitment to 'open government' – a combination of 'measurement with publicity' and 'the searchlight of published knowledge', they called it – but how far these devices would offset the concentration of bureaucratic power at the centre of the Webbian state is open to question (see chapter 6).[10]

For all their incessant and earnest reformist writings on the subject of the machinery of government, the Webbs were in many respects great admirers of the British civil service. Sidney Webb once described it as a national treasure (see chapter 3). Beatrice sketched in her diary a by no means unfavourable impression after her time on the Haldane Committee:

> This informal review of our bureaucracy leaves an impression of good temper and good manners, of native capacity and no systematic training, of philosophical indifference to ends, tempered by a moderately felt loyalty to the ideals of the British ruling class. Contempt for Parliament and a disdainful dislike for the newly imported 'business man', a steady depreciation of Parliamentary chiefs, are almost universal in the higher ranks of the civil service.[11]

It is a fair criticism of the Webbs – and of the wider Fabian tradition – that their concern was with questions of efficiency and accountability and not with the democratization of a socially unrepresentative higher bureaucracy. The idea that the class background of top officials might make them unsympathetic towards socialist aims or even disposed to obstruct radical ministers did not apparently even occur to them as a possibility, though other socialists were concerned about the implications of an 'unrepresentative bureaucracy' (see chapter 5).

Harold Laski has had a long-term influence on Labour thinking about the civil service which in some ways has probably been even more important than that of the Webbs. He certainly took up Webbian and Fabian ideas, being concerned at different times with the need to improve civil service training and to strengthen the role of the specialist, for instance (see chapter 3). But at the same time, his thinking had a more critical edge when it came to the problem of civil service power and the difficulties involved in exercising firm political control over the Whitehall machine (see chapter 2), and he was also worried by the problems posed by the narrow class background of the higher civil service (see chapter 5). His democratic credentials were impeccable. He served on the Donoughmore Committee on Ministerial Powers (1929–32), and as Kenneth O. Morgan puts it, 'became a fierce critic of the despotic implications of the quasi-judicial powers being annexed by faceless public servants in impenetrable government sanctums. . . . He should not be classed with the advocates of a juggernaut of faceless, centralized bureaucratic power.' He long championed the introduction of a system of Commons backbench committees to more effectively scrutinize government (see chapter 6). His caustic attacks on the Treasury ('it ought not to have taken a second world war to have persuaded the Treasury that Mr Montagu Norman's private prejudices are not part of the order of nature') and on the Foreign Office ('that nest of public-school singing birds'), and his insistence that Labour ministers needed to be armed by better policy preparation in Opposition and by *cabinets* of personal advisers, were themes that were to recur again and again whenever the party turned to the issue of the civil service (see chapter 2).[12]

Laski's output was prolific and his ideas certainly developed over time; inevitably it is easy to find apparent inconsistencies, contradictions and tensions in his thinking about the civil service. He was concerned about class bias and the Oxbridge stranglehold on recruitment but can be found praising *Literae Humaniores* as an ideal training for administrators. He changed his mind on the question of whether a civil service staff college was necessary and on the proper relationship of the generalist to the specialist official (see chapter 3). He wanted more outsiders with a 'capacity for ideas and . . . driving ambition' imported into Whitehall, citing Morant and Beveridge as examples of the type of man required, without seeming to realize that this might actually make the exercise of ministerial control over policy-making more, not less, difficult. And he could round off an article in an American academic journal like this: 'An Englishman may perhaps add one final reflection. There is no British institution of which all citizens are, on the whole, more proud or more justly proud than the civil service'.[13] As already mentioned, the war and the experience of the 1945 government changed Laski's perspective on the character of the whole political system, but nevertheless his more critical work in the 1930s and early 1940s must loom large in any account of Labour's approach to the use and reform of the civil service.

Webbian state socialism was denounced as a 'bureaucratic and Prussianising movement' by G. D. H. Cole. The philosophy of 'expertism and bureaucracy' was 'the road of reaction', he argued, depicting Guild Socialist ideas of workers' self-government as the 'road of democracy'. Workers' control should be the key organizing principle, not just for industry but also for public services. While technical experts could hardly be elected by a mass vote, Cole acknowledged, other managers and administrative officers should be chosen by the workers concerned. He envisaged that most administrative work in the future Guild Society would be carried on at a local or regional level and that the existing civil service would be broken up and reorganized into various functional Guilds.

The clerical staff employed in the administrative offices of the different Guilds would apparently choose their own departmental officers and 'only at the top should they be controlled by an authority elected on a wider franchise', Cole explained. This did, however, suggest that there were limits to the internal democracy of the Guilds.[14] In the 1930s and 1940s, Cole was to take up more of a mainstream Fabian position on the reform of the civil service (see chapters 3 and 5), and his general approach clearly places him in the anti-bureaucratic tradition of decentralist socialism. But it must be said that Labour has had strictly orthodox views on the constitutional acceptability of the idea of workers' control in the civil service. 'To subject major issues of policy to joint decision-making with the civil servants who happen to work on them would clearly be in conflict with parliamentary democracy', Tessa Blackstone has written, also ruling out giving the civil service work-force the final say or any power of veto over the implementation of policy decisions or changes to existing programmes.[15]

Labour governments have also had similarly conventional views on what the continued existence of a permanent and neutral civil service must mean for the rules governing officials' political activities (to the chagrin of those in the civil service unions who have campaigned for the relaxation of the restrictions imposed on them) even if this has meant overriding Labour Party (and TUC) conference policy. Until prohibited after the General Strike, some civil service unions – the postal workers' unions and the Civil Service Clerical Association (CSCA) – were actually affiliated to the Labour Party. In 1920 the CSCA conference voted to support Labour's nationalization policies and the postal workers agitated for workers' control in the Post Office; in 1923 the Union of Post Office Workers (UPOW) urged its members to vote Labour! Not surprisingly, this sort of thing worried the civil service top brass and Conservative politicians. After the Attlee government repealed the 1927 Trade Disputes Act, the UPOW but not the CSCA reaffiliated to the Labour Party. Significantly, *Socialist Commentary*, the journal of the Labour right, urged the civil service unions not to reaffiliate, arguing that the service's political neutrality had to be beyond doubt. In the 1920s, the 1940s and again in the 1970s, Labour governments faced pressure from the civil service unions to relax the restrictions on political activities. On each occasion, their response was the traditional Establishment one of handing the problem over to an independent committee of inquiry – whose recommendations have then usually disappointed the unions. Richard

Chapman's account of the Masterman Committee in the 1940s clearly shows the great influence of the then Head of the Civil Service, Sir Edward Bridges, over the way in which the issues involved were handled. Bridges was determined to protect the interests and traditions of the civil service as he saw them, and it seems that Labour ministers were happy to go along with his approach.[16]

G. D. H. Cole once advised that 'Socialists especially would do well to give their proposals for the reform and development of the public services a prominent place in their propaganda, in order to meet those critics who oppose Socialism on the ground that it means "bureaucracy" '.[17] And before 1964, Fabian critics of the civil service argued that Whitehall reform might be a precondition of a successful Labour government (see chapter 4). However, in office, Labour leaders have been institutionally conservative and have not pushed through radical reform of the civil service. Unlike some of their followers, they appear to have been reasonably satisfied with the Whitehall status quo and to have given administrative reform a low priority. In fact, Labour has never had a clear blueprint for civil service reform, different critics pointing to different 'problems' and sometimes making contradictory proposals for change.

Four persistent themes stand out when we look at the long-term development of Labour Party attitudes towards the bureaucracy and its reform. First, there is the Fabian critique, accepting the political neutrality of the civil service but suggesting that its *efficiency* needs improving. A line can be traced from the writings of the Webbs, Laski, Cole and others, through Fabian Society pamphlets of 1947 and 1964, to the bible of this school of thought, the Fulton Committee report of 1968. These all promote a familiar Fabian agenda for civil service modernization: changes in recruitment, training, organization and management (see chapters 3 and 4). A second approach to the civil service concentrates on the problem of bureaucratic *power* and alleged civil service obstruction of socialist measures rather than on the question of efficiency and leads to a concern with finding ways of strengthening the political impulse in government through devices such as ministerial *cabinets*, political appointments to the civil service and so on. It should be noted, though, that the question of whether there actually is a 'problem' of civil service power is the subject of some dispute inside the party – as we have already seen – with many Labour ministers denying that they experienced politically motivated civil service sabotage (see chapter 2). Third, there is the concern with the *class* composition of the higher civil service and allegations that the social and educational biases evident in its recruitment patterns skew its political sympathies to the right. But while the arguments for a more 'representative bureaucracy' have been periodically aired in Labour circles, Fabian ideas about efficiency and meritocracy have been more influential in shaping Labour's approach to the issue of recruitment to Whitehall, introducing a pronounced ambiguity on the question of elitism in the civil service (see chapter 5). A fourth strand of Labour Party thinking relates to Whitehall's *democratic accountability*. In office, Labour ministers have been unenthusiastic about suggestions for stronger parliamentary checks on the executive or more 'open government', their hostility reflecting statist conceptions of socialism, their assimilation to the traditions of executive-dominated government and calculations of political convenience in a competitive party system. But at the same time, there has always been an anti-bureaucratic strain of socialist opinion, and even if this has not historically had a major impact on Labour's general strategy so far as winning and using state power is concerned, it does underpin the arguments for select committees and freedom of information reform that have caused Labour ministers such disquiet (see chapter 6).

With the possible exception of the third, these approaches are not distinctively 'socialist', finding advocates and supporters beyond the Labour Party. Neither are they necessarily distinct, for figures such as the Webbs, Laski and Benn can be found espousing reform packages drawing on elements of each. However, there are possible tensions between these themes which are not always acknowledged by reformers. For instance, making the civil service a more professional, technocratic elite may well create new problems of ministerial control and democratic accountability. Moreover, opening up Whitehall to more penetrating parliamentary scrutiny and reinforcing the mechanisms of accountability will not necessarily strengthen the socialist resolve of Labour ministers or make it easier for them to implement their mandate.

The importance of some significant internal fault-lines in Labour Party politics is well known: left vs. right, party vs. (Labour) government, rank and file vs. leadership, and so on. Inevitably, these sorts of tensions and divisions have influenced the party's approach to the civil service. Opinion on the question of civil service power and obstruction, for instance, seems in some respects to reflect evaluations of the success or otherwise of Labour governments; this was less of an issue in the party after the 1945–51 government than after (and during) the 1964–70 and 1974–9 terms of office. And, historically, the left in the party has been more concerned with this issue than has the right (though after 1979 some figures on the right did endorse some of the criticisms usually associated with the left – see chapter 2). In part overlapping with the left/right distinction, the uneasy relations between Labour ministers and the party organization and activists in the 1960s and 1970s can be seen in Harold Wilson's public rejection of some of the criticisms of the civil service contained in the party's evidence to the Fulton Committee and in the Callaghan government's simply ignoring the criticisms and reform ideas of the party's Machinery of Government Study Group (approved by the NEC and party conference) (see chapter 4).

Henry Drucker suggests that the deep-rooted rank-and-file mistrust of the party's leaders also colours attitudes towards the mandarins:

> the problems of Labour ministers are increased by the suspicion of their supporters that unless they are seen to be having trouble with their civil servants they cannot be doing their jobs properly . . . If they satisfy their supporters' expectations, they have trouble using the machine effectively; if they use the machine effectively, they are suspected of betraying the movement. But they are sent to Whitehall to use it for the movement.[18]

Yet another significant distinction to draw is between socialist intellectuals and Labour's professional politicians, with the former usually being more critical of the Whitehall machine and more active in devising reform schemes, though often these have been just paper exercises because the party machine and/or the parliamentary leadership have not taken them up or made them a high priority (numerous examples of this will be seen throughout this book). The historical record indicates that when Labour is in office, the party's leaders pay much more attention to civil service advice and to the findings of government-appointed committees of inquiry on the question of reform of the Whitehall machine than to views and advice coming from party circles or sympathetic intellectuals.

The book is organized largely thematically rather than in terms of the particular historical periods around which studies of the Labour Party are often organized. Thus material on the Attlee and Wilson governments, for instance, will be found in several chapters. It seemed more sensible to structure the study in this way, rather than write a strictly chronological account, in order to bring out rather than blur the long-term development of ideas and practice relating to particular issues. The exposition and analysis in each chapter, however, takes a chronological form. Chapter 2 deals with the subject of civil service power: the relations between Labour ministers and the topmost mandarins, allegations of bureaucratic sabotage of Labour governments, proposals to reinforce Labour ministers' sources of political and party advice inside government, and the party's own policy preparations before it enters office. Chapters 3 and 4 are concerned with the long-running debate over Whitehall efficiency and the 'Fabian critique' of the civil service. Chapter 3 looks at the Attlee government and the civil service and at Labour reform thinking over the decades before 1945; chapter 4 deals with the 1960s and 1970s, looking at the run-up to and the aftermath of the Fulton Committee on the Civil Service. The issues involved in Labour's approach to civil service recruitment – class bias and meritocracy – are the subject of chapter 5. Chapter 6 examines party thinking about ways of strengthening Whitehall accountability through parliamentary reform and also the debate about secrecy and openness in government; the poor record of Labour governments in these matters will become apparent. Finally, chapter 7 is concerned with developments in the civil service since 1979 and Labour's reaction to them; looking ahead, the chapter also tries to preview the possible impact of a Labour government on the Whitehall machine.

2 Labour governments and the mandarins

Richard Crossman's first days as a cabinet minister in the 1964 Labour government were apparently a rather overwhelming experience for him. It took some time before he discovered the private washroom in his vast ministerial office. He was amazed to be told by his private secretary that if he put all the contents of his in-tray into his out-tray without a mark on it, then his paperwork would be dealt with by his staff and he need never see it again. He was worried that his officials would realize that he knew nothing about the subjects he had to deal with. He felt isolated. 'Already I realize the tremendous effort it requires not to be taken over by the Civil Service', he confided to his diary. 'My Minister's room is like a padded cell, and in certain ways I am like a person who is suddenly certified a lunatic and put safely into this great, vast room, cut off from real life and surrounded by male and female trained nurses and attendants.' Interestingly enough, ten years later an embattled Tony Benn was to use the same sort of image in *his* diary, describing how his permanent secretary 'treats me like a consultant psychiatrist would a particularly dangerous patient, and at any moment I expect him to ring a bell and a fat, male nurse in a white jacket will come in and give me an injection'.[1]

It would be wrong to suggest that these images were entirely appropriate for the individuals concerned, though it was certainly idiotic for Crossman to tell his permanent secretary, the redoubtable Dame Evelyn Sharp, that he must personally approve every decision made in his name by officials in the different corners of his ministry. Only by having mountains of files containing decisions for approval on one particular day brought up and piled high on every surface in his office could she convince him that this was impossible![2]

In earlier Labour governments ministerial encounters with the civil service machine also occasionally had their (unintentionally) comic – perhaps tragicomic? – aspects. In 1924, for instance, when J. H. Thomas arrived at the entrance to the Colonial Office, declaring that he was the new Secretary of State, the doorman's response was: 'Another shell-shock case, I'm afraid'. How senior officials reacted to him telling them that, 'I'm here to see that there is no mucking about with the British Empire' is not, however, recorded. Stephen Walsh, the former miner who became Secretary of State for War, is supposed to have told the generals, 'I know my place. You have commanded Armies in the field when I was nothing but a private in the ranks.' His wife would sit in his room in the War Office; when the Chief of the Imperial General Staff suggested that a confidential document was for the minister's eyes only, Walsh replied, 'Oh never mind mother. She's always there'. Sidney Webb, Colonial Secretary in the 1929 government, arranged a dinner for the whole of his administrative and clerical staff which took place in Lyons Corner House. The seating at the tables was arranged by drawing names out of a hat and the oldest and youngest officials were called on to make speeches. Webb's junior minister drily recalled this democratic innovation: 'Some say that this classless evening dinner went well, while others report a rather strained atmosphere. At any rate, the experiment was never repeated.'[3]

More often, it should be said, Labour's experience in office, as depicted by many socialist writers and some former ministers, seems like *Yes, Minister* without the jokes. Brian Sedgemore's *The Secret Constitution*, dealing with Tony Benn's 'power struggles' with his mandarins in the 1974–9 administration, or the various writings of (say) Michael Meacher and Lord Crowther-Hunt are cases in point, though Gerald Kaufman, a junior minister in the 1970s, managed a high quota of wisecracks in his book of advice, *How To Be A Minister*.[4] The opportunities, responsibilities, dilemmas and frustrations of office are no laughing matter, however, when one bears in mind the hopes pinned on Labour ministers and the expectations of Labour Party members and voters, not to mention the normative theory of the British constitution, that ministers, not civil servants, should have the final power because they carry the final responsibility to Parliament and public.

This chapter deals with the relations between Labour ministers and governments and the mandarins in five parts. There is a review of the party's experience in office under MacDonald, Attlee and then Wilson and Callaghan: do allegations of bureaucratic sabotage or obstruction hold up? Then, we look at the debate about strengthening the position of Labour ministers in relation to the Whitehall machine and the steps taken to introduce outside advisers and ministerial aides committed to the party. Finally, we examine the adequacy of Labour's policy preparations while in Opposition and the extent to which this factor might contribute to any problems later in office.

Assessing the influence of the civil service on Labour governments is not easy. To some extent, the experience of each minister is unique, depending on the personalities, circumstances and departments involved. Relations between ministers and their civil servants are highly variable and can change over time. In all governments – Labour and Conservative – some ministers dominate their departments or forge a fruitful relationship with their top officials, while weaker colleagues are more pliant.

The available evidence is often patchy, anecdotal and self-serving. There is a fair amount of folklore masquerading as analysis. Thus, civil servants routinely 'cook the minutes', according to their critics. As Crossman put it:

> Just as the Cabinet Secretariat constantly transforms the actual proceedings of Cabinet into the form of the Cabinet minutes (i.e. it substitutes what we should have said if we had done as they wished for what we did actually say), so here in my Department the civil servants are always putting in what they think I should have said and not what I actually decided.

On the other side of the argument, so to speak, ministerial machismo is ritually invoked. 'The first forty-eight hours decide whether a new minister is going to run his office, or whether his office is going to run him', Arthur Henderson famously told Hugh Dalton. 'I think that a minister who complains that his civil servants are too powerful is either a weak minister or an incompetent one', Denis Healey has declared. Labour prime ministers seem particularly fond of this black-and-white distinction between 'strong' and 'weak' ministers. 'I have always taken the view that Attlee took years ago', Harold Wilson said, ' . . . if a Minister cannot control his civil servants, he ought to go.'[5]

Some Labour ministers have acknowledged that things are not always so clear-cut. Tony Crosland, for instance, maintained that, 'It's a great mistake to think there's a continuous battle going on'. 'It's very rare that you meet real resistance or obstruction [from civil servants]', he explained. 'Generally I never found any problem in establishing good working relations . . . a Minister who doesn't do so is wasting a large fund of knowledge and expertise'. And from an earlier generation, Hugh Dalton – though in practice his relations with officials were often turbulent – also suggested that it was too blinkered to think in crude terms of 'ministers *versus* mandarins'. He subscribed to the Henderson dictum but thought that 'having established an independent personality, the Minister should try to get all the help he can – and it will generally be a lot – out of his officials'. The civil service certainly contained 'a few congenital snag-hunters', but there was also 'in the vast majority of cases' great loyalty to its (temporary) political masters. 'There should be a two-way traffic in ideas between a Minister and his Civil Servants', Dalton believed.

> It is best if a new Minister has *some* ideas about policy in his Department. But not, perhaps, too many or too precise ideas. If he has no ideas of his own, or does not quickly acquire some, the officials will gladly make a policy for him. But this is not a procedure to be unduly encouraged.
>
> Even, however, when the Minister has some ideas of his own, the officials can be most helpful in putting these into the best shape, whether for practical administration or for winning the agreement of Ministerial colleagues. The officials may even point out formidable difficulties, which are new to the Minister. He should face those in a calm and honest mood, but may sometimes usefully invite those who have indicated the difficulties to indicate also how these can best be surmounted or evaded.

Whitehall, he rightly pointed out, was not a monolithic entity: 'Often there is keen contention, and even ill will, between officials of different departments. And within each Department a group loyalty, though seldom a complete uniformity of opinion'. At the end of the day, Dalton endorsed the orthodox view that civil servants prefer a minister who allows reasonable discussion within the department and then makes up his mind, takes decisions and sticks to them.[6]

The dilemma faced by socialist ministers has been well described by Henry Drucker. Some, he observes, 'become so drawn into the playing of the Whitehall game as, almost, to forget what it is for'. He quotes Bruce Headey's finding that only 6 per cent of his sample of Labour and Conservative ministers in the late 1960s and early 1970s thought that it was their role to 'implement party policy or to take decisions in accordance with party policy'. (Headey was surprised to find the role conceptions of Labour and Conservative Cabinet ministers were so similar: 'It would be hard to imagine that thirty or forty years ago Labour leaders in particular would have omitted to mention as one of their main roles the implementation of party principles'.) The danger associated with this ministerial (or governmental) stance, Drucker argues, is estrangement from the wider movement and disenchantment among the party rank and file.

At the other extreme is the hostility and mistrust, the suspicions of a bureaucratic conspiracy, demonstrated, according to Drucker, by Barbara Castle and Richard Crossman (and, we might add, Tony Benn). These, he argues, 'remain acutely conscious of what their people want and of how foreign the cliques in Whitehall are to their constituency workers, but at the price of making very ineffective use of their position as ministers'. A socialist minister has to avoid these two traps: 'he has to avoid becoming a tool of the Whitehall clique, and he has to avoid so alienating that clique that he cannot use them to execute his policy and run his ministry'. 'Effective government, effective use of the Whitehall machine', Drucker continues, 'depends very centrally on the ability of ministers and civil servants to do their different jobs together' – something recognized by Crosland and Dalton in the quotes above, as well as by other successful Labour ministers such as Ernest Bevin. Writing of Bevin's time as Foreign Secretary in the post-war Labour government, Alan Bullock has made the point well: 'The view popular amongst left-wing members of the Labour Party that either a minister dictated policy or was mere wax in the hands of his permanent officials was naive . . . the most successful ministers were those who worked closely with their officials and profited from the interaction with them without allowing any confusion about the different roles they had to play'.[7]

THE EXPERIENCE OF OFFICE: 1924 AND 1929–31

From the party's first stints in office under Ramsay MacDonald and onwards, participants in and observers of Labour governments have been divided on the question of whether they are deflected from their radicalism by a conservative civil service machine. Beatrice Webb thought that Labour's debut in office saw Whitehall reacting in a textbook fashion. In 1924 she wrote how Sidney Webb at the Board of Trade found his officials 'polished instruments, waiting on him hand and foot, seemingly acquiescent in any practicable policy'. As the second Labour government took office five years later she was struck by 'the perfect smoothness of the British administrative machine – in the changing from a Conservative to a Socialist Government'. 'Of course the usual accusation brought by the outside enthusiasts is that the Minister is the tool of the Civil Service and that the Permanent Heads of departments are always against progress along the lines of political democracy and social and economic equality', she commented, adding however that 'S. [Sidney] does not find that his Permanents are reactionary'.[8]

On the whole, the civil service does in fact seem to have had little trouble in adjusting to the idea of a Labour government, both in 1924 and in 1929. MacDonald's biographer has told how in 1924 the service departments, particularly the Admiralty, tried to pursue their own policies free from political control – as indeed other governments frequently found – but so far as the rest of Whitehall was concerned, he wrote, 'All the available evidence suggests that the home departments accepted, and in some cases even welcomed, their new masters – in part, no doubt, because no important changes in policy were made'. The mandarins were also pleased that Labour did not disturb the organization, methods of working or personnel of the government machine. The Cabinet Secretariat and its head, Hankey, were kept on. Both times he became Prime Minister MacDonald resisted pressure to sack the civil service private secretaries he inherited from his Conservative predecessors in Number 10 and replace them with Labour supporters.[9]

It is clear, however, that some of MacDonald's ministers were not equipped or experienced enough to use properly the Whitehall machine that Labour took over. In 1924 only two ministers had ever sat in a Cabinet before. Haldane (one of the two) told Beatrice Webb that the trade unionists in the government 'simply accept everything their officials tell them.' 'Fortunately', he went on, 'we have a first-rate and progressive Civil Service.' During the second MacDonald government there were complaints that J. H. Thomas (in charge of unemployment) and Margaret Bondfield (Minister of Labour) were entirely in the hands of their top civil servants, but several other ministers, too, were carried by their officials. Robert Skidelsky's judgement is scathing: 'In general the Labour Ministers [of 1929–31] were propagandists with little knowledge of government. Their inexperience, lack of assurance and the sheer volume of work helped to make them slaves to departmental views'. MacDonald himself could be contemptuous, telling his principal private secretary in 1929 that few of his team were up to the job of directing their departments: 'The truth is we have not got the men'. He had not been long in Downing Street in 1924 before he wrote in his diary that he was beginning to see 'how officials dominate Ministers. Details are overwhelming & Ministers have no time to work out policy with officials as servants; they are immersed in pressing business with officials as masters'.[10] Some Labour ministers, though, were effective operators: notably MacDonald and Henderson at the Foreign Office in 1924 and 1929–31 respectively, Wheatley as Minister of Health in 1924, Morrison at Transport 1929–31, and Snowden at the Treasury in both administrations.

The Foreign Office and the Treasury – Whitehall's elite departments – were viewed as the chief bureaucratic saboteurs in some Labour circles. The influence of E. D. Morel and the Union of Democratic Control on Labour Party attitudes towards the diplomats was considerable; before he became Prime Minister MacDonald had made no secret of his own suspicion and hostility. Morel had long pressed for reforms to strengthen parliamentary control of foreign policy-making, 'democratize' the Foreign Office and break the stranglehold of the diplomatic service. Not surprisingly, the Foreign Office was rather anxious about the advent of a Labour government. In the event, it was relieved to discover that MacDonald (who became his own Foreign Secretary in 1924) was actually a better minister to work for than his insufferable Conservative predecessor, Lord Curzon. Labour critics were, however, confirmed in their views by the Zinoviev Letter incident, which torpedoed the government's election campaign and contributed to its defeat in October 1924. They were suspicious that anti-Bolshevik officials wanted to scuttle Labour's policy of *rapprochement* with the Soviet Union. Morel argued that the 'Red Letter' scare showed 'the powerlessness of a Labour Government to control the permanent officials of the Foreign Office and to protect itself against their incapacity or worse', a view apparently shared by some of the 1924 Cabinet but not by MacDonald. (The real culprits seem to have been the intelligence services, acting in concert with Tory Central Office, motivated by anti-Bolshevism and institutional self-interest.)[11]

Out of office, proposals were developed in the party to overhaul Foreign Office recruitment and organization and to strengthen the position of a future Labour Foreign Secretary in his department (see below), but Henderson in 1929 simply ignored them. That he had a firm political grip on his department could not be doubted, however, though senior officials seem on occasion to have tried to exploit the always uneasy relations between Henderson and MacDonald by communicating with the Prime Minister behind his Foreign Secretary's back. Henderson also had a clear view of his objectives, ordering that copies of *Labour and the Nation* be circulated around the Foreign Office so that officials would know what the party's programme was. Hugh Dalton later recalled his experiences of 'the Whitehall obstacle race' as Henderson's junior minister, but it would be quite wrong to argue that the government's foreign policy was subverted or knocked off course by obstructive bureaucrats.[12]

The Treasury, of course, became a favourite hate-object among socialist critics of Whitehall after 1931. George Lansbury denounced the department in the *Daily Herald* soon after leaving office: 'All through the life of the late Government Treasury officials obstructed and hindered the Ministers in their work. No one can deny this.' But he identified the real problem when he went on, 'Treasury officials act in this way because Cabinets allow them to do so.' The power of the Treasury under the second Labour government represented the failure of the party's political imagination and of ministers' political will. The problem was not that Snowden, the Chancellor of the Exchequer, was helplessly under the thumb of his officials – rather he was a stereotypical 'strong' minister – but that his views on economic and financial policy were completely in line with Treasury and Bank of England orthodoxy out of personal conviction and that his opinions were widely held and dominant in the Labour Party and the Labour government at that time. (The radical economic ideas of the ILP, Cole and Mosley did not impress the leadership.) If there were objections in Whitehall to a major public works programme to help combat unemployment – Ministry of Transport officials, for instance, ruling out a large roads programme as impracticable and ineffectual – these views were also shared by MacDonald and his colleagues. The Treasury and the civil service cannot be made a scapegoat for what was essentially Labour's own *political* failure.[13]

In the aftermath of 1931 most of Labour's parliamentary leadership continued to believe that the civil service was loyal to the government of the day whatever its political complexion, as Lansbury – who disagreed – complained. In his view, the civil service could not be relied on enthusiastically to implement a socialist policy. The second Labour government had had to work with officials who 'had made up their minds that Socialist policy if adopted would ruin the nation'. They had continually blocked ministers by bringing up reasons why nothing could be done or why ministerial proposals would not work. The Secretary to the Cabinet and the Permanent Secretary to the Treasury were now 'far more powerful than an ordinary Prime Minister', he alleged. The lesson he drew was that if a Labour government was to succeed, it needed at the top of the civil service officials who were completely committed to its programme.[14]

This was not how Herbert Morrison and Hugh Dalton interpreted their experience in office. 'I cannot remember a case where civil servants or municipal officers appeared to be running the show when it was not the fault of the politicians', was Morrison's robust view. In a memorandum written in early 1930 he had praised the 'loyalty, ability and sincerity' of the civil service.

> I have and am effecting some substantial changes of policy at the M. of T. [Ministry of Transport] and I have received every assistance once policy has been decided. . . . Provided Ministers know their minds, I do not know that there would be available much better technical advice, generally speaking, than we get in the state departments.

Out of office, Morrison's view was that, 'A high degree of administrative skill, organising ability, financial and economic astuteness, and even commercial prowess, is to be found in the ranks of the Civil Service'. He emphatically rejected charges of bureaucratic conspiracy or sabotage:

> The popular fiction that the civil servants are anxious to foist their own policy upon Ministers is not true in my experience. The civil servants like their Minister to do well; they feel personally humiliated if he makes blunders; they take enormous pains to give him all the facts and to warn him against pitfalls. If they think the policy he contemplates is wrong they will tell him why, but always on the basis that it is for him to settle the matter. And if the Minister, as is sometimes the case, has neither the courage nor the brains to evolve a policy of his own, they will do their best to find him one; for, after all, it is better that a department should be run by its civil servants than that it should not be run at all . . . Responsibility for policy rests upon Ministers whether they are weak or strong, and it is important that the civil servants should be the instruments, and not the masters of policy. They would have been just as loyal to a Conservative Minister; and that is well.

Anything like a political test for making administrative appointments and promotions was totally unacceptable, in Morrison's opinion.[15]

For his part, Dalton was willing to go along with the criticism that 'under the Second Labour Government the Treasury were always on top', but made it clear that he believed that a Labour government, no less than any other government, could count on the political neutrality and loyalty of the civil service. If civil servants acted like 'civil masters' the blame should be on ministers for not clearly laying down what their policy was. 'Some Socialists fear that, especially near the top of the service, class prejudice will show itself obstructive towards great changes. If so, the remedy is simple', he argued. There should be 'bumps and promotions'. Dalton was willing to go further than Morrison in backing the proposal that ministers should be accompanied into office by a number of politically committed and expert outside advisers, but he certainly did not envisage abandoning the model of a permanent higher civil service.[16]

The constitutionally orthodox assumptions of most of Labour's frontbench were most vigorously challenged by one of the party's leading left-wing intellectuals, Harold Laski, from whom came the strongest and most persistent warnings in the 1930s about the nature and consequences of civil service power. He was, of course, ever willing to take an easy swipe at the hapless MacDonald Labour governments: 'most Labour ministers fulfilled the Civil Service ideal of seeing most of the difficulties in the way of action even before they were embodied in memoranda for their consumption'. Rejecting the view that there was 'a conscious lust for power' on the part of officials, however, Laski argued that the real problems posed by the civil service were the result of the narrow class backgrounds and outlook of the top grades, the ' "negative" character of the Treasury mind . . . cautious, hesitating, opposed to wide innovation, accustomed to scrutinize prospects in somewhat narrow financial terms . . . more anxious not to make a mistake than to risk an adventure', and the existence in each ministry of a strongly held 'departmental policy' which most ministers came to accept as their own. He was quite prepared to accept that 'any minister who has known with any precision what he wants to do has been able, if he had the will to do so, to become the master of his officials'. The trouble was that this type of minister was exceptional and that 'the opportunity of the civil servant (from the highest motives) to place obstacles in the way of a Minister who differs from him is real'.

Writing in 1938, Laski argued that the neutrality of the civil service had not yet been tested by the need to work in support of a Labour government with a socialist programme of the kind he believed the party's 1937 *Immediate Programme* to be. Liberal and Conservative governments before 1924 had differed in degree, not kind. A socialist government would challenge the economic foundations of society and the traditional ideas for which the civil service had stood. Labour could not be sure that the mandarins would serve it with their customary disinterested zeal. Would the Treasury be able easily to work with a Labour government which had no sympathy with its traditional nostrums? Would the Foreign Office really swing whole-heartedly behind a minister with a socialist foreign policy? 'I do not for a moment suggest that the Civil Service would not meet such a test with adequacy', Laski observed. 'I note only that, so far, the need to meet it has not arisen'.[17]

THE EXPERIENCE OF OFFICE: 1945–51

Labour's experience after 1945 was to be the critical test for the Laski hypothesis. In a way, he was to provide his own answer for, revisiting the subject in his lectures *Reflections on the Constitution* in 1950, Laski was to be curiously silent on this point, perhaps because he recognized that the Attlee government had no reason to complain about civil service obstruction. In retirement, Attlee was asked about this by his former press secretary, Francis Williams: 'In earlier days many people used to suggest that a Labour government with a socialist programme would run into trouble with right-wing civil servants. Did you have any of that difficulty?' He replied:

> Never. I always found them perfectly loyal. So did all the others as far as I know. I never had complaints. That's the civil service tradition, a great tradition. They carry out the policy of any given government. If they think it's silly, of course they'll tell the minister so. If he decides to go ahead, then they carry it out. There may have been some whose advice to ministers was coloured by their own personal attitudes. I never encountered them. They were all anxious to do the best they could by a Labour government.[18]

The Marxist writer Ralph Miliband has responded by arguing that Labour's policies were not really 'socialist' at all. Labour ministers' tributes to the loyalty and co-operation of their officials 'may be less a comment on the conversion of those advisers to socialist principles than on the Government's failure to act upon these principles'. 'The notion that the programme of the Attlee Government was sufficiently "socialist" to confront top civil servants with a problem need not be taken seriously', he insists. 'Civil servants in Britain have never had to confront a government with a "socialist programme"; or at least they have never had to confront a government determined to carry out such a programme'. This approach to the problem is not very useful, however. It may fit in with a particular – and debatable – theory about the nature of the Labour Party's socialism, but it really evades the question. Miliband's redefinition of Labour's programme as 'not truly radical', it has been argued, 'effectively undermines the point by moving it away from an assertion which can be tested against the evidence to a hypothesis about what the Civil Service *would* do or would be *likely* to do *if* it were to be confronted by a radical government – which cannot be tested at all'.[19]

'On balance, evidence of civil service obstruction of the activities and policies of the Labour government is very hard to uncover', Kenneth O. Morgan has written in his authoritative history of the Attlee administration. It would be nonsense to claim that officials 'sabotaged' the policies of Dalton and then Cripps at the Treasury or of Bevan at the Ministry of Health; and Bevin was certainly not the Foreign Office's poodle.[20] Labour's ministerial team had the twin advantages of a five-year apprenticeship in government in the Churchill coalition and a bureaucracy ready to build upon wartime developments in economic planning and social reconstruction.

The period of the wartime coalition had been crucial both for Labour and for Whitehall. Only two of Attlee's 1945 Cabinet had not held government office during the war (Bevan and Shinwell). The party's leaders knew the problems and the debates on options from the inside, they understood the machinery of government and knew personally the leading officials. 'In fact, no postwar British Cabinet has been better prepared for power than Attlee's', Peter Hennessy has claimed. This experience had definitely not fuelled Laski-type suspicions of the bureaucracy, quite the reverse. Moreover, there had been a major transformation of the civil service during the war years. When the coalition broke up Cripps told Chuter Ede that

> all his officials in bidding him goodbye expressed the hope that he would be back. They added they were not allowed to speak as politicians but nevertheless their good wishes were with him. He thought the changed attitude of the Civil Service remarkable.

'By the end of the war a new administrative order was rapidly coming into existence', according to Paul Addison.

New peacetime departments were in place, new administrative procedures were at an advanced stage of preparation, and new mentalities were ingrained in officials. . . . The Labour manifesto of 1945, *Let us Face the Future*, was superimposed on an administrative revolution that was already taking place. In effect, the party was proposing to carry it through and extend it in a socialist direction. This helps to explain the speed with which the Attlee government was able to implement its remarkable legislative programme of 1945-8.[21]

The wartime developments in the official machine and in civil service thinking – reflecting a wider shift in elite as well as popular opinion – went far to render Laski's pre-war warnings redundant.

Labour's plans in key areas – economic planning, nationalization and the welfare state – were fairly vague. Without adequate blueprints, ministers inevitably had to rely upon civil servants to work out detailed schemes, which predictably reflected Whitehall's traditional methods of operation. Shinwell later complained that many of his officials at Fuel and Power were 'apathetic or antagonistic to nationalization'. If this was so, it did not hold up the momentum of the government's nationalization programme over its first three years, despite the fact that the relevant measures had to be devised almost from scratch as the/party had made no detailed preparations.[22] There were, in any case, 'many instances of radical impulses at work within the civil service machine', as Kenneth O. Morgan has pointed out. This was not just a matter of some of the key individuals advising ministers on economic policy in the Economic Section of the Cabinet Office and even in the Treasury having socialist backgrounds or progressive views. In a wider sense, there was 'in the Treasury, as elsewhere in Whitehall, a powerful commitment to economic change and planned reconstruction after the stagnation of the thirties, and the new initiatives of the war years', in Morgan's words.[23]

Left-wingers in the party frequently attacked the government's foreign policy, claiming that Bevin was disregarding socialist principles and carrying out the policy of his permanent officials. Laski, for instance, complained of him falling 'an immediate victim to the worst gang in the F.O.' and being 'fooled with fantastic ease by the professionals who capture him'. At the Labour Party Conference in 1946 and again in 1947, Bevin's critics protested that the class backgrounds of Foreign Office officials made them unsympathetic to a socialist foreign policy, proposing that obstructive diplomats should be removed and recruitment methods overhauled. He vigorously rebutted the charges:

> Now it is said that these men do not carry out my policies. I deny that. I beg of you not to try to introduce the wrong principle into the Civil Service. I have had a good experience now for six years. What the Civil Service likes is a Minister who knows his mind and tells the officials what to do. They will then do it. If it is wrong the Minister must take responsibility and not blame the Civil Service. That I am prepared to do.

The staff of the Foreign Office had apparently been relieved to get Bevin as Secretary of State rather than Dalton, whom they disliked on personality and policy grounds and whom they feared would want to get his own men into some of the key posts. But it would be a mistake to portray Bevin as some kind of puppet, with conservative diplomats manipulating the strings. 'Bevin's foreign policy was vividly his own', Kenneth O. Morgan has written; the stamp of his personality and ideas was unmistakable. He was fully backed up by Attlee and had the weight to get his way in Cabinet. Bevin's officials were not 'forcing their views insidiously on a reluctant or confused minister'. Foreign Office views and advice were in any case not uniform, as Morgan noted, but rather 'covered a very broad political and ideological spectrum'. If the government failed to pursue a 'socialist foreign policy', that was because of the hard facts of Britain's international situation – in which the Labour leaders, if not the party's rank-and-file, had been schooled during the war – and not because of Foreign Office machinations.[24]

The accounts of Labour ministers, detailed historical studies of particular areas of policy and the recollections of civil servants themselves all support Peter Hennessey's view that 'by and large, late-forties Whitehall approached the "team model" of ministers and officials pulling together in the same direction in an atmosphere of mutual respect.' Only during the devaluation crisis of 1949 is there much evidence that ministers had doubts about the loyalty of at least some of their officials. In 1946, when J. P. W. Mallalieu had attacked senior Treasury officials as all Tories in his column in *Tribune*, Sir Edward Bridges had complained to Number 10 that 'the propagation of this kind of stuff is bad for the morale of the Civil Service and is contrary to the public interest'. He also took up the matter with Dalton and eventually Mallalieu was persuaded to go along to the Treasury for a friendly chat with Bridges and to smooth ruffled feathers. Bridges took the opportunity to lecture him on the impartiality of the civil service, as he noted in the files:

I then explained that the experience and training of Civil Servants generally led them to adopt a view of political matters different from that of politicians of either Party. We looked at matters from the point of view of their effect on administration and that, from this standpoint, there were things in the programmes of both the major Parties which we disliked and others equally which we liked. Our attitude therefore became one apart from Party and although, of course, we took a great interest in political matters, we were not filled with suppressed desires to push policies either to the Right or to the Left.[25]

At times in mid-1949, however, it seems as if Labour ministers grappling with the sterling and foreign reserves crisis did believe that some of their mandarins *were* trying to push policy to the right. At one meeting of the Cabinet's Economic Policy Committee the officials were asked to leave the room, and according to Hugh Gaitskell, Cripps, the Chancellor, said, 'One of my difficulties is that my official advisers are all "liberals" and I cannot really rely on them to carry through a "socialist" [sic] policy.' Douglas Jay, a Treasury junior minister, told Dalton that 'not only are the officials not in sympathy with our policy, but that they are half expecting us to be beaten at the election, and are beginning to think in terms of a Tory Government and a Tory policy'. Dalton himself believed that 'officials served Ministers well so long as they thought the Govt. would go on. If they had doubts on this, they wavered and were tempted to make minutes for the record, to show to successors'. Gaitskell was also suspicious of the Treasury's motives and complained about the manoeuvres of 'the underground Civil Service'. Even Attlee, according to Dalton, was concerned that he was being served up from the Treasury and the Bank of England 'arguments which he thinks are fallacious on [the] evil effects of our public expenditure'.[26]

Some of this talk probably reflects the alarmism of weary (and in Cripps's case, ill) ministers under pressure. What is clear is that there were divisions of opinion at both ministerial and official levels over how to react to the currency crisis. Cripps was strongly opposed to devaluation of the pound. Some Treasury officials, including the permanent secretary, Bridges, along with the Governor of the Bank of England, were advising against devaluation and in favour of large cuts in public expenditure, involving changes in policy, to 'restore confidence'. The ministerial complaints noted above appear to have been about this group. Other key economic advisers, however, had for some time wanted devaluation and – given vital political backing by the younger economics ministers, particularly Gaitskell – their arguments finally prevailed. The lesson seems to be that ministers in the end took their own decisions on this matter though along the way there were some tough battles with deflationist Treasury mandarins.

Accounts of the in-fighting were soon circulating outside White-hall and were seized on by the civil service's left-wing critics. According to *Tribune*, for instance:

> Already civil servants are well-known to be suffering from that peculiar form of suspended animation which afflicts them when a General Election is in the offing. There is a hesitancy to advance with new plans. There is a reluctance to initiate, because at the back of the civil servant's mind is the thought that his present masters may soon be changed and the direction of today's work may be reversed. The higher the civil servant the worse the disease. So many of the top-ranking officials are ingrained with a Tory-consciousness that, in the hope of a Tory victory, they recommend action opposed to the spirit of this Government, and in accordance with the likely views of a Tory administration. Hence the pressure on the Government from its official advisers to make cuts in the social services before the Washington talks [preceding devaluation].

The left-wing backbenchers of the 'Keep Left' group, in a pamphlet published in January 1950, argued that 'devaluation could have been avoided if the Treasury and the Bank of England had followed a socialist policy last spring'. They blamed officials' 'liberal consciences' for preventing effective action being taken to check the flight of 'funk money' – the MPs wanted tighter exchange controls – and said that there should be 'changes of personnel' in the Treasury and the Bank. As in 1946, Bridges complained to the Chancellor and Cripps wrote to the authors, repudiating their remarks as 'wholly unjustified', as 'an implied attack upon myself as unable to control my staff'. Whatever his private feelings in July 1949, Cripps now asserted 'very definitely and specifically that the policy in this matter has been laid down by myself after full consideration and has been most faithfully carried out by my staff and the Bank of England'.[27]

There is no doubt that the Attlee government was heavily dependent on support and advice from the official machine in formulating and then implementing its policies. Sir Alec Cairncross, then one of the government's economic advisers, has argued that the Labour ministers were 'the reluctant pupils of their officials' because the economic problems they faced were not those they had expected and the solutions were not of their devising. 'On one economic issue after another . . . they were slow to grasp the true options of policy and had great difficulty in reaching sensible conclusions'. This is a perceptive judgement by a well-informed 'insider', but it is fair to ask whether in this respect the Labour government of 1945–51 was much different from its predecessors and successors of both parties. It is the duty of the civil service to ensure that ministers are fully apprised of the problems, constraints and options they face. But then it is also its duty to make the best of the policy ministers lay down and to put into effect their decisions, for which the ministers are responsible. And that is what the civil service in the Attlee years did. Hugh Dalton made perhaps the same point as Cairncross, but in a more positive way, when he recorded in his diary, following his return to office in 1948, how he was 'impressed . . . with the efficiency of the Higher Civil Service, making crisp sense of ministerial wavering diffuseness, and preparing admirable papers making it as easy as possible for ministers to choose between clear alternatives'.[28] This is not a picture of civil service 'obstruction' or 'sabotage' but rather of the civil service playing its proper and legitimate role in the system.

As Kenneth O. Morgan has noted, 'In return for its loyalty, the civil service was not subjected to any significant change.' The Attlee government brushed aside outside critics' calls for a large-scale restructuring of the service's recruitment, training, organization and management (see chapter 3). Whatever left-wingers such as Laski may have warned in the 1930s, Labour ministers in practice saw few major problems with the way Whitehall was working for them in this period. 'Any failures by the Labour government between 1945 and 1951 can hardly be blamed on pressures from the institutional framework that it inherited', Morgan rightly concluded. 'The civil service, like the monarchy and the House of Lords, cannot be made a scapegoat for the non-fulfilment of the socialist millennium'.[29]

THE EXPERIENCE OF OFFICE: 1964–70 AND 1974–9

Lansbury and Laski rather than Morrison and Attlee provided the (implicit) reference points for many in the party seeking to understand Labour's experience in office 1964–70 and 1974–9. The disappointing record of the 1964–70 government, according to Marcia Williams, the Personal and Political Secretary to the Prime Minister, could be attributed largely to Labour's 'defeats' in the 'battle . . . against the Civil Service'. 'Whitehall: The Other Opposition' was the suggestive title of a *New Statesman* article in March 1974 warning about the problems the new Labour government would face in trying to control the mandarins. The 1964–70 government, it claimed, had found itself 'baulked and its policies emasculated by the civil service . . . there is reason to hope that the civil service will be more strongly contested [*sic*] this time'. Even before the government fell in 1979, however, its left-wing critics were alleging that officials were impeding or actively sabotaging socialist policies. In a book published soon after Labour's defeat, explaining *What Went Wrong*, Michael Meacher indicted the process of government itself, condemning Whitehall's 'abuse of power and obstruction of democracy'.[30]

Such views were to become almost taken for granted on the left in the 1970s and 1980s, underpinning support for reforms designed to check bureaucratic and strengthen ministerial power and to increase government's democratic accountability. It has to be said, though, that there is no evidence that most Labour ministers and frontbenchers would go along with these accounts of life in Whitehall in the Wilson–Callaghan governments. Keith Middlemas, analysing the 1964–70 administration, has written how, 'Acquaintance with actual individuals in the mandarinate since 1964 had converted most Labour Cabinet Ministers, like their 1945–51 predecessors, to an admiration of the lucid professionalism and detachment of their officials'. Roy Jenkins gave a textbook description in 1971 when he recalled that, 'except in unusual circumstances', a minister does not have to 'batter his head against a brick wall of determined departmental opposition. If he knows what he wants to do he will not in general have much difficulty in getting his policy carried out'. After 1979, however, some ex-ministers on the right of the party did go some way to endorse the sort of criticisms more usually associated with the left. The civil service 'is a beautifully designed and effective braking mechanism. It produces a hundred well-argued answers against initiative and change', according to Shirley Williams. David

Owen recalled clashes with some of his staff in the Foreign Office who 'seemed to want to carry on conducting foreign policy on the lines that they thought right, irrespective of what ministers wanted'. And Joel Barnett, on the basis of his time as Chief Secretary to the Treasury, bluntly stated that ' "the system" can defeat Ministers'.[31]

Marcia Williams strongly believed that 'Ministers, and particularly Prime Ministers, should automatically suspect many of the activities of the Civil Service'. This drew a magisterial rebuke from Douglas Jay, whose own views reflected his service in wartime Whitehall and in Attlee's and Wilson's governments:

> The way not to approach the senior civil service is to assume *a priori* that they are a sinister and hostile conspiracy, to treat them as such, and then to adduce the resentment one has oneself created as evidence that one's suspicions were justified. This inferiority obsession is not unknown in the Labour Party . . .

It does seem to be the case, however, that a number of incoming ministers in 1964 *were* suspicious of the civil service, fearing that official attitudes would have been strongly coloured by thirteen years of Conservative rule. In fact, these doubts were largely unfounded. 'Most of the senior officials in 1964, far from being drenched with Toryism, recalled the Labour years of 1945–51 with real affection', judged Peter Hennessy. A contemporary observer wrote vividly:

> The formalities, the hierarchies, the architecture, the continuing background of the palace and its surroundings, all seemed to belong to a single conservative conspiracy of 'they': and to find that 'they' were divided, and that many of them were reformers and even Socialists, came as the same kind of shock as missionaries might feel when they find a remote tribe already believing in Jesus.

'There was good will for the incoming Labour Government', a Cabinet minister's civil service private secretary later recalled, contrasting the approaches of two of its key ministers: 'Jim Callaghan's great strength, after a slow start, was to learn to use it. George [Brown] never did'.[32]

Harold Wilson himself was clearly something like a permanent secretary *manqué*. Although as Leader of the Opposition before 1964 he had identified himself with fashionable modernizing thinking, and as a wartime 'temporary' he had apparently grouched about the dominance of the elite Administrative Class, as premier he displayed 'a profound reverence for the orders and mysteries of the civil service', according to Alan Watkins, writing in 1966. 'He would be most upset if he ever thought he had caused serious offence to a permanent secretary'. Bernard Donoughue, who was the head of the Number 10 Policy Unit 1974–9, also testified that Wilson 'was ever respectful of the sleek civil service machine. Having served early on in the Cabinet Office secretariat, his respect for the hierarchy, with the Cabinet Secretary sitting at the peak, was established for life'. Wilson's close relationship with Cabinet Secretary Sir Burke Trend was an important feature of the 1964–70 government, to the dismay of his old political allies and his 'Kitchen Cabinet'. Marcia Williams complained:

> It is the fact that he does have such an admiration for and such a working knowledge of 'the System' that he tends to lean over backwards in his relationship towards it. He gives it the benefit of the doubt. He doesn't really want to argue with it. He admires the way it is organized and its methods of working. He admires its efficiency and he is often myopic about its failings and its short-comings and its inefficiencies, and this is a great drawback.

The problem, Clive Ponting argues, was that Wilson's political style and his institutional conservatism reinforced each other. Absorbed into the Whitehall ethos, he came to regard the smooth processing of business through the official machine as the equivalent of successfully dealing with real problems. Other Labour ministers, too, criticized Ponting, 'settled down to the routines and rituals of Whitehall life, content to be in office'. And from 1966, he says, 'it became clear that in many senses the government was not governing but simply administering'.[33] It would certainly seem that Wilson's personal commitment to civil service reform was pretty shallow, the issue being hived-off to the Fulton Committee inquiry, whose eventual report was regarded as a missed opportunity by the really committed reformers (see chapter 4).

When it was put forward in the Labour Party's evidence to the Fulton Committee, Wilson scorned the idea that some ministers were tools of their civil servants because of the amount of information kept from them and because of the way in which interdepartmental official committees hammered out policies without a ministerial steer.[34] But this was exactly the sort of conspiratorial view of how the system operated against socialist ministers that was held by Richard Crossman, whose diaries, when they were published in the 1970s, seemed to bear out the standard left-wing criticisms of the bureaucrats. In the 1950s Crossman had talked about ministers being little more than public relations officers to their departments. In office, he constantly complained in his diary about his struggles with his departmental officials and particularly 'the Dame' (his permanent secretary at Housing, Evelyn Sharp), about how ministers were undermined on the Whitehall grapevine and their decisions pre-cooked and pre-empted by inter-departmental committees, and about the all-pervasive and malign influence of the Treasury. Of course, an important – but often overlooked – theme of the Crossman diaries is how clever and determined ministers (such as Crossman . . .) can triumph over this opposition. He certainly put his finger on some crucial problems when he bemoaned the effects of poor policy preparation in Opposition and of departmental fragmentation in Cabinet, but there are none the less some big question marks that must be put against Crossman's version of the experience of ministers in Whitehall.[35]

Crossman had had no experience of ministerial office at all (and precious little Shadow Cabinet experience) before 1964. As the incident cited at the start of this chapter shows – and this is seen throughout his diaries – he had simply no idea how to use the civil service machine properly in order to reach his political goals. His combative and contemptuous attitude antagonized his officials; he misinterpreted their actions and motives. He was amazingly ignorant of some of the basic features of the Whitehall set-up, confessing that neither he nor Thomas Balogh (supposedly a Labour 'expert' on the civil service) had known about the system of inter-departmental committees before entering government. This would suggest that he had never learned anything from talking to Attlee's ministers about their time in office or even that he had never read the second volume of Hugh Dalton's memoirs, published in 1957, in which that veteran former minister had sounded off about 'a jamboree of other Ministers' officials in an irresponsible Sub-Ministerial underworld' and denounced official committees as 'an indefensible excrescence on the British Constitution'.[36]

The same picture of ministers locked in combat with the Whitehall machine was described by Barbara Castle, in a talk to a seminar of senior civil servants published as a newspaper article, 'Mandarin Power', in 1973: 'I am suddenly moved into an atmosphere of ill-concealed hostility . . . the entrenched phalanxes moved in on me . . . the Permanent Secretary trying to wear me down . . . one person against the vast department'. The civil service possessed tremendous negative power: 'I thought, looking back at the Labour government, how effectively the civil servants impeded us by saying we could not do some of the things our successors are now doing with remarkable facility'. The Castle diaries, recording her day-to-day experiences and impressions as a minister, are however not so critical of the civil service as either 'Mandarin Power' or the Crossman diaries. She relates her doubts that her civil servants were too sympathetic to the Treasury view and so fought public expenditure cuts only half-heartedly, but there are many references to the loyalty and co-operation of officials and to the sense of solidarity, even camaraderie, in a crisis. 'Good government depends on the inter-relation of two things: a civil service with initiative . . . and activist Ministers', she noted at one point. She records her remarks over a farewell drink with her officials at the DHSS after being sacked by Callaghan in 1976:

> 'What I shall miss most is the comradeship . . . ' It was the comradeship of battle in which we all pulled and plotted together for victory. I told them I had never accepted the conventional criticisms of civil servants. It was their duty to tell the Minister frankly the dangers and snags they saw in her policy: 'It is far better that they should be voiced and faced in this room than for the Minister to encounter them for the first time at the dispatch box or in the press.' We needed strong civil servants and a strong Minister to digest their advice and make what use of it she saw fit.

Perhaps harassed ministers heavily dependent on their officials to stay afloat see virtues in the machine whereas Opposition lends a critical distance. Or perhaps in Opposition some left-wing Labour politicians feel the need to sound more critical of the mandarins than they privately are when in office. Whatever the reason, Barbara Castle turns out to be a less useful witness for the prosecution (of obstructive, anti-Labour bureaucrats) than might at first appear.[37]

Tony Benn, in his diaries from the 1964–70 government, certainly complains about 'the Civil Service network' and about problems with his officials but he only really developed a full-blown critical analysis of bureaucratic power after he had moved sharply to the left in the 1970s. Indeed his technocratic thinking in the 1960s led him to criticize the civil service for its lack of dynamism, ideas and initiative, and to back the Fulton Report, without apparently seeing that a more professional and expert bureaucracy might also be a more powerful one. In the 1980s Benn was to condemn Treasury thinking – 'It has its own policy. I suppose you could argue that the economic failure of Britain since the war could be attributed primarily to the Treasury because they've [sic] always been in power' – but at one Cabinet committee meeting in the late 1960s, he had suggested that all civil servants should be judged in their annual reports on the basis of whether they had economized on public spending – the 'Treasury view' with a vengeance![38]

Benn's thesis, as it was presented after 1979, was that civil service power has grown to such an extent that it threatens the working of British parliamentary democracy. Outlining (in a lecture in 1980) the 'process of civil service containment successfully practised against both Conservative and Labour governments over the last thirty years', Benn argued that

> it would be a mistake to suppose – as some socialists have suggested – that the senior ranks of the civil service are active Conservatives posing as impartial administrators. . . . The problem arises from the fact that the civil service sees itself as being above the party battle, with a political position of its own to defend against all-comers, including governments armed with their philosophy and programme.

In a BBC radio interview he explained: 'The deal that the civil service offers a minister is this: if you do what we want you to do, we will help you publicly to pretend that you're implementing the manifesto on which you were elected'. Whitehall preferred consensus politics: 'they are always trying to steer incoming governments back to the policy of the outgoing government, minus the mistakes that the civil service thought the outgoing government made'. 'It is not a coincidence that governments of both parties appear to end up with policies very similar to each other, and which are in every case a great deal more acceptable to Whitehall than were the manifestos upon which they were originally elected'. The techniques the civil service used to get its way included setting the overall framework of policy within which problems and options were considered; the manipulation of information; mobilizing against ministers on the Whitehall grapevine; mobilizing external pressures (press leaks, the IMF, the EEC); and so on. Major reforms were needed to open up government, restore parliamentary control and secure effective ministerial control over the civil service.[39]

Benn's difficult relations with his civil servants in the 1974–9 government were well leaked at the time, but he was then, of course, unable to speak out in the way he did after 1979. His allies and supporters on the Labour left, however, were free from the constraints of office and able to develop and publicize their own critique. Brian Sedgemore, Benn's PPS at the Department of Energy 1977–8 (who had, incidentally, been a civil servant at Housing when Crossman was the minister and who thought that 'what Crossman wrote was a brilliant description of what was going on'), drafted the vitriolic alternative first chapter to the Expenditure Committee's 1977 report on the civil service which was backed by all except one of the Labour MPs on the committee but voted down by the rest of the members. Sedgemore saw the problem of civil service power as linked to the development of corporatism and argued that both were threats to democracy. He accused civil servants of usurping the role of their political masters and of seeking to govern the country according to their own interests, values and backgrounds. 'Some bureaucracies, unlike our own, have actually governed effectively and efficiently. Whereas the French bureaucracy has sometimes proved itself undemocratic and effective the British bureaucracy has proven to be undemocratic and ineffective in the post-war years', he asserted. 'Our own bureaucracy is more dangerous than some other bureaucracies because it is an intelligent and hard-working bureaucracy'. Committed to the maintenance of the status quo, Whitehall had 'obstructed the radical Selsdon-man policies of the last [Heath] Conservative government' and had 'frustrated the more socialist policies of this Labour government'.

> Civil servants at the Department of Industry have been culpable in frustrating the interventionist industrial policies of the current government. In this case political bias may have played a part. . . . The Department of Trade contains civil servants who are steeped in nineteenth century Board of Trade attitudes . . . [and who] are also known to be hostile to any meaningful form of industrial democracy although it is Labour Party policy. . . . The Home Office, the graveyard of free-thinking since the days of Lord Sidmouth early in the nineteenth century, is stuffed with reactionaries ruthlessly pursuing their own reactionary policies . . . some Foreign Office officials interpret being a good European as being synonymous with selling out British interests. The Vichy mentality which undoubtedly exists in some parts of our Foreign Office does not to the best of our knowledge and belief reflect the views of Her Majesty's ministers.

As for the Treasury, it 'had messed up everything over the past 25 years'. In the Commons in January 1979 Sedgemore went on to make specific allegations of civil service obstruction and sabotage directed against Tony Benn at the Departments of Industry and Energy, providing more details in 1980 in his book *The Secret Constitution.*[40]

From the start of its work it was clear that the party's Machinery of Government Study Group, set up in 1976, had already made up its mind and went along with this sort of approach. As an agenda paper prepared in Labour's Research Department indicating the scope of the group's inquiries put it:

> The publication of the Crossman memoirs [*sic*] has underlined the crucial *political* role played by the Whitehall machine in the *formation* of Government policy – often completely at variance with policy-making within the Party; and too, in frustrating the *implementation* of policies hammered out by the Movement. . . . The Whitehall machine, it is clear, is an important political force in its own right. Yet it is one which, on the evidence, is not at all sympathetic to Labour's call for 'a fundamental and irreversible shift in the balance of power in favour of working people and their families.'

A subsequent Research Department paper argued that the

> slant of [civil service] power, whilst not directly conspiratorial or overtly anti-reformist, is certainly ideologically towards the maintenance, albeit with improved operation, of the existing socio-economic system. . . . A variety of tactics can be and are used by civil servants to isolate and weaken a Departmental Minister who breaks with the broad Whitehall consensus or who seeks major changes in the power structure affecting class relations.

Top civil servants' class backgrounds and close, almost collusive, links with big business (including secondments and moving into the private sector on retirement) were held to be important factors here. In the event, the group's report, approved by the NEC and party conference in 1978, rather eschewed a hard-edged class and ideological analysis, actually repeating Fulton-style proposals for *greater* interchange between Whitehall and industry. But it did insist that there was a problem of civil service power – analysing the dimensions of this in a familiar manner – and that reform was necessary in order to strengthen ministerial control of policy-making and accountability to Parliament.[41]

What are we to make of these analyses of the role and power of the civil service in relation to the Labour governments of the 1960s and 1970s? Is the power of a conservative civil service a convincing explanation for the failure of the Wilson and Callaghan administrations to meet their objectives? The short answer must be: no, it is not. The failures of those governments were *political* in origin rather than due to bureaucratic subversion. 'The conspiracy theory of civil servants working against radical ministers will not stand up', as a Fabian Society study group on the machinery of government convincingly argued in 1982.

> It is doubtful if the civil service as a whole has a conscious political position of its own to defend. A united government can rapidly secure the support of the civil service in carrying through major and sharp changes of policy, and a strong minister – with the support of the Prime Minister and his colleagues – can impose his will on the government machine.

Lord Crowther-Hunt, who believed that the power of the civil service *had* grown, nevertheless admitted that 'for the most part civil servants do seem to change course when the electorate throws out one party and gives a majority to the opposition instead'. Government departments '*will* be changing directions as far as the major policies are concerned'. That 'successive governments do make major changes of direction and policies', he thought, was 'testimony to the fact that either civil servants have been co-operating fully with ministers or that ministers have successfully overcome them'. An example he gave from the 1974–9 period was the emergence of schemes for devolution to Scotland and Wales. Civil servants were opposed to devolution, but so too were most Labour ministers and MPs. The government's devolution proposals, he argues, 'represented the triumph of a handful of ministers both over their colleagues and over the government machine as a whole'. The schemes had their defects, but these could have been remedied if ministers had really wanted them to be.[42]

Tony Benn's experience at the Department of Industry 1974–5 suggests that when a Labour Prime Minister and Cabinet are clear about what they want, they do not find the civil service blocking their way, though as in that case, a departmental minister out of step with his political colleagues may well choose to complain of civil service obstruction. Officials at the Industry Department and elsewhere in Whitehall were clearly unhappy about key aspects of the interventionist industrial policy set out in Labour's programme and which Benn was committed to. More importantly, the party leadership was also unhappy about that policy but had been unable to block it in Opposition. If Benn and his policy had had the confidence and the backing of the Prime Minister and the Labour Cabinet the story would have been different. But, as his permanent secretary pointed out, and as Benn recognized himself, he was a radical minister in a non-radical government. Benn does in fact acknowledge that 'all the issues concerning the role, power, influence and authority of the civil service . . . take you right back to the alliance of mutual loyalty and support between Number 10 Downing Street and the mandarins' and believes that 'any major reform of the work of the civil service would require a major change in the powers of the prime minister'. The problem is the structure of power as a whole and not just the power of the civil service. Frances Morrell, Benn's special adviser and an influential member of Labour's Machinery of Government Study Group in the 1970s, also admitted that when a Prime Minister's wishes conflicted with the wishes of a departmental minister, officials could be placed in a difficult position. Her argument that 'it cannot be the primary responsibility of public officials to ensure that manifesto pledges are carried out when ministers decide otherwise' was, however, clearly intended to put the Labour Cabinet in the dock for the abandonment or watering-down of the party programme.[43]

One problem, then, is that Labour governments are not necessarily united entities, so that what might at first appear to be bureaucratic obstruction of a minister is in fact something rather different. Indeed, the Labour government's divisions about EEC membership and the Cabinet's 'agreement to differ' prior to the 1975 referendum also raised this question of whether the loyalty of civil servants was to their departmental minister or to the government as a whole, when these were pulling in opposite directions. And conversely Whitehall itself is not in all respects a united entity. Shirley Williams insisted that 'it is simply wrong to describe the civil service as a collectivity as being either pro-Conservative or pro-Socialist'. Each department had its own ethos and outlook, usually reflecting its last major achievement or reform. Thus the DHSS – champion of the National Health Service – 'has a tendency to seem to defend Labour Government achievements rather than Conservative Government achievements', while the Home Office, with a pronounced law-and-order perspective, tended to be a 'Conservative department' when it came to major reforms, she argued. Furthermore, it would be wrong to see each individual department as a monolith. Brian Sedgemore, a supporter of Tony Benn, admitted that at the Department of Energy there was harmony between Benn and officials on the oil side, most friction with civil servants arising on EEC and nuclear power issues.[44] It would seem that life in Whitehall is not lived in a state of permanent conflict and struggle between ministers and civil servants. Analyses that focus on adversarial relations between ministers and governments on the one side, and the civil service on the other oversimplify and distort. Relations are complex and fluid, and the lines of division are more often than not to be found not *between* the political and bureaucratic elements in government but *within* them, as alliances of ministers *and* officials compete with each other to advance particular goals or defend common interests.

The Treasury, as we have seen, has long been a favourite bogey figure for the Labour left in seeking to explain the failures of economic policy of Labour governments, and the 1960s and 1970s were no exception. After 1964 the ill-fated Department of Economic Affairs failed to break the Treasury's predominance over economic policy, handicapped as it was by an ill-thought-out division of functions between it and the Treasury and by a lack of direct executive powers on key issues, primarily because of *political* decisions giving priority to the defence of the exchange rate which ensured that the Treasury would inevitably come out on top in the inter-departmental struggle. Whitehall 'welcome[d] restoration of fiscal and monetary orthodoxy after the end of 1967', as Keith Middlemas noted, but it was the inescapable facts of Britain's economic situation rather than bureaucratic fiat that dictated policy. Roy Jenkins, Chancellor 1967–70, seemed to see eye to eye with his senior officials but he was certainly not their stooge.[45]

David Coates argued that 'Treasury conservatism stood as a major barrier to Labour Party radicalism' in the 1974–9 period. There is evidence that senior ministers and their political aides sometimes suspected the motives of senior Treasury mandarins, but the Labour government took its own decisions rather than rubber-stamping the Treasury's. Joe Haines, Harold Wilson's press secretary 1974–6, recalled a constant struggle 'against being suffocated by the civil service', Whitehall's 'contempt' for the government's manifesto and its 'instinct for coalition', and accused the Treasury of attempting 'to make the Government put its policies totally in reverse, abandon its manifesto commitments and commit suicide' by trying to 'bounce' it into introducing a compulsory pay policy in 1975. Had they succeeded, he says, 'it would have been a civilian coup against the Government'. But the point is that the Treasury failed: at the crucial moment, the Prime Minister apparently wobbled, but his key Number 10 political advisers steadied him, and the Chancellor then changed his mind and abandoned his own officials' proposals, and the result was that Labour's pay policy was a voluntary rather than a statutory one.[46]

A year later, during the 1976 IMF crisis, there were claims (believed by some ministers and Number 10 advisers) that some Treasury officials were secretly briefing the US Treasury and the IMF in order to increase pressure on the government for large public spending cuts. Additional pressure for expenditure restraint or cuts came, it has been suggested, through manipulation of the statistics on which ministerial decisions were based. Behind the public expenditure figures and the public sector borrowing requirement (PSBR) were numerous assumptions and estimtes, and there were suspicions that the Treasury inflated PSBR forecasts to create a crisis atmosphere and panic ministers into large cuts. Denis Healey has said that if he had been given accurate figures in 1976 the government would never have needed to go to the IMF at all, but he does not blame the Treasury for this – outside forecasters did not have a better record. Treasury officials, it is clear, were deeply divided on the issue of public spending cuts in 1976 – there were 'hawks' who backed the IMF line and wanted very large cuts, but they were a minority; other officials opposed cuts or at least came round to accept them but not on the scale the IMF wanted (in the event, this was the course the Cabinet adopted).

Interestingly enough, Joel Barnett unconsciously echoed the worries of Labour ministers in 1949 when he felt in early 1979 (and Callaghan and Healey apparently shared his suspicions) that the Treasury, perhaps sensing that the writing was on the wall for the Labour government, was submitting papers on public spending cuts that would have been more suitable for Conservative rather than Labour ministers. It should be pointed out, however, that the introduction of cash limits in 1976, which led to massive underspending against targets (at times on a scale matching the Cabinet's planned cuts), received strong political support from Labour's Treasury ministers Healey and Barnett, support which enabled Sir Leo Pliatzky, the senior official in charge of public expenditure, to overcome opposition to these from within the Treasury itself. On the wider questions of economic theory and management, it would appear that there was a spectrum of opinion in the Treasury, from unreconstructed Keynesians through to monetarists; there was no monolithic 'Treasury line'. As Prime Minister, Callaghan was evidently rather wary, if not mistrustful, of the Treasury, setting up his highly secret 'Economic Seminar' – a small group of senior ministers, officials and Number 10 advisers – to tighten his political grip on the key economic discussions and decisions (most Labour ministers only discovered the existence of this group from the press after the government had left office!). Overall, the conclusion has to be, as Martin Holmes argued, that 'Treasury advice, 1974–9, though influential was far from decisive with the government'. Joel Barnett rightly believed that any blame for the government's economic record had to be placed firmly on political shoulders.[47]

In his Godkin Lectures at Harvard in 1970, Richard Crossman asked himself the question:

> If the Labour Government [of 1964–70] has made mistakes and suffered failures, would I attribute these failures and mistakes to the Civil Service? My answer is 'no' . . . I would say that normally when a Government fails it is not because the Civil Service blocks its plans, but because the Government team has not had a clear enough sense of direction. A Government which really knows where it is going, a Government which has a series of measures ready, prepared, well thought out, has to hand . . . an instrument which will enable it to carry out all it wants.

In the 1930s, Laski too had seen that unless a government had come in knowing what it wanted to do in some detail, it had to 'trust to the ingenuity of the civil service to improvise a policy after office has been taken'. It was hardly surprising that departments should, in those circumstances, be able to impose their own orthodoxies upon unprepared ministers. A party's programme had to be more than just wishful thinking. As Laski put it, 'This predicates, of course, for the modern political party something like a civil service of its own. It must have at its disposal not merely men who can write well-sounding propaganda leaflets'. However, Labour's policy preparations in Opposition before 1964 were characteristically flimsy. The party had no detailed plans worked out to deal with the sterling crises it encountered immediately on taking office. Almost as soon as he entered the Cabinet in 1964, Crossman was complaining that 'what we lacked was any comprehensive, thoroughly thought-out Government strategy. The policies are being thrown together.'[48] This weakness was compounded by the fact that, after Labour's thirteen years out of office, the 1964 ministerial team was largely ignorant of the techniques of governing (the 1974 Cabinet was, however, very experienced). Further, Wilson's regular reshuffles meant that too many ministers were switched between departments just as they were beginning to become effective in their posts. None of this can be blamed on the civil service: Labour's mistakes were its own.

The party *did* develop detailed economic and industrial policies in Opposition before 1974, but it was obvious from the start that the main party leadership were unhappy about these. Add in the post-OPEC oil price rise and the deflationary reactions of other western states, together with the failure of the Social Contract to reduce inflation while the government delivered its side of the bargain with the unions in the shape of rapid increases in public spending in 1974–5, and the non-achievement of party policy goals and the 1974–9 government's problems can be explained in political terms and without scapegoating the civil service. The government seemed to be just reacting to events from 1975 onwards. In the summer of 1977 Tony Crosland complained in his diary, 'Now no sense of direction and no priorities: only pragmatism, empiricism, safety first, £ [*sic*] supreme'.[49] Labour had been there before, in the 1964–70 period, as numerous similar quotes from the Crossman diaries would show. Labour ministers rather than officials bore the primary responsibility for that state of affairs, and they deservedly paid the price for it.

REINFORCING LABOUR MINISTERS

The idea that, in order to supplement the information and advice coming from the civil service machine and to develop a stronger political control over policy-making, Labour ministers need political allies in their departments can be traced back to the inquest into the first MacDonald government. Before Labour took office in 1924, MacDonald had been warned by UDC-ers in the party that at the Foreign Office he 'must have someone he could trust in charge of the private secretariat, of publicity, and of Russia'. He had ignored this advice and, suspicious of its role in the Zinoviev Letter affair, the party's International Advisory Committee in early 1925 proposed sweeping changes in the organization of the Foreign Office. Action was said to be necessary because of 'the profound distrust of the personnel of the Foreign Office entertained by the Labour Party . . . the entire absence of anyone in high position in the Foreign Office or Diplomatic Services who even remotely understands the mentality of Labour', and by the lack of anyone except the overworked Foreign Secretary and his junior minister to form a link between the Foreign Office and the party. Aiming to 'strengthen the influence of the political chiefs over the permanent Civil Service', the committee proposed that in the next Labour government the Foreign Secretary's principal private secretary should be 'a member of the Party of sufficient ability and authority to control the official Private Secretaries and should be in such a position that everything passes through his hands'. The parliamentary under-secretary should rank above the permanent under-secretary and see all papers submitted to the Foreign Secretary. The head of the publicity department should be 'a Labour man, probably a journalist'. A new Foreign Office department should be established to deal with League of Nations business, including in a senior position 'a political supporter of the Party with knowledge of international affairs'. Finally, the next Labour government 'should be prepared at once to put in charge of Embassies or Legations . . . diplomatic representatives who are in sympathy with Labour, whether there is a vacancy or not'. The committee recommended that similar steps be taken in other departments, and particularly in the service ministries.[50]

MacDonald reacted strongly to this radical memorandum, setting out his views in a letter to Arthur Henderson:

> In essence this is the American system of the spoils to the victor with a vengeance, and is a complete reversal of all of our ideas regarding the Civil Service. . . . If the Labour Party were to give its indication to the Civil Service that it had no confidence in its impartiality and that it would on assuming office post outsiders into controlling positions . . . we would raise such a hornet's nest inside the Service that, so far from promoting efficient and loyal service, we would destroy both. . . . A Civil Service upon its honour may work; but a Civil Service told quite frankly that we have no confidence in it would never work at all . . .

MacDonald intervened and after two meetings with him the committee watered down its proposals. A redrafted memorandum suggested that the Foreign Secretary's private office should be reorganized under an 'official' and an 'unofficial' or 'political' private secretary. The former would, as hitherto, be a permanent official and in charge of all communications between the Foreign Secretary and the Foreign Office staff. The latter should be a party member, responsible for maintaining contact between the Foreign Secretary and all persons and organizations outside the department. The proposal that a new Labour government should replace official representatives abroad by its own supporters and sympathizers was also ruled out as one likely to set 'an undesirable precedent' and be of 'less practical use than is supposed'.[51]

Despite this opposition from the party's leader, the International Advisory Committee had in fact identified a genuine problem and its solutions have, in one form or another, been supported by Labour reformers ever since. There were, however, no new departures in the staffing of the government machine when Labour returned to office in 1929. As in 1924, MacDonald introduced Rose Rosenberg into Number 10 as a personal and political private secretary responsible for links with the parliamentary party and with the press, but he retained Baldwin's principal private secretary, a career official from the Foreign Office, Robert Vansittart. Henderson, as Foreign Secretary, worked through a team of upper-class intellectual experts: Hugh Dalton, his junior minister, Philip Noel-Baker, his PPS, and Lord Robert Cecil, appointed as a prototype special adviser on League of Nations affairs.[52] After 1931 though, Labour's reliance on the civil service machine was criticized by advocates of a resolute socialist approach.

'The protective armament of a civil service is always the doctrine of maximum continuity', warned Harold Laski. 'Where there is a wide departure from this continuity, it is probable that experiments in personnel will be essential to carry it through successfully'. Noting Henderson's experience at the Foreign Office, Laski appears to have been the first to have suggested the introduction of something akin to the French ministerial *cabinet*. As he conceived it, the minister's *cabinet* would be 'a small number of experts of his own upon whom he could rely to push forward his own policy with a knowledge and energy at least equal to that brought to its examination by the regular departmental officials'. In addition to being a check upon official advice, the *cabinet* would make possible closer ministerial and party inter-relationships. Laski also favoured the use of politically committed outside experts, preferably associated with the party's policy preparations in Opposition, to challenge departmental thinking. While rejecting the 'spoils' system, he recommended that ministers should be prepared to make 'drastic changes' in the personnel of their departments to overcome deliberate obstruction or ill-will, such as special appointments from outside, accelerated promotion from within the civil service, and even the compulsory retirement of officials out of sympathy with new policies. These measures would, he thought, be particularly neces-

sary to change the aristocratic tone of the Foreign Office and where
new departments had to be created rapidly. He hoped, though,
that changes in the civil service would be minimal in character.
Praising the Whitehall tradition of loyal and efficient service to the
government of the day, Laski warned that 'nothing is more dangerous in any society than a deliberate effort to make officials men
who are wedded to a particular political outlook'.[53]

It was just such a step that George Lansbury appeared to propose
when, convinced that the failures of the 1929–31 government were
in part due to civil service sabotage, he called for a degree of
commitment to a Labour government's objectives going beyond the
norms of a career civil service: 'when a Labour Government comes
to power it will need as its leading men in all departments men
who . . . understand our policy, who believe in it, and are willing
to work night and day to make it succeed'. Herbert Morrison, who
accused Lansbury of opening the door to an American-style 'spoils'
system, with its dangers of muddled administration, corruption and
jobbery, better represented the outlook of the bulk of Labour's
parliamentary leadership in the 1930s. At the party conference in
1936, Morrison went as far as to declare that anyone who made
local council administrative appointments on the basis of political
favouritism 'ought to be cleared out of the Party bag and baggage'.[54]

The first of Laski's proposed 'experiments in personnel' (ministerial *cabinets*) was slow to get off the ground. Hugh Dalton backed
the idea of ministers bringing in with them 'persons in whom they
have confidence and who have special knowledge of the problems
of the Department and of the Party's policy', whose job would be
'to assist the Minister, and to co-operate with, rather than to
replace, the permanent officials in preparing and carrying out
policy, and in suggesting ideas'. During the wartime government
he appointed Hugh Gaitskell as his *chef de cabinet*. Attlee used
Douglas Jay as his personal economic adviser for a year after 1945,
but ministers in the 1945–51 administration relied upon their regular
civil service private offices. A 1947 Fabian report on the reform of
the higher civil service rejected the suggestion that ministers should
have a number of personal assistants of their own choosing, arguing
on the basis of wartime experience that 'these assistants interfere
with the working of departmental machinery without necessarily
invigorating it'. Nor did the Attlee government see the importation
into Whitehall of politically committed outside experts of the type
Laski had envisaged.[55]

Laski's proposal for a greater ministerial say in civil service appointments and promotions was taken up by Evan Durbin who, in 1944, made the ingenious suggestion that civil servants' security of tenure in particular posts be removed. It would then be possible for a minister to remove an official on the grounds of unsuitability for a particular post without necessarily reflecting on his or her capacity for other duties. Such officials would remain at their substantive rank but be transferred to work elsewhere in Whitehall. More far-reaching still were the ideas contained in a paper to the Fabian Civil Service Group that drew up the 1947 report mentioned above. Its (anonymous) author took issue with the ideas that the civil service should be apolitical and that a 'spoils' system was undesirable or dangerous. 'To claim that the Civil Service must be apolitical so as to hold the balance between Right and Left is to deny the Government of the day an instrument to its purpose', he insisted. The analogy with the American 'spoils' system leading to inefficiency and corruption was not apt, he claimed, as these phenomena had quite different causes. What came next went far beyond what Laski or Durbin had proposed:

In this country there is now, and will be in future, a real and deep cleavage, certainly in the economic field, between the theories of the Government and the only Party that might provide an alternative. In these circumstances, to change part of the higher personnel of the Civil Service with the colour of the Party in power is not a spoils system so much as a system whereby the theories of either Party may, in fact, be given an all-out trial within the limited span of a particular Parliament.

I should like to see, say 20% at the lower levels and 10% at the higher levels, brought into departments at the discretion of the Ministers concerned. I think it would be most undesirable if these were grouped directly about the Minister in the role of his personal assistants. . . . Persons recruited in this way should . . . take their place in the machinery of the Ministry, where they would serve as a leaven. . . . There should be little difficulty in finding the necessary places, and those selected by a former Minister would retire automatically, unless their appointments were confirmed by the new Minister. Provided that full employment conditions are maintained in the managerial class, I do not see why those displaced should find difficulty in securing other employment . . .

There is a further advantage to my suggestion. A Minister is constitutionally responsible for every act of his department, and by the method I suggest he could have greater confidence in those acts of which he could have no personal knowledge. Moreover, before he became a Minister he would be on the lookout for good people . . . [56]

If Lansbury's vague ideas about the need for top civil servants who believed in the government's programme had been denounced as a move towards a 'spoils' system, it takes little imagination to envisage what the likes of Herbert Morrison would have made of *this* scheme. Perhaps fortunately for the Fabian Society, its Civil Service Group firmly quashed this proposal. In a way the paper's basic premiss was flawed – though perhaps this was not apparent at the time it was written – because in the post-war period there was to be a large area of common ground between the main parties as to the main features of economic policy, with the Conservatives adapting themselves to the Keynesian–welfare state politics practised by the Attlee government. By institutionalizing the post-war consensus, the Whitehall mandarins could thus be seen to be – and were – loyal to the purposes of governments from different parties, and this did much to undermine the paper's argument for a British version of the 'spoils' system. In any case, it was obvious that ideas like these were completely alien to a party leader and Prime Minister who could say, as Attlee did in the Commons:

> We always demand from our civil servants a loyalty to the State, and that they should serve the Government of the day, whatever its political colour. That undertaking is carried out with exemplary loyalty. Any departure from this system would mean the adoption of a spoils system, and that would destroy our Civil Service.

Attlee made no change to the procedures under which ministers were largely excluded from civil service promotion decisions, while discreet consultations generally ensured that personal incompatibilities were taken into account. Developing ideas he had formulated in the 1930s, he merely encouraged his ministers to make better use of their junior ministers, a practice which faced very real constitutional, political and administrative obstacles.[57]

Despite the success of the Attlee government in implementing its reform programme without Laski-style 'experiments in personnel', the issue of political control over the civil service was again raised in Labour circles as part of the critique of Britain's machinery of government developed in the late 1950s and early 1960s. Richard

Crossman led the way, calling for the appointment of a small 'Brains Trust' in each department, a mixture of civil servants and outsiders acting as the minister's eyes and ears. Thomas Balogh argued that 'the American system which replaces the Heads of Divisions with politically trusted experts whenever the party in power changes has worked much better than the British', but, shying away from the full implications of this claim, suggested, as 'a compromise', that ministers be supported by private offices and expert advisers recruited from outside and sharing their political beliefs. 'Far from regarding outside appointments as in some sense immoral, or to be concealed, we regard them as desirable, indeed essential, if a new government on coming to power is to have vitality and is to succeed in devising, presenting and executing new policies', argued another Fabian Group on the Civil Service in 1964. 'We believe that it is high time that an end was put to the error of pretending that governments can change but none of their servants or advisers ever should'. As in the case of the 1947 group, even stronger and more politically explicit arguments had been advanced in the Fabians' private discussions:

In very few large organisations outside central or local government . . . is one man expected to be able to take charge and carry out new policies without making any changes in his advisers, particularly when they have been closely involved in policies now discredited . . .

The argument against excessive patronage remains valid . . . Nevertheless, the opposite extreme we have in the U.K. today (i.e. having no political appointments at all) is an artificial one. It is only appropriate when there is little change in basic approach to policy with changes in minister, i.e. for ministerial changes within a particular administration or for departments where there is no political disagreement over policy. But where policy is the subject of bitter party controversy, and a change of Government is intended to mean a major change in policy, it is questionable whether the people behind the old policy are the best people to help a minister formulate and implement the new one . . .

The injection of new blood . . . would be of some benefit to both political parties but it would be of particular benefit to the Labour Party. For the 'non-political' approach tends to be a Conservative approach and the greater the power of the permanent Civil Service to dominate policy, the less will be the likelihood of radical change.[58]

Following the Fabians' recommendations, the Labour Party's evidence to the Fulton Committee, aiming to 'strengthen the Minister, the "temporary politician" in his department in relation to the "permanent politicians", his Civil Servants', proposed that two types of temporary political appointment should be explicitly recognized: politically committed experts in particular subjects and a limited number of personal assistants (up to four), forming a ministerial *cabinet*. The pronunciation alone would be French: this British *cabinet* would have neither the size nor the power of its French counterpart. Its members would take no administrative decisions themselves, rather their role would be to keep in touch with what was going on in the department and thus enable a meaningful political intervention in the early stages of the evolution of policy, to brief the minister on items on the Cabinet agenda, to liaise with other ministers through their *cabinets* (developing a political network to parallel officials' inter-departmental links), and to transmit the political impulse from the minister to his department, providing a point of contact and complementing the work of the existing private office.[59]

'If I had thought that we ought to have a *cabinet* system, I would have done it by now', said Harold Wilson in 1967, distancing himself from his party's evidence to Fulton. In Opposition, Wilson had ruled out any idea of large-scale recruitment of outsiders into the top levels of Whitehall and had been sceptical about the introduction of *cabinets*, pointing out the dangers of a false division between the political team and the departmental officials, and saying that in his experience as a minister it was better to work through the civil service private office, a view which Richard Crossman, abandoning his earlier support for a ministerial 'Brains Trust' came to share. In the 1964–70 government, a number of ministers and the Prime Minister brought in a small number of personal aides, but there was no systematic pattern of recruitment and no formal *cabinet* system emerged.[60]

'I'm rather against the idea of bringing in a series of *eminences grises* or Rasputins or court favourites to advise a Prime Minister', Wilson had declared before entering Number 10. Nevertheless, some of the members of Wilson's 'Kitchen Cabinet' did attract notoriety, especially Marcia Williams, who headed the Political Office, responsible for links with the parliamentary party and the party in the country and for personal and political correspondence. Two other key figures around the premier were Thomas Balogh, an Oxford academic, a Wilson adviser since the 1950s and a member of the party's Finance and Economic Policy Committee, who served as Economic Adviser to the Cabinet 1964–7, and Sir Solly Zuckerman, Chief Scientific Adviser to the Ministry of Defence since 1960, who was appointed Scientific Adviser in the Cabinet Office. Zuckerman, a more experienced bureaucratic operator – 'house-trained' in the Whitehall phrase – fitted in more smoothly than Balogh. The latter often complained to Wilson that he was denied access to Cabinet papers necessary for his work by the civil service. The most important of the Prime Minister's advisers and confidants, as we noted earlier, was, however, a career official, Cabinet Secretary Sir Burke Trend. Crossman observed their developing relationship, and by 1967 was describing Wilson as 'tightly integrated into the Whitehall set-up' by Trend and the government as a 'Wilson–Burke Trend axis'. While the Prime Minister's Number 10 staff remained small, the Cabinet Office was greatly strengthened.[61]

At the Ministry of Defence, Denis Healey established the small Programme Evaluation Group (PEG) to provide him with a check on the advice coming up to him through the regular channels of the services, scientific staffs and the civil service. Including high-flying 'insiders' in mid-career, and operating in tandem with the secretary of state's private office, the PEG was apparently regarded as a fifth column by the chiefs of staff and a large part of the M.o.D. administration – and was sometimes kept in the dark by them – but was considered 'immensely valuable' by its client, the Defence Secretary.[62] Probably the closest thing to a *cabinet* to be found in Whitehall at that time, it is surprising that it did not form a model for other ministers to copy. Instead, those ministers who did appoint advisers did so on an *ad hoc* and individual basis.

The so-called 'irregulars' – temporary, expert officials serving on a contract basis or on secondment from an outside employer – were often economists with Labour sympathies occupying high-level advisory positions, such as Robert Neild and Nicholas Kaldor at the Treasury and Christopher Foster at the Ministry of Transport. Brian Abel-Smith, a social policy expert at the LSE, had a similar role as an expert adviser at the DHSS, while John Harris, formerly secretary to Hugh Gaitskell and the Labour Party's Director of Publicity 1962–4, worked as a special assistant to Michael Stewart (until 1965) and then Roy Jenkins (1965–70), concerned especially with press liaison. The creation of new departments – Economic Affairs, Overseas Development and Technology – provided additional opportunities to bring outsiders (economists, scientists, technologists and industrialists) into advisory and administrative positions. Most outsiders entered Whitehall at grades several ranks down from the most senior civil service levels, for sensible reasons, as the Fabian Society pointed out in its evidence to Fulton:

> To have recruited more than a very few irregulars at grades above Under Secretary would . . . have been a dangerous challenge to good working relationships with regular officials. Even the few above this level were placed in new departments. To put an outsider into a Deputy or Permanent Secretary post in an established department would be a doubtful move as he would not be in the 'club' of top men and would not have the Whitehall knowledge to support his great responsibilities.[63]

As in previous (Labour and Conservative) governments, the interventions of ministers and the Prime Minister in senior civil service postings in the 1964–70 period centred on personalities rather than on political factors. When Barbara Castle tried to move her permanent secretary at the Ministry of Transport in 1966, she failed. Other Labour ministers did not always secure the appointment of the particular permanent secretary they wanted, chiefly because of the need of the Head of the Civil Service, when advising the Prime Minister, to take account of the requirements of different departments and the long-term interests of the civil service as a whole.

Like Attlee, Harold Wilson identified junior ministers as an important political resource, claiming that giving them a stronger political role would assist their chief more than establishing a *cabinet*. Reorganizations and amalgamations (and the consequent reduction in the number of departments) led to the creation of teams of four or more ministers in many departments, permitting the greater delegation of ministerial functions to junior ministers. The Prime Minister appointed a number of junior ministers with designated responsibilities for specific subjects such as sport, the arts, disarmament and London housing. The Wilson government also saw experiments with 'mixed' committees of junior ministers and officials working together on particular subjects, for instance science and technology. Although the experiences of junior ministers were still highly variable, their role in the 1964–70 government was in many cases much more significant than in previous administrations, and so strengthened the position of Labour Cabinet ministers.[64]

As we have seen, the experience of the 1964–70 government

rekindled the traditional suspicions widespread in the Labour Party that the civil service diverts Labour governments from pursuing radical policies. The equally traditional proposals for providing ministers with alternative sources of information and advice and for keeping them in touch with the party were brought out and dusted down after 1970. The appointment of ministerial advisers or *cabinets* found support right across the party. Consciously echoing the work of Labour's International Advisory Committee in 1925, a Fabian Foreign Policy Group examined ways of providing political advice to a Labour Foreign Secretary. Supporters of the Fulton Report such as John Garrett and Robert Sheldon proposed that ministers should have a personal *cabinet* of expert policy advisers and that junior ministers should be given greater policy and management responsibilities. Marcia Williams thought that

> Labour should . . . start earmarking eager, enthusiastic, able young men and women to be trained in the work they must do when they accompany future Ministers into the departments. Their function must be to ensure that political assessments of policy can be as accurate and as good as the flow of Civil Service advice.

Barbara Castle was strongly in favour of ministers having political support inside their departments: 'the loneliness of the short-distance runner must be alleviated by a political "cabinet" '. Tony Benn and his left-wing advisers, such as Stuart Holland, also backed these ideas. Benn ruled out the adoption of the American system of appointing political sympathizers to senior civil service posts but he argued that the appointment of political, economic and trade union advisers was essential to break down ministerial isolation, strengthen the political impulse within government and maintain closer links between a Labour government and the Labour movement. Holland went so far as to talk of a 'counter-Whitehall structure' of *cabinets*, with regular meetings of special advisers in parallel with civil service inter-departmental committees. There were senior Labour figures opposed to this thinking, however. Jim Callaghan, for instance, thought *cabinets* 'just inflated the egos and ambitions of Ministers', according to Benn's account of an NEC meeting at which supporters of the idea failed to get it incorported into the party programme.[65]

During Labour's period in Opposition after 1970, personal assistants, financed by the Rowntree Trust, were introduced into the offices of some shadow ministers; in 1974 some of these were able to move across in Whitehall as ministerial special advisers. Marcia Williams also proposed the creation of a 'self-contained top grade advisory unit within No. 10'.

> This is more necessary for a progressive government than a Conservative government since the Conservatives can rely on the Civil Service being tuned in to what they want to do. But the Labour government must have a small core of highly qualified, highly expert individuals to initiate policy and ideas which can filter down through the machine. This unit should also assess decisions coming up through the machine via the departments for the Prime Minister's approval.[66]

When Labour returned to office in 1974, the Number 10 Policy Unit, under Bernard Donoughue, was created to act as these extra eyes, ears and hands for the Prime Minister. 'Until Harold Wilson created the Policy Unit in 1974 there was no systematic policy analysis separate from the regular civil service machine and working solely for the Prime Minister', Bernard Donoughue has noted. The Number 10 Policy Unit was a group of half a dozen or so economists and experts in social and industrial policy, all with Labour sympathies, designed to provide a political, party-oriented and personal advisory service to the Prime Minister. The Unit worked closely with the Number 10 private office staff, the Cabinet Office, the Central Policy Review Staff, and – less successfully – with ministerial special advisers. It aimed to keep in touch with thinking outside government through contacts in universities, industry, trade unions, pressure groups and Labour Party headquarters. Ground rules agreed with the Cabinet Secretary granted it unique access to Whitehall networks: the Unit's members were authorized to make direct links with departmental officials and to attend and/or receive the papers of official committees. Bernard Donoughue himself, the Prime Minister's Senior Policy Adviser 1974–9, attended Cabinet committees and some meetings of the full Cabinet. A Downing Street press release announced that the Unit would 'assist in the development of the whole range of policies contained in the Government's programme, especially those arising in the short and medium term'. An internal memorandum approved by the Prime Minister described its role in detail:

> The Unit must ensure that the Prime Minister is aware of what is coming up from departments to Cabinet. It must scrutinise papers, contact departments, know the background to policy

decisions, disputes and compromises, and act as an early warning system. The Unit may feed into the system ideas on policy which are not currently covered, or are inadequately covered . . .

The political dimension to the Unit's work was stressed: 'The Prime Minister has assumed responsibility as custodian of the Labour manifesto. The Unit must assist in that role, making sure that the manifesto is not contravened, nor retreated from, without proper discussion and advance warning'. James Callaghan has recalled how the Unit would analyse for him the political implications of policies and also look to party interests: 'they were trying to make sure we did the opposition down if we could'. The Policy Unit was a successful innovation at the centre of government. Created by Wilson, it was retained by Callaghan and – in a modified form and, of course, with new staff – by Thatcher. It was accepted by the higher civil service. Strengthening the Prime Minister's position in the policy-making process, it played a crucial role in the Labour government's crises of 1975, 1976 and 1979.[67]

The 1974–9 Labour government extended and institutionalized the practice of ministers bringing advisers from outside the civil service into their departments. The total number of special advisers working in Whitehall as temporary civil servants was usually around twenty-five or thirty, spread around departments mainly in ones and twos, though four or five worked in the DHSS and six or seven in the Number 10 Policy Unit. Guidelines issued by the Prime Minister limited them to two per Cabinet minister. Not all ministers appointed advisers, some apparently feeling no need for them or preferring to rely for political support on their junior ministers and PPSs. Special advisers performed a variety of functions: examining civil service policy submissions for politically sensitive problems and to extend the range of options from which the minister could choose; 'progress chasing' on decisions; briefing the minister on non-departmental items on the Cabinet agenda; thinking about long-term policy and making a political input to departmental planning; liaising with the party and with interest groups (including the trade unions); helping to handle the media and gingering up civil service drafts of speeches and statements.[68] Special advisers thus performed, in some degree, the functions of policy research, political liaison and departmental contact suggested in Labour's evidence to Fulton as the main roles of a ministerial *cabinet*. Broadly speaking, whereas some advisers contributed impressive subject-expertise (e.g. Brian Abel-Smith at the DHSS), others were more general political aides and party linkmen (e.g. Jack Straw at the same department). Some of the advisers were recruited from academic posts, others came from Transport House, others were researchers working for Opposition spokesmen – the Rowntree Trust's 'chocolate soldiers' – or were specialists in particular subjects, with Labour Party connections.

The results of the special adviser experiment were inevitably mixed. Labour ministers relied for policy advice primarily on the career civil servants in their departments, but special advisers were able to supplement and complement the work of officials in a number of ways. First, advisers were able to keep in touch with the party, including NEC sub-committees, both in terms of day-to-day issues and in longer-term policy development, in a way not possible for a neutral career bureaucracy. Second, briefing from special advisers on Cabinet business outside the area of their minister's departmental responsibilities contributed to improving the quality of Cabinet debate in the 1974–9 government. Donoughue argues that having economic policy analysts as special advisers enabled non-economist ministers to participate intelligently in Cabinet discussions of economic policy.[69] Third, advisers could provide alternative ideas on policy to those presented by the department; ideas, moreover, developed within a framework of political values shared with the minister.

On the debit side, it is clear that some advisers, lacking specialist subject-expertise, and relatively junior in both age and status, were quickly marginalized in their departments, contributing little to policy-making and soon drifting out of their jobs. A second drawback, it is commonly noted, is that there were too few special advisers. In Bernard Donoughue's opinion,

> with ministers, if there is only one [special adviser], there almost might as well be none. There is so much paper, so many people to keep your eye on and just retaining access to and confidence of ministers is virtually impossible on top of meetings and everything else.

Finally, as Pollitt put it, 'the advisers as a group largely failed to develop an *esprit de corps*, or more functionally, an effective interdepartmental net to parallel that of the Civil Service', thus weakening their impact.[70]

This innovation must be put in perspective, then. Special advisers were too few in number to supplant the mass of career bureaucrats and had no place in the administrative chain of command implementing decisions. They were not a 'counter civil service'. Yet it would be going too far to dismiss them as a 'minor cosmetic'.[71] Special advisers provided, at their best, political support to Labour ministers in forms which other resources – career officials, junior ministers and PPSs – could not. Senior officials came to welcome the contribution that they could make. Labour critics of civil service power were able to point to the experience of special advisers when arguing that a full-blown *cabinet* system could be made to work.

Although special advisers did not take over essential *ministerial* functions, some commentators saw their proliferation as evidence that Cabinet ministers were failing to use their existing resources of political support, particularly their junior ministers, as fully as they might. In fact, in terms of identifiable roles and the delegation of defined departmental responsibilities, the position of junior ministers in the 1974–9 government was an advance on the position in 1964–70, let alone in the Attlee period. Much depended on the style of the top minister and on his or her willingness to delegate authority, but some Labour ministers – such as Barbara Castle and Tony Benn – clearly saw their teams of junior ministers, together with their special advisers, as vital allies in running their departments. Giving junior ministers a bigger role in policy-making and involving them in the work of departmental and inter-departmental committees of officials were ideas widely supported in the party. However, the constitutional convention of ministerial responsibility and problems of political and bureaucratic relationships and of prime-ministerial patronage remained as major stumbling-blocks to further increasing the scope and authority of junior ministers in general: factors not always fully appreciated by Labour reformers.

As its analysis of civil service power became more pointed, Labour's left in the late 1970s began to press for further steps to reinforce ministers' positions in their departments. Brian Sedgemore, in his alternative first chapter to the Expenditure Committee report of 1977, urged that 'steps be taken to re-establish or possibly establish for the first time political power and authority in this land'. Ministers and the Cabinet had to be 'given weapons to take on the civil service'.

> Whether through the appointment of powerful ministerial back-up teams or 'cabinets', chosen by Ministers and including Members of Parliament if Ministers so desired and to whom civil servants at Deputy Secretary and Under Secretary level would report and be accountable, or through developing the role of

political advisers, or through political appointments of top civil servants at Under Secretary level and above, or through other devices Ministers must inject more party political clout into the upper echelons of the administration.

The party's Machinery of Government Study Group was thinking along the same lines. Its report recommended that the special adviser system be developed further so that each minister would have a 'private political office', including specialist and political aides, but did not say how large this unit should be. Frances Morrell wanted the number of special advisers increased but opposed any move towards giving them an executive as opposed to an advisory function. Tony Banks, Judith Hart's special adviser, thought that while 'it would be nonsense to suggest that the present small number [of political advisers] are capable of correcting the inbuilt anti-Socialist bias of the Civil Service their presence alone constitutes an important break-through'. He envisaged a ministerial political office of twelve or more advisers – only something of this size could provide effective ministerial support and really alter the balance of power in Whitehall, he argued. But ministers should not only have more political advisers, the party's Study Group believed, they should also be able to determine crucial top-level civil service postings to ensure that they had confidence in their senior officials. A Research Department paper argued that 'if loyalty to a Departmental Minister is to become a reality and not merely a deferential cosmetic, it is essential that all top official appointments . . . should be subject to the express approval of the Minister himself'. The Study Group's report said that a minister on accepting office should have the right to remove his permanent secretary if he so desired and that he should be directly involved in appointments at Deputy and Under Secretary levels and be able to seek the transfer of officials should he feel it right.[72]

These proposals were approved by the NEC and endorsed by the 1978 conference, but were simply ignored by the Callaghan government. If they had been acted upon, then it seems likely that the Labour government rather than Mrs Thatcher's Conservative government would have been accused of politicizing the higher civil service. Although what was apparently envisaged in 1978 was not a party political test, it might well have looked like one or been portrayed as one by the government's opponents, especially if (say) Tony Benn had proceeded to remove his senior civil servants. The Labour government was not prepared to even think about any changes in the established practices and procedures relating to filling Whitehall's top jobs, however. Moreover, such proposals would have involved some diminution of the power of the Prime Minister, which would not have been attractive to Callaghan, even if, after the usual consultations, he apparently invariably accepted civil service recommendations on senior appointments and promotions. But this issue did not go away. After 1979 the arguments in the Labour Party about the mistakes of the Wilson and Callaghan administrations breathed new life into this long-running controversy about reinforcing socialist ministers, and the impact of Mrs Thatcher's premiership on the mandarins and the debate about Labour's response posed the old questions in a still more acute way.

PREPARING FOR POWER: LABOUR'S POLICY-MAKING IN OPPOSITION

Richard Crossman was quoted earlier (p. 44) to the effect that Labour's problems and failures in office were not the result of civil service obstruction but were due to ministers' lack of clear and well-thought-out plans. The 'battering-ram of change' in British politics, he argued, was the system of mass parties, dynamized by the doctrine of the mandate. Essentially, this meant that once a party won an election and formed a government, it had the right and the duty to put into effect the promises it had made in its manifesto. Crossman believed that 'it is *after* the election in its effect on the Civil Service, not *during* the election in its effect on the voter, that the mandate plays its most essential role'. A minister could most effectively override civil service resistance by saying that he was committed by party policy and by the manifesto. Consequently, it was important that policy was fully worked out by the party when in Opposition. As he put it in a lecture in 1972:

> The point of the manifesto is not to persuade the voter. The point of the manifesto is to give yourself an anchor when the civil service tries to go back on your word. If a politician enters Whitehall without a manifesto, without a programme, he is lost; and they will tell him what to do, although the only point of his being there is to be a catalytic irritant in the departments.
>
> But for them to be eager, the party must have a policy: not just an idea, but a detailed policy which they cannot emasculate or castrate or pervert, because the politicians know what they want to do. Anything you haven't worked out in some detail

they will change. And very properly. Why shouldn't they since they know more about it than you? Your only hope then is work in opposition. So what Labour should be thinking about now in opposition is not slogans which will sell us to the electorate but policies which, when we have got into office, will hold us steady next time.[73]

This idea was not new. As we also noted earlier, Harold Laski had pointed out the importance of thorough policy preparations in Opposition in the 1930s. A socialist government must take office knowing what it wants to do and how it proposes to get it, he maintained.

> It is essential that the large principles and the main details of socialist schemes should be firmly outlined before the party takes office. Unless this is done, the processes of investigation, consultation and defence against error, which are the normal routine of the Service, will prevent the rapid taking of important decisions. There is nothing at which the Civil Service is so skilful as in persuading a Minister who is vague about his policy that it is much better to let sleeping dogs lie. Unless he enters office knowing definitely what he wants to do, he will either do nothing at all, or do merely what the Department wants.

A party needed a 'civil service of its own', Laski thought, so that it could be equipped with something more than declarations of intention, the broad heads of proposals or pious hopes. Behind a party's programme there needed to be 'solid investigation', with the party organization able to serve up detailed proposals in such a form that there could be no question of delay after the election while the official machine ponderously set about trying to 'clothe ministerial policy in concrete terms', giving vested interests and its opponents time to mobilize against the government. A reforming minister must

> not merely have [a] plan in his head; he must have lived with it, argued about it, considered it in such a way that his sense of its implications is deep-rooted enough to withstand the official scepticism he may encounter. He must be prepared, that is, for action and not for investigation, He must have a plan to be criticized, not a direction to be explored.[74]

The MacDonald Labour governments, seen in this light, were a model to avoid. They lacked a clear short-term programme with a set of ordered priorities. Their commitments were misty and vague, with the means of achieving their desired ends not spelt out. Mac-Donald's Labour Party was, frankly, utopian and propagandist, not practical and hard-headed. 'It was not fit for the kind of power it was called upon to exercise', as Skidelsky has brutally put it. After 1931 Labour started to wake up to these deficiencies. Tawney saw the need for clear priorities: 'Labour programmes [are] less programmes than miscellanies – a glittering forest of Christmas trees, with presents for everyone'. 'The business of making programmes by including in them an assortment of measures appealing to different sections of the movement must stop', he insisted. 'The function of the party is not to offer the largest possible number of carrots to the largest possible number of donkeys.' Dalton's view was: 'Let us have no more MacDonaldite slush and floral phrases, meaning nothing definite'. Important work was done in the 1930s by the NEC's policy sub-committees and by unofficial socialist think-tanks such as the New Fabian Research Bureau and the informal XYZ club of financial and economic experts, but there was nothing like a Laski-style 'Labour Party civil service'. The party's research department had only four staff (including two clerical assistants) in 1940.[75] Great strides were made in producing a feasible party programme but there were still many gaps and the specifics of policy commitments were not always fully developed.

The classic illustration of this lack of preparedness is, of course, Labour's nationalization programme. Kenneth O. Morgan has written of the 'intellectual void' at the heart of the party's proposals for nationalization. The Attlee government certainly entered office in 1945 with a precise list of industries to be taken over by the state. Morrison's work in the 1930s had provided a general organizational model: the public corporation. But that was about it. 'The details of organizational structure, finance, the compensation of private stockholders, pricing policy, the system of consultation with the workers, the relation to the consumer, domestic and industrial – all were left studiously vague', Morgan has noted. In a scene worthy of *Yes, Minister*, it has been claimed that when Manny Shinwell, the Minister of Fuel and Power, went to the Transport House files for the party's detailed blueprint for coal nationalization, all he found were two copies of a pamphlet by James Griffith, one of them a translation into Welsh! Similarly, the party was committed to economic planning but there had been relatively little advance work done on the practical issues involved or on the design of the appropriate government machinery and instruments for socialist planning. Without a positive scheme of their own, ministers simply continued wartime controls and left the construction of the (ineffective) planning machinery to be improvised by the mandarins. Labour's plans for the welfare state were just as vague, the relevant parts of the 1945 manifesto being largely lifted from the Beveridge Report.[76]

Looking back in the mid-1960s on the lessons of the Attlee government, Richard Crossman roundly condemned its 'failure to do its homework in the years before it achieved power'. Was the 1964 government any different? Crossman's January 1965 diary entry suggested not: 'it is clear once again that a socialist Opposition in this country comes into office with very half-baked plans'. There were various study groups and working parties set up by the party in Opposition but, on the whole (Crossman's pensions group being a notable exception), these produced, in Headey's words, 'prescriptive documents rather than detailed guides to action'. A fatal weakness was the absence of any party preparations for dealing with a balance of payments crisis and a run on the pound. The party had done some relatively detailed work on policy in the mid-1950s, it is true, but after 1959 a deliberate decision was taken to adopt a broad-brush approach. As Richard Rose has put it, 'In the five years prior to the 1964 general election, policy-making was more concerned with the politics of opposition than with plans for governing'. In an effort to defuse the party's factional disputes, the stress was put on criticizing the Conservatives and articulating agreed party values. In a confidential internal memorandum in 1960, the research department downplayed its policy work and emphasized that it needed 'to do more, not less, propaganda'. *Signposts for the Sixties*, the party's 1961 programme, explicitly ruled out providing a detailed guide to action: 'Since the situation will almost certainly change between now and the election, raising new problems and offering new opportunities, we would regard it as folly to anticipate . . . the party's election manifesto'.[77]

Harold Wilson, for all he was to say in retirement about governments primarily being frustrated 'because they have not worked out with sufficient precision when they were in Opposition what it is they want the civil servants to do', as party leader after 1963 was happy to go along with – indeed, took to new heights – this unspecific, sloganizing approach. The consequences were soon apparent in government. Labour was committed to the repeal of the 1957 Rent Act, for example, but, characteristically, reliving Shinwell's experience in 1945, Crossman, the Minister for Housing, could find only 'one slim series of notes' at the party's headquarters, so that he was inevitably in his civil servants' hands when it came to devising the government's own rents legislation. As far as Labour's plans for a Land Commission were concerned, which Crossman described as 'a subject completely beyond comprehension' for most of the ministers on the relevant Cabinet committee, he commented that 'at first glance in Whitehall the Party policy was seen to be unworkable or futile'. The government only persisted with the proposal because it was in the manifesto, the outcome being more or less a complete failure in terms of the party's original intentions. The party was pledged to introduce an 'integrated transport policy' but the problem was that nobody knew what this meant, least of all successive Labour Ministers of Transport. Similarly, the fate of the DEA (Department of Economic Affairs) and the 'National Plan', and the whole conduct of economic policy after 1964, demonstrated that, behind the rhetoric, there was little substance to Labour's work in Opposition on economic planning. And where there was a detailed blueprint available, as with Crossman's radical plans (worked out in the late 1950s) for pensions reform, matters were left to drift and nothing was achieved in office.[78]

The party launched a massive policy-making exercise when out of office after 1970 – with nearly 1,000 individuals serving on over eighty NEC sub-committees and study groups, and a 56,000-word programme produced in 1973 – but it is not clear that it did itself much good with these efforts. For a start, the detailed work done on industrial policy and public ownership was very divisive within the party (and, according to opinion polls, unpopular even with Labour voters), the internal rows culminating in Harold Wilson vetoing the proposal to nationalize twenty-five leading companies. And then, while the party happily entered into major new spending commitments, it rather glided over the problems involved in financing them. To be sure, an NEC paper in 1973 said that the question of expenditure priorities should be tackled while in Opposition, to ensure that Labour went into office with a 'systematic sense of social priorities and a viable public expenditure strategy which can withstand the pressures of economic circumstances'. 'Within the lifetime of any government there will be times when tough decisions have to be made on public spending', it sagely warned. 'There will be an inevitable tendency for [Labour] ministers to become preoccupied with short-term problems and to have too little attention and energy to devote to the purposeful planning of priorities'. Hence, 'the opportunity must be grasped now, while still in Opposition, to concentrate our minds on the expenditure options available to us'. But Joel Barnett, Chief Secretary to the Treasury after 1974, is scathing on Labour's preparations.

> We in the Shadow Treasury team . . . did little or nothing about how much, or rather how little, total public expenditure would be available, and how it should be divided in terms of priorities. If Denis Healey had worked out a plan for a Parliament, I am bound to say he kept it a secret from me. We naturally discussed the likely immediate economic situation we would face, but medium- and long-term planning on the allocation of resources rarely, if ever, entered into our thinking and discussions.

Barnett concluded, 'The 1974–79 Labour Government had a difficult economic and financial task rendered impossible by pledges foolishly made without any serious thought as to where the money would come from'. It would, however, be unfair to pin all the blame for this on the NEC and shadow-ministerial teams that were beavering away on substantive policy areas, when, clearly, the shadow Treasury team was not doing *its* job properly of at least preliminary work on relating individual spending commitments to the overall picture. On the related issue of tax policy changes, the story is equally dismal, a major study of the subject showing how plans to introduce a wealth tax were not well thought out either in principle or in detail – the party's work being described by one Labour minister as 'very informal, very haphazard and very superficial' – and no progress being made in office.[79]

Many commentators and 'insiders' agree that a major reason for the poor performance of Labour governments is poor policy preparation by the party when in Opposition. Why and how does this happen? There are a number of reasons. First, there is the peculiar structure of Labour Party policy-making, with authority divided between Conference, NEC and the parliamentary leadership in the Shadow Cabinet. Resolutions may be approved by Conference and become party policy without any detailed research being done. The way in which different proposals may be spatchcocked together into 'composite' resolutions at Conference is another problem. 'The end result of policy-making under the present procedure can be unclear, internally inconsistent and sometimes actually contradictory', an NEC sub-committee has admitted. Then there is the question of relations between the NEC and the parliamentary leadership on the Opposition front bench. Shadow ministers sit on the relevant NEC sub-committees developing party policy but do not usually chair them, and these bodies report to the NEC and not to the Shadow Cabinet or the party leader. This is not a recipe for a fruitful partnership between those making policy and those who will have to implement it later in office when there are ideological strains and conflicts between the two groups, as in the 1970–4 period, for instance. The fact that different sub-committees can have different political balances only complicates the picture further (for example, before 1974 the Finance and Economic Affairs sub-committee was dominated by right-wing parliamentarians, but the Public Sector Group – working out far-reaching public owner-ship proposals – had a left-wing membership, with MPs in a min-ority).[80] Given the political balancing acts needed to evolve Labour's programme, it is not surprising that some policies rep-resent compromises or fudges that are quickly shown to be unwork-able after the election. Less easy to forgive is the way in which some fundamentally important issues are not properly addressed because they are taboo subjects for one section or another of the party – incomes policy being the classic example.

A second problem is the lack of proper co-ordination of Labour's policy-making in Opposition. The NEC does not knit together the output of its various sub-committees and working parties into a coherent whole or set clear priorities. That no one properly per-forms the Treasury function – costing policy proposals before they are adopted – is, as we have just seen, another glaring weakness in the party's preparations for office. Evaluation of the constraints of the parliamentary timetable and of the overall machinery of government implications of the party's programme is also perfunc-tory, when it is done at all.[81]

Third, there is the problem of the party's limited research capa-bility. Labour's research department is small, the number of researchers fluctuating between eight and seventeen in the period since 1950 (this is something like half the size of the Conservative research department which itself is overstretched and can do rela-tively little in-depth policy research). Because these staff must also service the NEC's committee network and work on party publi-cations and other routine functions, it has been estimated that only around one-fifth of their time is actually devoted to 'research'. In the 1970s some Labour frontbenchers were able to employ their own research assistants (funded by the Rowntree Trust) and after 1979 the so-called 'Short Money' provided funds for Shadow Cabi-net advisers (allowing each member of the Shadow Cabinet at least a half-share(!) in a researcher). To adapt the well-known phrase, it is surprising not that Labour Party policy research is not done well, but that it is done at all. One consequence is clear, however, and that is that the party lacks a research back-up able to 'develop and argue practical solutions to a degree of robustness which can withstand the sheer competence of an incoming minister's first civil service brief', in the words of a former Labour ministerial special adviser.[82]

Over the years various proposals have been made to beef up the party's research effort, with talk of an enlarged research department, better links between party headquarters and the advisers working for Labour frontbenchers (in and out of office) to form a 'Labour Party civil service', an independent (but closely linked) socialist think-tank, and even a formal 'Department of the Opposition', staffed by civil servants on secondment. The Fabian Society has long been unable to conduct much policy research: Shirley Williams once candidly describing its work as 'amateurism taken to its highest level'. The appearance in 1989 of the Labour-oriented Institute for Public Policy Research was a belated response to the influential right-wing think-tanks which had had a notable impact on the policy agenda and the thinking of the Thatcher government in the 1980s.

There are, however, some problems involved in the search for ways of strengthening Labour's policy research resources. There is the objection (though some might see it as a recommendation) that the party might be inhibited from adopting a radical programme and that a bureaucratic caution might be introduced into party policy-making; the civil service, it is said, is already too powerful and too conservative a force: why should the Labour Party do its work for it first? A full-blown Department of the Opposition seems a non-starter in the British context because of fears about possible politicization of the civil servants involved. Perhaps most important of all is the problem of power within the party. To the extent that the difficulties Labour experiences in framing a coherent and properly worked out programme in Opposition are the result of the party's structure and internal politics, it is not clear that simply recommending more research or more researchers is the answer. To whom would the extra staff be responsible: the NEC, the Shadow Cabinet, the leader, the PLP? Even with the present set-up there have been strong tensions, as when in the late 1960s and 1970s the research department's 'party' and left-wing image set it at odds with the parliamentary leadership. In the early 1970s, Wilson, Callaghan and Jenkins opposed an overhaul of party organization because they did not want to see Transport House become more powerful. Labour's internal struggles could mean that co-ordinating the work of the different researchers and staffs scattered around the different parts of the party would not be easy. And a move towards a more rational and informed approach to party policy-making would seem to involve a major reform of the workings and role of Conference – political dynamite in a party which is traditionally deeply conservative when it comes to its own cherished institutions and practices. Neil Kinnock's post-1987 Policy Review, which gave a bigger say than in previous Opposition policy-making exercises (in the 1970s and early 1980s) to parliamentarians and shadow ministers in drawing up policies, and the ideas emerging from it about continental-style policy commissions and the reform of Conference, suggest that improving a Labour Opposition's preparations for office depends at least as much on political will and, ultimately, on reorganization of the party's structures as on boosting research support.[83]

The party's problems in putting together policies in Opposition – and the possible or desirable 'solutions' – are not, then, quite so straightforward as proponents of what we might call the Crossman/-Laski approach often tend to assume. It is worth bearing in mind that there are those in the Labour Party (as in other political parties) who believe that Oppositions should not try to set about constructing extensive and detailed packages of policies to be ready for implementation on day one of the new regime. This can actually be dangerous and futile, they argue. It can generate electorally damaging splits and disputes, and it can hand free ammunition to the party's opponents (work on costing spending commitments being seized on with particular relish). A party's research resources are never going to match the information and expertise available in the civil service; an Opposition cannot be sure it has considered all the possible pitfalls nor be fully aware of all the practical difficulties in the way of its proposals. Circumstances can change, throwing up unanticipated problems and opportunities for which the manifesto offers no guidance and which perhaps make some existing commitments no longer appropriate. As Barbara Castle noted in her diary early in the life of the 1974 government: 'The NEC must not assume that every modification of party policy by a Labour Government is a sign of betrayal rather than a closer knowledge of the facts'.[84]

Suspicions not just of a supposedly hostile or conservative civil service but also of the possibility or likelihood of 'betrayal' by the party's own leadership are embedded in Labour's theory of the mandate (or 'manifestoism' as Henry Drucker has labelled it). Barry Hindess has made some telling criticisms of the Labour left's approach to party policy-making. Viewing policy as something which is to be determined by one body (Conference) and then put into effect by another (a Labour government), and conceiving of the problem of implementation as simply a matter of how to tie the hands of the parliamentary leadership, avoids rather than resolves the real problems, he believes. The campaign in the late 1970s and early 1980s to 'democratize' the party, he suggests, was really aimed not at opening up the process of policy debate within the party but at holding the leadership to the (left-wing) programme worked out by Conference and the NEC. The party does need to work at policy, Hindess argues, but it would be wrong to suppose that outside bodies can or should draw up detailed blueprints for governments to act upon independently of the particular conditions and constraints they will face in office. Similarly, Jones and Keating take issue with the idea of specifying the programme in detail and giving the power to determine policy to bodies that do not carry responsibility for decision-taking in government. 'Indeed,' they point out, 'it can be argued that, in constructing a chain-of-command from the activists cadre into the heart of the state machine and expecting one end of the string to move when the other is pulled, the Labour Left have fallen into one of the basic errors of the classical management school'.[85]

Richard Rose, who has systematically analysed the conditions for successful 'party government', concedes that 'An opposition party need not specify in great detail how every one of its manifesto pledges will be realized'. But, he goes on, 'Unless it has done substantial homework about how to realize its intentions, its policies will not be a programme for action, but rather a description of the world as they [sic] wish it to be'. A party can take its schemes only so far, however, and can develop its proposals only to a certain stage, as even Harold Laski was aware. A socialist party can do a good deal, he thought, to prepare detailed policy proposals before it takes office and to equip itself with its own expert advisers.

> But, when all allowance has been made for such preparedness as this, it does not really meet the pith of the problem. A socialist government, unless it desires deliberately to provoke revolution, cannot ride rough-shod over the vested interests it proposes to attack. It must test its proposals against the facts which come

into its possession when it takes office; and it may have to adjust them in the light of the new circumstances, not least their possible international repercussions, thereby revealed. It has to discuss, negotiate, conciliate, that it may attain the maximum possible agreement to its plans . . .

And Laski was clear that 'a policy which was separated from official experience would almost certainly be ignorant and, not seldom, disastrous'.[86]

Improving Opposition policy-making, then, is not a question of duplicating Whitehall in Walworth Road, trying to prepare policies to the same degree of administrative detail as the regular civil service departments, nor trying to pre-empt the future and having contingency plans in the party files for all possible eventualities. The record suggests that Labour could prepare better for office, but it is best to be realistic about just what it is possible for parties in Opposition to do. Robinson and Sandford got it about right in their study of tax policy-making, and their argument has a wider application:

> What is desirable in the parties is a clarification of objectives; some consideration of alternative means of achieving the objectives before a choice is made of a particular tax; and enough detailed consideration to ensure the practicality of the tax – i.e. that the objectives can be attained at an acceptable cost, in efficiency, or equity, or resources used in administration and compliance. Without research assistance adequate for this purpose (which implies both a capacity to assess economic effects and to anticipate the practical problems of day-to-day administration) a Shadow Chancellor is likely to be less well-prepared for office and more inclined to the rash commitment.[87]

The purpose of party policy-making in Opposition should not be to make Labour ministers into automatons nor to make the civil service redundant. There is no easy way around the problems of government and there is no easy way around the civil service. Labour governments and ministers have got to know what they want to do and to have done some serious work on their plans before entering office, but then they still need to work with and through the civil service machine to reach their objectives. Better preparation in Opposition and reinforcement by outside advisers can help strengthen the position of Labour ministers, but it would be wrong to think that these are simple and straightforward remedies and, even with them, it seems probable that the relationship between Labour governments and the mandarins would continue to be a problematic and controversial subject.

3 The Attlee government and the reform of the civil service

This chapter is as much concerned with what did *not* happen to the civil service during the 1945–51 period as with what *did* happen. Before 1945, a far-reaching reform of Whitehall had been seen on the left as an inevitable and vital task for a socialist government. Harold Laski, for instance, never tired of calling for reform on the Northcote-Trevelyan scale in order, as he saw it, to adjust the government machine to meet the challenge of contemporary problems and the needs of the 'positive state.'[1] But the changes the Attlee government introduced simply did not add up to the fundamental reform programme Laski and others had wanted and deemed necessary.

Even with the benefit of hindsight – the knowledge that the 1945 government's massive accomplishments were achieved largely through and with the traditional Whitehall personnel, structures and techniques – other commentators cannot conceal their surprise and disappointment at the way in which the civil service emerged unscathed from the Attlee years. 'The Missed Opportunity', Peter Hennessy called the chapter of his monumental book *Whitehall* which covered the period of the Attlee administration. Why, he asked, did the 1945 Labour government fail to reform the civil service 'as an integral part of its programme and as a necessary part of its success'? The Second World War had obliged the British government to find new men and to improvise new methods almost overnight but with impressive results. Yet, in Hennessy's view, 'the reform Hitler forced on Whitehall was undone by the peace because neither the politicians nor the senior Civil Service tried or cared to devise its peacetime equivalent'. He claims that this represents 'probably *the* greatest lost opportunity in the history of British public administration'.[2]

Writing from a committed socialist perspective, Richard Crossman bemoaned the 1945 government's 'uncritical reliance on White-hall' and complained that 'it did not occur to Mr Attlee that the election of a Labour Government pledged to radical social reform required any radical changes in the civil service'.

> How much more humane and imaginative our post-war recon-struction would have proved [he wrote] if government depart-ments had been invigorated by an influx of experts with special knowledge, new ideas and a sympathy for the Government's domestic and foreign policies. But the Premier dismissed such suggestions as Left-Wing claptrap. Once again, as after 1918, the best of the temporary civil servants returned to their peace-time occupations, and the old Establishment ruled unchallenged over a bureaucratic empire which had been both enormously enlarged and dangerously centralised during the war.

For Crossman, this was one of the negative lessons of 1945 and its result was that 'in 1951 the Attlee Government quietly expired in the arms of the Whitehall Establishment'.[3]

If the Attlee Labour government failed to shake up the Whitehall bureaucracy this was certainly not for want of preparatory socialist theorizing or contemporary political prodding. There is plenty of evidence of both. From the Webbs onwards, a long line of socialist intellectuals had portrayed the civil service as an inefficient vehicle for a progressive government and had advocated changes in its recruitment, training and organization. And during the war and immediate post-war years after 1945 proposals for the reform of the machinery and personnel of government achieved a somewhat wider constituency, being taken up in the press and at the parlia-mentary level and, to some extent, winning support among key figures in the leadership. Yet, despite this, there was no thorough-going reconstruction of the civil service machine after 1945. Indeed, when the civil service and the machinery of government came on to the agenda again in the 1960s, would-be Whitehall reformers very largely repeated the criticisms common twenty (and more!) years previously and propounded reorganization schemes that would also have been familiar to the earlier generation(s) of reformers. But in the 1960s as in the 1940s, a Labour government frustrated rather than fulfilled these hopes of administrative reform.

'A CIVIL SERVICE OF A NEW KIND'?

If Labour is going to have its fair share of the Government of this country in the future, the party will have to take a very keen interest in the efficiency and general well being of the Civil Service, for that Service is the instrument upon which it will have to depend for the execution of its policy.[4]

So warned a prescient writer in the Labour Party's monthly discussion journal *The Labour Magazine* in March 1929, just three months before the second MacDonald government took office. That appeal, it must be said, fell largely on deaf ears. Outside a small Fabian circle, there was at that time no serious or sustained interest in the Labour Party in the problems of civil service efficiency and organization.

What early socialist thinking there was about the adequacy of the administrative machine for the tasks of modern government had developed as part of the wider pre-First-World-War campaign for 'national efficiency', which drew in figures from across the political spectrum, including Conservatives and Liberal Imperialists as well as bureaucratic socialists of the Fabian school, most notably the Webbs. The cult of the expert, the need for specialized education and training and for a closer relation between government and science, dissatisfaction with the machinery of government (local as well as central) – these and other themes which were to become the staple fare of later reformers and modernizers were central to the 'ideology of national efficiency'. Where the Webbs differed from some other campaigners was in basing their plans for the collectivist society of the future firmly on the expert bureaucrat rather than on the importation of businessmen and the methods of private business into public affairs.[5]

The importance that the Webbs attached to these questions is shown by their pinpointing 'the lack of administrative science and the shortcomings of our administrative machinery' as actually being the most formidable obstacles to the adoption of a programme of social reform. 'Our governing class', they argued, ' . . . do not yet seem to have realised that social reconstructions require as much specialised training and sustained study as the building of bridges and railways, the interpretation of the law, or technical improvements in machinery and mechanical processes'. The link between administrative and social reform was also made by Beatrice Webb, who was an influential member of the Haldane Committee which reported in 1918, when she noted that 'the subject matter of the machinery of Government Committee is immense and the importance of the questions raised vital to the success of the Equalitarian state'.[6]

The Webbs' writings were brimming with ideas for the more efficient organization and conduct of government which, even when they might have had little immediate practical impact, have had a powerful long-term and indirect influence. The separation of policy from day-to-day administration, which they saw as an essential reform, was reflected in the creation of public corporations to run the nationalized industries and lies behind the schemes for hiving-off, accountable management and the establishment of executive agencies put forward since the 1960s. The repeated calls for (and the faltering steps towards) better trained and more expert officials obviously echo Webbian preoccupations. The Haldane principle of organization according to function rather than clientele, with which they are so closely associated, still governs administrative cartography in Whitehall. Attempts to introduce 'output budgeting', to utilize cost-benefit analysis and to develop performance indicators and management information systems in Whitehall are eerily foreshadowed in their *Constitution for the Socialist Commonwealth* (1920) where, as Samuel Beer has pointed out, 'some pages read like an early prospectus for PPBS (Planning Programming Budgeting System)'. And Beatrice Webb can be found happily explaining the idea of an 'efficiency audit' to a fellow-member of the Haldane Committee.[7]

The Webbs believed that the greatly extended functions of the state in the future socialist commonwealth would require 'a Civil Service of a new kind', equipped for original research and investigation and trained in the use of statistics and modern administrative techniques. They called for 'the systematic organisation . . . of comparative statistics of output or results'. Government departments would have to abandon their traditional function of being 'inhibitive of what was bad rather than stimulative of what was good'. They envisaged that 'control departments', charged with tasks of inspection, costing, audit and research, would monitor the administration of public services and nationalized industries and report to MPs and the public on their performance. And although later Fabian critics were to be fierce in their denunciations of the 'all-rounder' and the 'amateur', the Webbs supported the development of a unified cadre of generalist administrators, moving from department to department and acquiring invaluable 'inside' knowledge of the working of the government machine.[8] (The Webbs' generalists would, however, seem to be rather different creatures from the products of the Fisher reforms being introduced into Whitehall as they were writing, in being trained scientific bureaucrats even if not subject-specialists.)

A 'Civil Service of a new kind' was, however, never on the cards during the 1924 and 1929–31 Labour governments. Their limited tenure of office, the short-term horizons imposed by their always precarious parliamentary position and the constant pressure of other urgent problems and, not least, the desire for constitutional 'respectability' and the lack of interest in administrative questions shown by most Labour ministers and by MacDonald as Prime Minister made a Webbian-style administrative revolution simply inconceivable.

There was little chance of Whitehall being seriously disturbed by those of MacDonald's Cabinet ministers who *did* take public administration seriously – most notably Sidney Webb and Lord Haldane. As a socialist theorist Webb had long argued the need for administrative reform but as a minister he was fairly ineffective and was favourably impressed by the service he got from his officials. In any case, his ministerial posts never gave him direct access to the levers of power over the civil service in the Treasury, though one suspects that it would not have made a great deal of difference if they had, for as a frontbencher in the 1920s he took pains to defend the civil service against its critics. For instance, while Willie Graham, Financial Secretary to the Treasury in the 1924 government, questioned the power over senior Whitehall appointments of Sir Warren Fisher as Permanent Secretary to the Treasury and Head of the Civil Service, and criticized its consequence in the displacement of departmental specialists by 'general managers' at the top of the service, Webb's view was that there was no practical alternative to Treasury control of a unified civil service and he defended the role of the official head of the Treasury in Whitehall postings. The mandarins had nothing to fear from a man who could say, 'I cannot help feeling that we have got a treasure in our Civil Service, and we want to keep it'.[9]

It is an interesting comment on Labour's institutional conservatism that the only proposal for administrative reform to be made during the 1924 government came from one of its newest recruits, the former Liberal Cabinet minister Lord Haldane, though it goes without saying that he had little opportunity in his ten months as Lord Chancellor to implement the far-reaching proposals of his 1918 report on the machinery of government. Haldane's sole achievement was in fact to win Cabinet approval for the creation of a 'Committee of Economic Enquiry', modelled on his beloved Committee of Imperial Defence and reflecting the Haldane Committee's call for better governmental arrangements for 'investigation and thought, as preliminary to action'. He envisaged an expert advisory body for the Cabinet on economic and (civil) scientific and technical questions, though there was civil service opposition to such a wide-ranging remit and a clear concern in Whitehall not to see the regular officials' and departments' monopoly of advice to ministers seriously threatened.[10] In the event, the Labour government fell before the plan could leave the drawing board, though Baldwin's Conservative government took up the proposal and set up a Committee of Civil Research which in practice operated very much on the sidelines of government.

On his return to office MacDonald replaced the Committee of Civil Research in January 1930 with the Economic Advisory Council, but this new body was something very much less than the sort of expert and powerful Economic General Staff seen as essential by critics of Treasury and Bank of England orthodoxy. The idea of an Economic General Staff had been floated by William Beveridge at the end of 1923, had been taken up by the Liberal Party in its 'Yellow Book' of 1928 and was championed by progressive economists such as Keynes. *Labour and the Nation* had promised a 'National Economic Committee' to act as the Prime Minister's 'eyes and ears on economic questions'. But the hybrid scheme that finally emerged in 1930 was bound to fail, combining as it did only a tiny (albeit impressively qualified) staff with a representative council membership of businessmen, union leaders and economists who could be guaranteed not to agree on the key economic issues of the day. Indeed, to J. H. Thomas it was a recommendation that if such a body had existed in 1929 'it would have stopped many of our impossible Election promises'. And certainly – as in 1924 – senior civil servants were anxious to prevent the creation of any real rival to the Treasury or anything that could be construed as duplicating the work of existing departments. There are suggestions that MacDonald might well have been looking to establish a counterweight to Snowden and the Treasury – if so, he was unsuccessful – but the council was also born of his political need to be seen to be doing something in the face of the economic crisis the government faced, and his desire to respond in an 'above-party' or 'national' fashion. In fact, Mosley's resignation in 1930 removed the only figure inside the second Labour government with bold ideas about overhauling the executive machinery of government (at ministerial and civil service levels) to tackle unemployment – ideas which MacDonald and a Cabinet committee under Snowden dismissed as unworkable.[11]

On a different front, although in the 1929 government Henderson had a firm ministerial grip on the Foreign Office he did not push through the major reorganization its Labour critics wanted. As we have seen earlier (chapter 2), the party's International Advisory Committee was in a vengeful mood towards the Foreign Office after the Zinoviev Letter incident and it had drawn up a detailed plan designed (among other things) to both democratize and make more efficient the foreign services. It proposed 'a career open to the talents from the bottom to the top' by eliminating the class distinctions between diplomatic, consular and clerical posts, and alongside this would go a reorganization into a series of specialized regional services: Far-Eastern, Middle-Eastern, East European, and so on (see also chapter 5). The latter idea made no headway, however, and as Foreign Secretary Henderson emphatically rejected the merger of the diplomatic, consular and commercial classes.[12] Not surprisingly, the Foreign Office continued to be sniped at but even partial implementation of the IAC's agenda had to await the Eden–Bevin reforms of the 1940s (which went nowhere near far enough for radical opinion at that time).

There were other ideas for civil service reform floated in the 1920s by Labour supporters which could have yielded useful results but which were also not taken up when the party was in office. Harold Laski, for instance, was concerned that the narrow social base of the administrative class of the service could skew the advice ministers received, and he wanted to widen its recruitment (which he recognized was contingent on democratizing the educational system) and to make more determined efforts to promote able officials from the lower grades. Officials should be put in touch with new ideas by a system of sabbaticals and by more contact with universities and research bodies. Younger officials should be brought into senior positions more rapidly and the retirement age-limit lowered to try to counter the tendencies towards rigidity of thinking at the top levels. New blood should be introduced from outside Whitehall by means of 'special appointments to a small number of technical posts'. E. P. Harries, quoted earlier on the need for Labour to take the question of civil service efficiency seriously, felt that the government machine would not be able to take over and run nationalized industries without a considerable influx of experts and technicians specially recruited from industry, and he wanted to see greater interchange of staff between the central bureaucracy and local government and private business in order to broaden experience and break down the engrained Whitehall point of view.[13]

The absence of any programme of nationalization made Harries' proposals appear somewhat premature, but he had none the less put his finger on an important problem which was in fact to be met with the public corporation device rather than by changing the character of the core civil service. More generally, his and Laski's other proposals simply had no political steam behind them at this time. In terms of their (lack of) impact on the Labour party and Labour government (or indeed any other government) in this period they are thus no more than a footnote to a non-event; their significance comes as part of the longer-term development of socialist thinking about the problems of civil service and government reform. For when, in the 1930s and early to mid-1940s, socialists returned to these problems, this legacy of ideas and experiences from the Webbs onwards was to have an important, if perhaps sometimes subliminal, influence on their approach.

WHITEHALL AND THE DEMANDS OF THE 'POSITIVE STATE': PRE-WAR AND WARTIME CRITIQUES

'The post-war world will call for adjustments in our administrative technique at least as far-reaching as those which reformed the [Civil] Service nearly three-quarters of a century ago', argued Harold Laski in September 1941 in the *New Statesman and Nation*, firmly putting Whitehall reform on the post-war reconstruction agenda then starting to take shape even though the outcome of the Second World War was still in the balance.[14] Indeed, Laski implied that civil service reform might well be a *precondition* of meaningful social and economic advance after the war. In view of recent positive evaluations of Whitehall's wartime record,[15] it is significant that Laski's judgement at the time was scathing. 'There has been a lack of imagination and audacity, an unwillingness to take the risks of innovation, when the times called for these qualities', he wrote. 'The departments have known how to construct a powerful case against doing anything; they have rarely shown zeal for decisive experiment. They have been silent before powerful interests. They have shown a tragic unwillingness to accept new responsibilities'. The pre-war bureaucracy had been no better, having in the 1930s 'a record in the field of social and economic matters in which timidity was a virtue and innovation a horror from which every sound official was taught to shrink.' British officials compared unfavourably with the energetic and enthusiastic US New Dealers. As Laski put it:

> The unstated assumptions of most of the Departments were in keeping with the prevailing temper of British government in the inter-war years. The permissible boundaries of state-intervention had been reached. New experiments would be economically unsound and administratively unwise. The Service was, on the whole, satisfied and complacent. Great action would have disturbed the even tenor of its ways.

Since 1919, he asserted, Whitehall had lacked 'both the capacity to see the problems before it in their full proportion, and the courage to tackle them with resolution'. The central problem was that the civil service was increasingly out of kilter with the needs of the times. It was 'an admirable instrument for the *laisser-faire* state', but 'now we have moved into a society which will live or die in proportion to its capacity to plan, we need administrative expedients on a scale far wider than the present direction of the Service appears to be aware'. Laski's article finished with some very pointed advice to his own party and its leaders then in government in the wartime coalition that Whitehall could not and should not be left to reform itself:

> It is important, above all for the Labour Party, to remember that every great impetus to administrative reform has, in the past, come from outside the Service. On its record so far in the war, it does not seem likely that the source of renovation will be different in the future.

These last remarks were important because, as it happened, Laski was writing at the start of a seven- or eight-year period (from around 1941–2 to around 1948–9) which did in fact see considerable outside pressure to reshape the civil service – a campaign in which Labour supporters were to be well to the fore. But, for the most part, the outsiders' pressure was simply absorbed by the Whitehall machine and what reforms there were were initiated and firmly controlled by the insiders – senior mandarins and ministers, including Labour ministers. One important reason for this is that for all the exhortation by Laski and others, a thoroughgoing reform of the government bureaucracy never became part of the Labour Party's official programme. Consequently, the party's leaders entered office with no definite and properly worked-out scheme for the reorganization of Whitehall. Their experience in the coalition government served mostly to reinforce their already existing caution and pragmatism in their attitude towards these questions. Thus after 1945 it was hardly surprising that they should rebuff outside critics of the civil service, confident that the machine they now knew so well could work in the way they wanted and that any adjustments needed were best made under general ministerial superintendence by the permanent technicians of government in the civil service.

Laski was always something of a thorn in the leadership's side, which might well have coloured assessments of his thinking, but it is important to point out that, while he was one of the most publicly prominent socialists arguing for an overhaul of the civil service in the 1930s and 1940s, he had no monopoly of ideas and proposals in this respect. Other figures, notably G. D. H. Cole and W. A. Robson, could be found canvassing reforms too, and also relevant in this context was the work done on economic planning in the party in the 1930s, which raised, even if it did not resolve, important questions about the administrative machinery of a socialist government.

The new generation of socialist economists rethinking Labour's economic policy in the mid-1930s, such as Evan Durbin and Hugh Gaitskell, were clear that 'the Civil Service would not be fully equipped to provide the necessary advice' to successfully execute an incoming Labour government's economic programme.[16] Supporting the development of economic plans at the ministerial level, it was envisaged, must be some sort of expert secretariat or a specialized planning commission, including regular officials, socialist outsiders and economists. The Economic Advisory Council was rejected as administratively ill-conceived and because of its association with MacDonald. But there was no agreement in the party on the details of a replacement. Laski, for instance, would have no truck with an Economic General Staff. He had written a Fabian pamphlet in 1931 on *The Limitations of the Expert*, and was fearful of the anti-democratic implications of a technocratic approach to policy-making: 'Not even an oligarchy of economic experts, supposing them to be agreed, is entitled . . . to have the sovereignty of the State transferred to its hands'. Attlee, however, insisted that though a Labour government 'should not require advice from experts as to what policy to pursue', the absence of a 'general staff' was a 'serious defect in our governmental machinery'. 'In order to carry through a co-ordinated plan of reconstruction', he argued, 'there will be required a well-equipped and diversified staff at the centre to work out the main lines of the plan which is to be implemented in the departments'.[17]

The Prime Minister, Attlee pointed out, had no department, only private secretaries and the (then) very small Cabinet Secretariat. But though some in the party favoured a Prime Minister's Department 'to give more informed and vigorous direction to government', it was difficult to reconcile this idea with plans endorsed at the 1933 conference to put a future Labour premier under close Cabinet and party control.[18] Cole, in one of the fullest discussions of the machinery of government options for organizing planning, called for a central statistical office and proposed to locate the central planning machinery under the Prime Minister in a Prime Minister's Department. Neither Attlee nor Morrison was impressed by his scheme, however, and the whole question was simply allowed to get lost in the NEC committee network so that the party never actually prepared a blueprint indicating how it would organize the planning which was central to its economic strategy.[19]

More generally, throughout the 1930s a variety of ideas for the reform of the civil service was floated by a trio of socialist academic experts in government and public administration: Laski, Cole and W. A. Robson. The details were sometimes rather hazy, but there was considerable common ground.[20]

The style and the cautious cast of mind of the traditional mandarin elite might have been appropriate for a largely regulatory state, it was argued, but were not suited to the social-service-providing and interventionist state. 'The Treasury mind is a negative mind', argued Laski. 'All the evidence goes to show that modern administration requires the positive mind capable of creative innovation, and able to conceive long-term schemes which do not necessarily bring an immediate financial return'. As Robson saw it, the need was to secure

> a more constructive type of individual in the various [public] services, so that when a go-ahead policy is ordered, it will not meet with the unconscious obstruction caused by the sort of official who, with the best will in the world, can see only the difficulties and dangers of the situation rather than its possibilities and opportunities.

The way to get this new type of official was fairly simple, he thought:

I am sure that I could devise a series of examination tests which would distinguish the cautious, negative, obstructive type of individual from the positive, constructive, problem-solving, planning type for whom there is so great a need at present.

There were calls for greater mobility between Whitehall and the outside world and for greater flexibility within the civil service. Cole argued that 'any rapid growth of socialization or State economic control' would necessarily involve 'a considerable amount of recruitment from outside the ranks of the Civil Service, and by methods different from those by which the Civil Service is ordinarily entered'. Robson looked forward to able outsiders joining the civil service at mid-career, who 'should infuse official life with a continuous stream of stimulating ideas derived from unofficial sources'. Transfers and interchange between different branches of the public service – the civil service, local government, the diplomatic and consular services, public corporations – should become the norm, it was suggested, to widen the experience of officials, give them a broader outlook and break down the exclusive caste spirit at the top of Whitehall. It should be made easier to pension off inefficient officials or those unable to adapt themselves to the new methods and tasks. Promotions from the lower classes of the civil service would both broaden the class base of the higher grades and make better use of talented individuals who would otherwise go to seed doing routine jobs.

Of these three socialist reformers, only Laski addressed the issue of the divisions between specialists (scientists, engineers, technicians and so on) and generalist administrators, which so preoccupied Fabian reformers in the 1960s and 1970s. In 1926 he had said that 'the one big innovation for which I am above all anxious is that technical experts shall be deliberately considered for the highest Administrative posts', but in the 1930s, as noted above, he was very much concerned to keep the expert in his (clearly subordinate) place. The 'administrator must predominate over the technician', he insisted in a review of the Tomlin Report. 'As a general rule it is the former, and not the latter, who should attain the highest administrative posts. . . . The unanswerable defence of this standpoint is that it safeguards the attainment of proportion in administration'. Certain passages in *Parliamentary Government in England* could not have been better written by the most ardent defenders of the Whitehall status quo:

the confinement of the highest posts . . . to men whose training is, in the best sense, humanistic, has . . . been the salvation of the service . . . as between two able men, the specialist is less likely to become a successful administrator in the modern State than, say, one who has been trained in the Honours school of *Literae Humaniores* at Oxford.[21]

It must be said that there was nothing particularly *socialist* about these ideas and proposals, though they were often presented as necessary for a successful programme of economic planning and social reform. Eatwell and Wright's general comment about Labour discussions in the 1930s about the reform of government is applicable here: these proposals 'were designed to achieve sensible reform in the machinery of government rather than replace one sort of machinery by another (socialist) sort'. But whatever their advocates' intent or purpose, these were clearly not the sort of issues to quicken the pulse of the party leadership (when they got any attention at all). Dalton was the exception rather than the rule when, in *Practical Socialism for Britain*, he addressed the subject of civil service reform. Even then he gave only one page to the matter, referring to 'some minor weaknesses in our Civil Service'. The defects he singled out were:

a tendency, which politicians should have checked, for a few high officials to take too much upon themselves; a tendency sometimes to run in ruts, and to exaggerate difficulties; some excess of Departmental self-consciousness; some slowness in all inter-Departmental mechanisms; occasional honest incapacity, especially among the older men, to change direction readily when policy changes; a tendency, much more marked in some Departments than in others, to damp down initiative in the junior ranks.

Dalton's view was that 'such weaknesses as these may be largely remedied by active political chiefs', and the only structural reforms he mentioned were the 'fusion' of the diplomatic and consular services and more frequent interchanges of staff between different Whitehall departments, and between central government, local authorities and public enterprises, to 'quicken the circulation of ideas, extend individual experience, and dig men out of their ruts'.[22]

But to the party leadership, including Dalton, other machinery-of-government issues were apparently more important than the niceties of civil service organization and reorganization, hence the controversy over parliamentary reform and emergency powers (see chapter 6) and the discussions about the functional regrouping of departments and the need for Cabinet reform to create a small policy-oriented Cabinet free from day-to-day administrative burdens.[23] The NEC did issue a report on parliamentary procedure but, as in the case of planning machinery noted above, there was never any statement of official party policy on the future shape of the civil service or on the question of the departmental and Cabinet structure. So, although some of the relevant issues were raised in a piecemeal fashion within the party in the 1930s, the opportunity was missed to mount a formal Haldane-style exercise to settle the 'first-order' questions about the parliamentary and Cabinet context within which the civil service would operate under a socialist government and which would largely determine the sort of civil service required.

Whitehall's socialist critics may thus not have succeeded in the 1930s in getting their ideas incorporated into Labour's official programme, but with the outbreak of war and the threat to national survival their strictures were given an extra edge. Indeed, from different points on the political spectrum there was a flood of criticism of the government machine and the civil service over the organization of the war effort. The setbacks of the period up to the end of 1942 were one factor here, but the looming problems of post-war reconstruction also raised questions like those posed in the 1930s about the administrative capabilities of the British system of government. The press carried articles about the need for reform of the administrative machine. The Select Committee on National Expenditure suggested in 1942 the reorganization of the Treasury, the creation of a standing select committee on the civil service and a civil service training college. The National Administrative College Group, pressing for improved management training, won the backing of leading figures in many walks of public life and in the different parties. A Liberal Party committee brought forward proposals for civil service reform, and a PEP broadsheet on the machinery of government and the civil service was a particularly influential contribution to the public debate.[24] On the left, Laski used his column in *The New Statesman* to carry his ideas about government reform to a wider audience, and he and others missed no opportunity to develop and expound their pre-war critiques.

Laski's best-remembered piece from the war years is his Introduction to J. P. W. Mallalieu's spirited polemic '*Passed To You, Please*', published in 1942. In his book Mallalieu (who became a Labour MP in 1945) complained of muddle, waste and red tape in Whitehall. The civil service was inflexible, remote from ordinary people, had no knowledge of how industry was run and lacked proper administrative training. 'The ruling class, at least in this country, has a curious belief in the amateur, whether in sport, or in running an industry', Mallalieu argued, and in the civil service the expert 'tends to be treated as a necessary hack rather than as a colleague'. 'Such defects, under Socialism, would be even more disastrous than they are under capitalism', he insisted.[25]

In his Introduction to Mallalieu's book Laski accused Whitehall's dominant administrative class of lacking imagination and audacity and of being unwilling to experiment: 'they regard all principles to which they are unaccustomed, all experience alien from their own, as dangerous and impracticable'.

> Innovation on a grand scale, utter frankness, relentless attack upon obstructive interests, rapid adaptation to the unexpected, the ruthless rejection of men who do not rise to the occasion . . . are pretty exactly the qualities against which the main genius of our Civil Service has been directed.

He went on to make twenty suggestions for civil service reform including: more recruitment of outsiders with 'special qualifications' into the administrative class; the division of the Treasury, with a separate Ministry of Personnel taking over its establishment functions; the creation of a civil service staff college; an end to the rigid division between the civil service and the local government service, with transfers between the two becoming the norm and not the exception; the dismantling of the barriers between the administrative and the scientific and technical sides of the civil service, permitting the most able specialists to be considered for the highest administrative posts; and finally he proposed a major shake-up of the diplomatic service and the Foreign Office.[26]

Over twenty years later a new generation of Whitehall critics and reformers were to find a contemporary relevance in this short essay of Laski's, seeing it as something like a rough first draft of the Fulton Report.[27] There is a great deal in this interpretation (see chapter 4), but it should be borne in mind that Laski's was by no means the only voice calling for civil service reform at this time in terms that would become fashionable again in the 1960s. In addition, it is important to point out that Laski had in his Introduction to *'Passed To You, Please'* abandoned one key feature of his pre-war thinking and that he was very soon to backtrack on one of the central reforms proposed in it. In the 1930s, as noted above, he had praised the dominance of the generalist over the specialist in Whitehall and disputed the claims of the 'expert'. Now he recanted: 'I have become convinced that the subordination of the specialist to the general administrator . . . is a profound mistake'. He argued first that the civil service should look out for and nurture administrative talent in the ranks of its scientists and open up to them the way to the top departmental jobs, and second and more generally that government policy-making in the 'positive' state should be much more informed by the results of scientific research and intelligence (meaning both the natural and the social sciences). The establishment of a Staff College for the training of higher civil servants would seem to fit in with this more technocratic approach to government, and certainly Laski's initial view when the Select Committee on National Expenditure proposed one in 1942 was to welcome the idea as 'long overdue'. But by 1943 he had changed his mind, arguing that it would be wrong to segregate civil servants in their own possibly narrow and ingrown establishment, and that their post-entry training should instead involve some time in a university, taking relevant social science and law courses, together with placements outside the service (in local government or Parliament, for instance). Describing the aim of training as producing officials with 'flexible' minds and able to transfer without difficulty from one type of work to another suggested that Laski wanted to modify but not abolish Whitehall's generalist tradition.[28]

Like Laski, G. D. H. Cole continued in wartime to press the case for civil service reform to adapt to what he anticipated would be the greatly extended functions of post-war government (especially in the economic sphere). Again, the criticisms were similar to those voiced in the 1930s, particularly that putting too great a value on 'playing for safety' and 'keeping out of hot water' (a stance which Cole at least recognized was largely the result of the ever-present possibility of parliamentary scrutiny and questioning) fostered timidity and a desire to evade responsibility when the need was for 'a new spirit of creative adventure'. The higher civil service, he complained, was 'conservative and averse from change, more apt to envisage difficulties than opportunities, and disposed to let well alone'. Cole's remedies were also pretty much in the mainstream of contemporary 'reformist' opinion. For instance, he wanted a less cloistered civil service with greater mobility and interchange with other parts of the public service at all levels. Changes in recruitment and promotion practices were needed to open up the higher administrative ranks to promotees from the lower grades and to specialists and technicians ('somehow, the ring which corners the best jobs has to be broken'). And while he felt that Whitehall recruits should be drawn from a wider range of academic degree subjects – particularly sciences and social sciences but perhaps also from relevant postgraduate courses – Cole rejected the idea of a civil service staff college (which would presumably have a 'relevant' curriculum) and opted for post-entry training via bursaries for further university study on the grounds that officials needed less, not more, isolation from the world.

Cole was particularly convinced that 'the present civil service system . . . is entirely unfitted for the control or operation of productive enterprises or economic services, or for the undertaking of major tasks of economic planning – e.g. planning for full employment'. The implication was that a Labour government would therefore need to build up a new 'second Civil Service' of a functional character, concerned with tasks of economic planning and the management of 'socialized' industries. This new breed of public servants would have to be experts in economics, technology and science rather than having the traditional mandarin background in 'greats', and Cole believed they would have to be drawn largely from the existing technical and managerial personnel of private industry. This new public service would exist alongside the conventional civil service, with which there would be regular interchange, but Cole envisaged that in the new functional service there would be less security (no jobs for life) and much more flexibility to move people in and out (including relaxing the normal Whitehall inhibitions about interchange with private business).[29]

While Laski and Cole's detailed analyses were being presented in the form of lectures to Fabian audiences, talks to conferences and articles in academic journals, similar arguments were being aired in the pages of *The New Statesman*, particularly in 1941 and 1942, reaching a wider left-wing audience and contributing to the general pressure for change. (Sometimes Laski wrote in his own name, but other articles had no byline – though W. A. Robson, for one, is known to have contributed anonymously to the magazine on the civil service.)[30] In March 1941, for instance, the magazine was urging the need to make leading officials 'take more risks, assume more responsibility, and break down departmental and inter-departmental barriers', and complaining that the traditional mandarin was far from being the sort of 'hustler, animated by an unconquerable will to get things done' that was needed in wartime. The Labour movement, it suggested, had fought so long against victimization and unfair dismissals by capitalists that it had a rooted objection to sacking anyone:

> Consequently, when Labour men get into Government, they do not, in general, sack any of the regulars who they find in control of their departments, or even bring in outsiders, more in sympathy with wartime needs, to take charge of important emergency work. They tend to leave the established machine as they find it, and to hope that, if they hustle about themselves, issuing orders right and left, their own energy will somehow transmit itself to their departments, and their orders get carried out as fast as they give them.
>
> This does not happen: it cannot happen as long as the old personnel is left undisturbed.

There was no need to 'sack the lot', however, but ministers should dig down below the top ranks in their departments to find the energetic, younger staff who could do the job properly. As the state's administrative role grew, it needed 'in the places of authority men of courage and initiative . . . it cannot afford to make shift with routineers'. Other articles contrasted the brilliant, reforming civil service of 1906–19 with Whitehall's mediocre record in the inter-war years, attributing it in part to the baleful influence of Warren Fisher as Head of the Civil Service:

> The result was a number of heads of departments who can always find good reasons for doing nothing: and a service which can subject any new proposal to a withering fire of criticism, but not one that can willingly entertain new ideas, much less originate them and carry them through.

The civil service, the *New Statesman* argued, needed both a different spirit and different leaders if it was not actually to hamper first the war effort and then post-war reconstruction.[31]

As in the 1930s, though, despite the obvious importance of these ideas for a party proposing to more actively use the state's administrative machine to achieve its programme, there was a complete disjunction between the proposals developed in socialist intellectual circles and the official response of the Labour Party. A machinery of central government sub-committee of the NEC's central committee on reconstruction problems held a few desultory meetings from late 1941, considering papers by Laski (on devolution, parliamentary committees and the position of the Prime Minister) and Morrison (on parliamentary procedure) which fell well short of anything like a properly considered and agreed party blueprint for the reform of government.[32] That no such plan emerged during the war years is all the more surprising given that some individual senior Labour figures did latch on to the fashionable outside reform thinking and seemed prepared to use their positions inside the government machine to promote reorganization proposals.

Stafford Cripps led the way, calling in June 1942 for 'another Haldane'. A firm believer in Webbian scientific administration, Cripps also appears to have seen public discontent with the organization of government as a lever that he could use in a bid to replace Churchill as Prime Minister. In Opposition in the 1930s he had, controversially, seen drastic parliamentary and governmental reorganization as probably necessary to overcome capitalist opposition during the transition to socialism. The Cabinet Secretary, Sir Edward Bridges, was concerned that Cripps the minister might be unduly influenced by socialist intellectuals such as Laski and Kingsley Martin (editor of the *New Statesman*), but in fact his thinking about the civil service seems to have been more strongly influenced by PEP's (1940–1) inquiry into the machinery of government (PEP's secretary became his private secretary when he entered the Cabinet). Churchill was unenthusiastic about an inquiry and senior mandarins were aghast at the idea of a Haldane-style review dominated by 'outsiders', thus Cripps' proposal was only given the go ahead when he had been persuaded by Sir John Anderson (Lord President of the Council but also significantly a former permanent secretary) to agree to an 'insider' operation. Cripps had triggered off a process of internal machinery of government review that was to last in one form or another for ten years, but a practitioners' focus on the immediate and the practical, eschewing reflection on general questions of a constitutional nature or anything like root-and-branch change, was to be the predictable outcome of the method adopted: Whitehall's classic combination of a committee of officials working to a committee of (busy and preoccupied) ministers (chaired in the wartime coalition government by Anderson and including, for Labour, Cripps and Morrison – whom Bridges also amazingly thought would be excessively influenced by the 'theoretical' views of Laski and the *New Statesman*).[33]

Attlee, who had held Haldane-type views on administrative questions since the 1930s, had as deputy Prime Minister chaired the Cabinet meeting in August 1942 which had authorized the establishment of the Anderson Committee. In December of that year he circulated to the committee his own proposals for civil service reform and, in view of what happened – or rather what did not happen – after 1945 when Attlee formed his own government, it is worth spelling out just what they were.

First, Attlee wanted the machinery of government committee to consider 'the desirability of establishing a Civil Service Staff College'. Its function would be to develop 'initiative and flexibility of mind' by exposing officials to a wider range of experience from public organizations outside the regular civil service and to methods based more on business principles as practised in industry (Attlee felt that this was important because the relation of the state to private enterprise would be pressing after the war and knowledge of routine Whitehall methods would not be enough). An important feature of Attlee's plan was to allow for the earlier promotion of those passing through the college with distinction. Second, he advocated more interchange of staff between Whitehall departments and between central and local government; it would be more difficult to arrange transfers between business and the civil service, though he thought these too would have their advantages. Third, he argued that 'the changed content of much Government business demands . . . not only alterations in the government machine, but also changes in methods of financial control'. He criticized the Treasury's 'Gladstonian' traditions – 'saving half a crown, while millions are passed with less difficulty' – as tending to waste, and thought that the way forward was to improve internal departmental financial controls. Finally, Attlee proposed a reconsideration of the position of the Permanent Secretary to the Treasury as Head of the Civil Service. The financial side of the Treasury should be under the Chancellor of the Exchequer and a permanent secretary expert in financial matters, while a separate permanent secretary dealing with establishments and personnel should be directly under the Prime Minister as First Lord of the Treasury (assisted by a junior minister taking over the functions of the Financial Secretary). He emphasized that he would not wish to establish a Prime Minister's Department.

> The Prime Minister can of course look to all departments for advice and assistance, but in my view requires something more than Private Secretaries for carrying out his functions. In my view this second Permanent Secretary to the Treasury, while being head of the Establishments Branch, should also be something equivalent to a chef de cabinet to the Prime Minister.[34]

Senior Treasury officials defensively minuted that there was nothing new in the points Attlee raised and his initiative came to nothing. Although the ideas *were* largely derivative and far from revolutionary, that Attlee was prepared to put them forward at all was significant. Here was the leader of the Labour Party and the deputy Prime Minister – and not at all the sort of maverick figure that Cripps seemed to be at this time – endorsing some of the key proposals of Whitehall's outside critics. But the drawback was that this was a one-off intervention and crucially absent was the sort of follow-through in the bureaucratic politics of the Whitehall arena necessary to translate these ideas into practical schemes or – outside Whitehall – any attempt to incorporate this thinking into the party's programme as part of the preparations for a future Labour government (Attlee seems to have paid no attention to the struggling party sub-committee on the machinery of central government).[35]

Moreover, continued experience in office seems to have made Attlee – like other Labour ministers – into a pragmatic 'insider' so far as the administrative machine was concerned. His 1944 view that 'we must see to it that, in the machinery of Government as well as other things, we utilise to the full the valuable lessons that we have learned in the war' thus suggested a process of adaptation that would be firmly rooted in notions of what was practical and realistic developed by those Whitehall insiders – ministers and senior officials – who had run the wartime machine and who would also run the peacetime one rather than any Laski-style commitment to the imposition from the outside of a programme of far-reaching changes of the sort advocated by socialist theorists from the 1930s onwards. Peter Hennessy has rightly emphasized the importance of the experience of the wartime coalition for understanding Labour's approach to government after 1945:

> Attlee and his ministers, despite being a radically intentioned government, did not embark on a reform of the Civil Service because they knew the wartime machine personally and liked what they saw. They had seen the recent administrative past and it had worked.[36]

OUTSIDERS' PRESSURE AND INSIDERS' RESPONSE: THE 1945 LABOUR GOVERNMENT AND THE CIVIL SERVICE

For Labour's leadership, which had seen the workings of the civil service from the inside, the administrative lessons of the war years may have been reassuring but there were those in (and outside) the party who believed that the coming to power of the first majority Labour government in 1945 did in fact raise some pretty fundamental questions about the suitability of the Whitehall machine for the achievement of socialism. As an *Observer* editorial put it, a few months after Attlee's ministers had entered office:

> One point frequently overlooked in the discussion of Socialism is the nature of the tools for the job. If the Government is to make nationalisation work, it can only do so through the energy and ability of the Civil Service. To that Service our fortunes are increasingly committed: muddle, lethargy and dilatory methods in the Departments of State can do far more harm to Socialism than any blunder of the Ministers themselves. Never was a Government so dependent on its officials as one which brings to Whitehall continual increase of burdens and responsibilities. How is it to use for its purposes an organisation designed for quite different ends?

That the civil service 'was born to serve the Victorian State' posed a special challenge for the new socialist government, the paper thought. 'Ministers have not only to reshape the national economy . . . they have to reanimate and remould the Civil Service to their new purposes. Success in one will be useless without success in the other'.[37]

Six months into the new government the *New Statesman* was also wondering 'whether the civil service machine . . . is in need of larger adaptations to its new functions than are in contemplation at present':

> The scientists and technicians have had their pay and status improved; but they are still dissatisfied. Little has been done to break down the sharp division between the Whitehall 'desk-and-carpet man' and the public servant 'in the field', as inspector or regional officer. The Civil and Local Government services still stand entirely apart, with only the most exiguous possibilities of interchange. Some thought is, no doubt, being given to these matters; but are they being considered on the right scale? They are all issues arising out of, and closely affecting, the transition from a 'private profit-making' to a broadly 'socialist' society. They must be promptly considered if there is not to be a danger of the Government's excellent legislative record coming to grief in the no less important matter of administrative efficiency.[38]

Writing in *Tribune*, J. P. W. Mallalieu's view was similar: 'new tasks are calling for new men and new methods. . . . . [The] present Government, as its nationalisation programme extends, must provide not only new methods for recruiting and training Civil Servants but also a new machine for them to work'. In the words of 'An Ex-Civil Servant' in another *Tribune* article, reform was necessary because the civil service 'was supposed to serve the political system we are just about to consign to perdition'. 'Labour Ministers have been too willing to defend their established Civil Servants', he complained, cataloguing the numerous defects of the service: red tape, inter-departmental rivalries, the neglect of the expert, the stress on the right sort of social background, lack of ideas and initiative, hostility towards the public. 'Labour needs a dynamic Civil Service', was the view of this former insider. 'Put a premium on knowledge, initiative, good ideas, efficiency; pension off the dunces'. He proposed to 'let as many officials as possible have their own say – at the cost of having to bear the responsibility for what they decide', but it was not clear how this was to be reconciled with 'upholding the political responsibility of the Government, [and] every iota of parliamentary control and criticism'.[39]

Calls for civil service reform also came from those former wartime 'temporaries' among the new intake of Labour MPs whose experiences in the bureaucracy had convinced them that changes in Whitehall had to be on the agenda. 'With the advent of a Labour Government the efficiency of the Civil Service becomes of great importance', argued one such figure, Arthur Skeffington, in *Socialist Commentary*, hitting out at what he saw as:

1. Lack of drive and initiative. Fear of responsibility.
2. Old-fashioned and slow methods of work.
3. Isolation from and indifference to the public. Bureaucracy.
4. The undemocratic nature of the Service itself.

Two other former 'temporaries', Hugh Gaitskell and Evan Durbin, had made the link between economic planning and Whitehall reform in the 1930s, and were to move rapidly up the political hierarchy after 1945. Gaitskell, who had worked in the Board of Trade and as *chef de cabinet* to Dalton during the war, argued in his maiden speech in Parliament that 'reinforcements' should be brought into the civil service from 'the younger generation' and that, as the existing staff of the service was not adequate for the task of promoting industrial efficiency, the government should set up a committee to look into the question of 'an economic and industrial Civil Service'.[40]

Durbin, who had been personal assistant to deputy Prime Minister Attlee and who on election to Parliament became Dalton's PPS at the Treasury, had more fully developed ideas and had (anonymously) made some biting criticisms of the civil service in an article published in the *Political Quarterly* in 1944. He condemned the amateurishness and intellectual isolation of the service, the lack of systematic training, the poor quality of establishments work and the influence of the Treasury over senior promotions. The administrative capacity of the topmost mandarins was 'remarkably low', he suggested.

> They are intelligent, charming (for the most part) and conscientious men, but they are not men of imagination or action. They are slow, cautious and obstructive. They are 'shrewd' but not wise, dependable but not creative. They are, too often, cynical rather than realistic. They are small men.

As for the lower ranks of the administrative hierarchy, 'they are not bouncing with vitality in the way that a group of young scientists, or young socialists, or young doctors, appear to be'.

Durbin's proposals for change were wide-ranging. 'More scientific methods of selection' involving a 'modern combination of intelligence tests, practical tests and psychiatrical examination' should be introduced. He wanted a proportion of posts at senior levels (perhaps one-quarter of Assistant Secretary posts) open to outsiders to 'break down the cloistered separateness of Whitehall – the "place apart" '. A civil service staff college, placements outside Whitehall and a system of sabbaticals would widen experience and – on the lines of the 'passing out' exams of a military staff college – assessments of performance during training should be a factor in determining promotions. To break the power of the Treasury over the civil service, an enlarged and reformed Civil Service Commission should be given responsibility for recruitment, training and the supervision of promotions (including advising the PM on toplevel appointments). Whitehall's failure to define and delegate spheres of responsibility chafed: 'It is never easy to find anyone who is finally responsible for anything'. Durbin acknowledged the constraints of a parliamentary and a Cabinet system, but felt that Parliament's machinery of supervision was out of date and ill-suited to modern conditions. Officials should be allowed more discretion and parliamentary inquiry limited to 'larger questions and the prevention of corruption'. Co-ordination was essential but so too was drive and independent action.[41]

Let Us Face the Future, the party's 1945 manifesto, had promised 'the better organisation of Government departments and the Civil Service', but had made no specific commitments.[42] It soon became clear, however, that the outsiders' criticisms and reform-thinking had little resonance in the only quarter which could actually deliver, as opposed to write about, administrative reconstruction. For not only senior civil servants but also key ministers at the heart of the Labour government were unconvinced by the reformers' arguments. An incident during the first autumn of the government was revealing.

In October 1945 Morrison (in the chair), Dalton and Cripps met on the machinery of government committee to consider an official paper (which had actually been prepared for submission to ministers in the wartime coalition) which argued that no fundamental changes were needed in the organization or functions of the centre of the government machine. The existing arrangements worked well to meet the needs of co-ordination; the Treasury's approach to the control of public spending was sound; and the Treasury should continue to control the civil service. The report was approved but then, to their evident dismay, officials unearthed Attlee's December 1942 note to the wartime machinery of government (MG) committee, which had apparently been overlooked and which had included a proposal to split the Treasury. A draft was prepared for Morrison to send to the Prime Minister pointing out the disadvantages of such a move and (in early November) Attlee conceded that that section of his wartime memorandum 'needs reconsideration in the light of experience'. However, he continued, ministers had had before them a report which was 'an examination by persons from within the machine. It would have been interesting to have had an outside expert in organisation on the [Official MG] Committee'. 'I think that the [Treasury's] Establishment Branch wants looking into', he minuted, 'and that a review of methods of business would probably be rewarding in the light of outside practice.'

On (not) splitting the Treasury, officials were clearly relieved that Attlee had been brought into line: 'This is what we wanted to secure' as Sir Edward Bridges, now Permanent Secretary to the Treasury and Head of the Civil Service, put it. But they were not so keen about the Prime Minister's other points. Bridges minuted that the wartime MG committee had deliberately decided to mount an insider review. It would have been inappropriate, he thought, for an 'outside expert in organisation' to have been brought on to the official MG committee, and outside business experience was simply not relevant for Treasury establishments work. As for the other aspects of Attlee's 1942 note – relating to training, interchange and Treasury financial control – the civil service view was that these had been settled in a satisfactory manner. For instance, the Assheton Committee had dealt with training (and had included outsiders, Bridges tartly noted), though in the event it had rejected the establishment of a civil service staff college. Here, too, Attlee did not press his wartime views.[43]

After this episode Attlee was to be found strongly defending the existing arrangements for Treasury control of the civil service. In correspondence with Henry Legge-Bourke, a Conservative MP with a bee in his bonnet about the issue, Attlee emphatically rejected removing control of the civil service from the Treasury, defended the role of the Permanent Secretary of the Treasury in advising the Prime Minister on senior appointments and repudiated the suggestion that officials from other departments tried to fall in with Treasury views rather than those of their ministers.[44]

In fact, Attlee's approach as Prime Minister to the civil service and the machinery of government was pragmatic and undoctrinaire; he had moved away from his earlier Haldane-type views. Even when he was prepared to float what in the Whitehall context were radical ideas, he would drop them if senior colleagues objected. A good example of this was the fate of a minute he circulated in November 1949 at a time when ministers on the MG committee were considering possible post-election departmental reorganizations. There was agreement on authorizing officials to consider the redrawing of departmental boundaries in the fields of transport and civil aviation and health, housing and planning. But when Attlee – looking for ways to cut both the size of the Cabinet and the number of civil servants – raised questions about whether there was a case for a single Minister for Socialized Industries, and for the amalgamation of the Foreign Office and the Commonwealth Relations Office into a single External Relations Office, ministers on the MG committee – Morrison (in the chair), Cripps, Addison, Alexander, Ede and Tomlinson – were quick to point out the drawbacks, record their doubts about whether the ideas were desirable or practicable, and rule out any further investigation of them.[45]

For all the (admittedly vague) talk of an Economic General Staff in the 1930s, and despite the importance of 'planning' in Labour thinking, no central planning staff was created in 1945, what limited economic planning there was being handled through the standard Whitehall device of inter-departmental committees and with very few economists (socialist or otherwise) involved – something which did not appear to greatly trouble ministers, however. The appearance of the Central Economic Planning Staff in 1947, combining insiders, outsiders and economists, was a step forwards, but this was soon absorbed into the Treasury (when Cripps became Chancellor) and never developed into a proper long-term planning unit as opposed to dealing with short-term *ad hoc* problems. Ironically in view of post-1931 socialist suspicions of it, there was no doubting the primacy of the Treasury in the economic policy-making of the Attlee government.[46] The sort of bureaucratic innovations – of machinery and of personnel – needed to break the grip of the Treasury or of the traditional generalist civil servant dominant in it and in the rest of Whitehall may have been attractive to socialist critics in the 1930s but were not seriously considered by Labour ministers in the 1940s.

Whenever outsiders attempted to put civil service reform on the agenda during these years, ministers never roused themselves to grapple with Whitehall's inevitably defensive and blocking reaction. In February 1946, for instance, a Labour backbencher, Geoffrey Cooper, wrote to Attlee, drawing a parallel with Roosevelt's New Deal and his appointment of the Brownlow Committee on Administrative Management and arguing that, with Parliament now passing legislation that constituted 'a complete change of policy', an investigation into the efficiency of the 'executive instrument' of British government had become imperative. He proposed a select committee, including MPs with experience of 'scientific methods of business organisation' and of industrial management. 'Fundamental reorganisation' was required, Cooper insisted, and he warned that 'To ignore the necessity or to allow any reorganisation to take place piecemeal . . . will be disastrous to the Socialist legislative programme it is intended to carry through.'[47]

Whitehall moved smoothly and irresistibly to scotch Cooper's initiative.[48] Sir Edward Bridges convened a special meeting of permanent secretaries to discuss the issue and, as in 1942, top civil servants were resolutely opposed to an external review or inquiry and favoured just the sort of process of *ad hoc* adjustment Cooper thought inadequate. (It is interesting to note in passing one exception to the rule: Evelyn Sharp – Richard Crossman's future permanent secretary and then one of Whitehall's rising stars – apparently suggested in 1947 a 'very powerful Commission' on the machinery of government, but Bridges disagreed, wanting to keep these matters under the control of the insiders.)[49] Recommending rejection of Cooper's call for a select committee, Bridges proposed a review by a small group of civil servants, 'who, after all, can tell better than any outsider where the shoe pinches without any long process of collecting evidence', as he minuted Dalton. 'This task will be undertaken in no spirit of complacency', he continued, raising the standard objection to the claims made for the relevance of scientific methods of business management: 'the problems of Government organisation are inherently different from those of business. You cannot solve the problems of the Civil Service simply by applying business techniques.'

Bridges got his way and, in the event, a handful of top-level official working parties on civil service organization were set to work. Covering accommodation, recruitment, training and business efficiency in departments, they submitted reports between October 1946 and July 1947.[50] The business efficiency working party did actually consult outside businessmen who had been wartime 'temporaries', but its efforts have been harshly judged by recent writers. It is difficult to disagree with Chapman's view that some of the recommendations in its first report, on ancillary services, were 'disappointingly low level'[51] for a high-powered group which included some of Whitehall's leading figures (Barlow, Brook, Douglas, Maud, Nicholson, Padmore):

> Vacuum cleaners should be provided on an increased scale for the cleaning staff as supplies permit. . . . It is essential that the messenger services should be so organised that the discharge of their prime duties – carrying papers, and ushering visitors – is not hampered by subsidiary jobs like tea-making.

To be fair, its final report went on to deal with the higher organization and working of departments and to consider the bigger questions of management efficiency. In some departments, it considered, it might be right to appoint a 'Chief Executive' to relieve the permanent secretary and mark the importance of the management function (such a figure, it noted, need not be a business outsider for within the civil service there were men with the necessary qualities). But officials (and the business outsiders they had consulted) were adamant that there was no single or simple means of promoting greater efficiency in government: there were many defects and problems with the existing departmental machinery, but there was no single cure available which was universally applicable throughout Whitehall.

Peter Hennessy's judgement on this whole exercise is damning:

Bridges 'had carried off *the* classic manoeuvre of professional self-preservation when, for once, the odds seemed stacked in favour of significant and lasting reform'. The 'perils of allowing the British Civil Service to conduct itself as a self-regulating organisation' could hardly be more clear. But Bridges' political masters had let him get away with this negative approach – how had the politicians performed? 'In a word, appallingly,' argues Hennessy, 'even allowing for the huge weight of problem-solving and decision-taking that bore down upon Attlee and his colleagues in those early postwar years'.[52]

This is not how ministers saw matters at the time, however, as Hennessy acknowledges: 'The key to understanding the lack of result is not timidity . . . but self-confidence. Ministers, just as much as Whitehall's "higher divinities", knew they were running a machine that had worked in wartime and would continue to do so in the peace'. As should be clear by now, there can be no suggestion that devious mandarins were thwarting reform-minded ministers. The views of a Geoffrey Cooper were shared neither by Attlee and his colleagues nor by Bridges and his. Hennessy's view is that Bridges' working parties achieved 'precious little of substance', but when their reports went up to ministers on the MG committee in January 1948 Cripps – now Chancellor of the Exchequer – was impressed:

> The reports of the four working parties are a notable achievement. They show that the Civil Service is alive to the need for changes in organisation, outlook and procedure to meet new conditions and that it has formulated a programme as to the lines on which development should take place over the immediately ensuing years. . . . If the recommendations of these bodies are effective, we shall have gone a long way towards adapting the organisation of the Civil Service to the new and heavy responsibilities which our Government has placed upon it.[53]

The events surrounding the preparation of an abortive White Paper on the future of the Civil Service offer a further insight into 'insider' thinking about these problems during the first years of the Attlee government.[54] The initiative came from Evan Durbin – Dalton's PPS – who wrote to the Chancellor in June 1946:

> There is much ignorant and prejudiced criticism of the Civil Service current in the Party and in the country.
> In addition there is, among sensible people, a genuine concern

that the selection, training and promotion of Civil Servants should be reformed in ways that will adapt the Service to the more active and positive work that it will be called upon to do in an increasingly socialist society.

In my view this criticism and concern should be met by the publication of a White Paper on the whole problem.

As a wartime 'temporary', Durbin had had strong views about the need to overhaul the bureaucracy. Now, he felt, 'there is a good story to tell. A great deal has already been done'. New methods of selection were being tried; on training, the main recommendations of the Assheton Report had been adopted and in part implemented; opportunities for inter-class promotion into the higher grades were now considerable. A White Paper, Durbin suggested, should include proposals to speed up this process of adaptation. It would be easy, he thought, to write a White Paper that would 'go far to satisfy the critics'. There could then be an informed public debate rather than continued ignorance and prejudice. Senior Treasury officials, including Bridges, were attracted by the idea, he told Dalton.

Dalton gave the go ahead and a forty-page draft was prepared in the Treasury in the summer and autumn of 1946. On recruitment, the relevant section of the draft White Paper insisted that the Civil Service Selection Board (CSSB) tests were not intended 'to test social graces', but rather 'what they aim to do is to measure the force of character, the resourcefulness, the potentiality as members or leaders of teams and the general good sense and all-round ability of . . . candidates'. Successful candidates, it pointed out, now 'represent a wider field of ability and social background' in both the Home and the Foreign Services. On training, a civil service staff college was explicitly ruled out. Owing to the urgent requirements for administrative staff, the draft admitted, central training was 'for the present' limited to full-time courses of two-and-a-half weeks for Assistant Principals. And training (in the widest sense) for the highest posts, it was argued, best took the form of inter-departmental transfers, sabbaticals, and secondments and interchange with organizations outside Whitehall. The section on the structure of the civil service noted the greater opportunities for promotion from the lower to the higher classes of the service and claimed that a start had been made on modernizing the structure on the professional and technical side. But it was silent on the key question of the distinction between generalists and specialists, though the government was described as wanting to maintain and develop the wartime fluidity in the selection of staff for higher posts, seeking out talent wherever it could be discovered.

'It will be seen that the task of rebuilding, adapting and refashioning the Civil Service to meet the needs of the future is being tackled from many sides at once', the draft White Paper concluded. Much remained to be done, of course, but the government intended to 'press forward continuously with the reforms and improvements which have already been initiated'. The document may thus have ended on an upbeat note, but it actually gave little away. It apparently acknowledged the outside critics' argument about the need for reform to meet new conditions and problems, but the message was that this was a process already under way and that the government's approach was a sound one. It is possible that though its self-congratulatory tone might have backfired with committed reformers, a broader audience might well have found it a reassuring prospectus. As the White Paper was never published, however, Durbin's judgement about it assuaging outside critics was never tested. In October 1946, just when he was starting to raise detailed queries about the draft and was telling officials that he wanted production of the White Paper deferred, he left the Treasury (in March 1947 he was appointed a junior minister at the Ministry of Works). Durbin had only been the Chancellor's PPS – and so not officially a member of the government – but his departure effectively killed off the project. In November a meeting of Treasury officials chaired by Bridges decided that further work on the draft should await clarification of certain issues, particularly the future of CSSB. Dalton at this time was railing about the use of 'psychiatrists' and had put a question-mark against the new recruitment procedures, but Glenvil Hall, the Financial Secretary, whom he asked for a report on the subject, was favourably impressed on his visit to CSSB and advised it should continue.[55] As far as the proposed White Paper was concerned, though, the impetus had been lost. The draft stayed in the Treasury's filing cabinets. The issue of the future of the civil service did not go away, however. At the official level Bridges' working parties were beavering away, and at the political level ministers' attention was starting to be focused on the size of the civil service as parliamentary and other outside critics began to highlight this as an issue as well as the general question of civil service (in)efficiency.

The issue of the size of the civil service was in fact an uncomfortable one for Attlee's ministers because although they recognized that some of their policies would necessarily involve increases in the number of civil servants, they were also sensitive to parliamentary allegations about a bloated bureaucracy (including questions from maverick Labour MPs about 'the increase in non-productive labour now drawing state salaries') and were concerned to reduce the manpower demands associated with rationing, controls and other functions hanging over from the war. The Treasury had asked government departments in January 1946 for forecasts of their future size and the alarm bells began ringing once it became apparent that the number of civil servants was growing at an unexpectedly rapid rate over the first half of the year. Bridges favoured a firm line with ministers: 'if we are to do with fewer people, we can do fewer things'. Attlee's response was in November 1946 to establish a Cabinet committee on civil service manpower chaired by Home Secretary Chuter Ede, backed up by an official committee at permanent secretary level chaired by Bridges, with a remit to review the whole question and to set and monitor staffing levels for departments. As an interim measure, departments were instructed to treat their staff level of 1 January 1947 as a maximum figure which could not be exceeded without special authority.[56]

The manpower committee's report went before the Cabinet in April 1947. The total of non-industrial civil servants was expected to rise from 713,000 in October 1946 to a peak of 740,000 in April 1948 before starting to fall back, it indicated. There was little scope for substantial savings of staff through administrative economies; numbers were not inflated in relation to the tasks falling on the service. Any arbitrary cut in the size of the civil service would depend upon policy decisions to reduce services and eliminate programmes. The corollary was that ministers should defend the size of the civil service and 'its contribution to the public good' in the face of outside criticism.[57]

Attlee soon obliged. He took exception to the civil service being labelled 'parasitic', he told one questioner in the Commons. And in June 1947 he defended civil service manpower levels at some length. The government recognized the importance of limiting the demands which Whitehall made upon the available manpower and was committed to avoiding waste and making the most economical use of staff, he insisted. But at the same time controls, rationing and other work connected with the aftermath of the war continued for the moment to absorb large numbers of officials (though these were expected to decrease over time), while the state had also shouldered new social and economic duties which inevitably entailed some increase in the size of the civil service. The Prime Minister had obviously taken to heart the manpower committee's injunction to speak out in defence of the civil service:

> I think that we all believe that our Civil Service is the best in the world and that it has in its ranks very many men and women of great ability whose devotion to the public interest is unsurpassed. The Civil Service has never failed to be a faithful servant, not only to successive Governments but to the country as a whole. But a good servant is better for having a good and understanding master, and I regret the fashion, now current in some quarters, of speaking slightingly of the Civil Service as though its members were less useful members of the community than other people. If attacks of this kind continue unanswered, we cannot expect to recruit energetic and able young men and women to the Service who will take a proper pride in their important tasks; we shall then fail to build up a Service which will be efficient, economical and responsive to the needs of the country as a whole. The research worker in a Government laboratory, the postal worker and the clerk in a labour exchange, or the administrator in Whitehall, all these are making their contribution to the common end. We shall not get the best out of the Service unless we give them the support and credit they deserve.[58]

For the rest of its term in office, however, the government continued to be concerned about this issue. The crises of 1947 – first coal and then sterling convertibility – led the Treasury to emphasize even more strongly the need for manpower economy and to keeping within departmental manpower ceilings, and the pressure for civil service economies was kept up after the 1949 devaluation. In November 1948 the ministerial and official committees on civil service manpower were wound up and the Treasury resumed full responsibility for controlling the size of the civil service. There had been some speculation in the press and in Parliament in mid-1947 about a planned 10 per cent cut in the civil service, but ministers maintained that this was never an official target, merely a hypothetical figure put to departments in order to gauge the implications for services and to encourage the search for staff reductions. However, the overall number of non-industrial civil servants *was* reduced, falling from 711,000 in October 1948 to 684,000 in April 1950 (which, allowing for some individual increases, represented a gross fall of 5 per cent), according to a report to the Cabinet by the

Chancellor of the Exchequer, though this saving was not on the scale ministers had expected and predicted in 1947, when a reduction of 100,000 had been mentioned.[59]

While the government was struggling to contain the growth of the civil service, Whitehall's outside critics and would-be reformers continued to plug away at their now well-established themes – and to meet with the same lack of success. In August 1947, for instance, the House of Commons Estimates Committee issued a report on the nuts-and-bolts subject of Organisation and Methods in government departments which also included a call for a major reorganization of the administrative machine. These questions, the committee argued, 'should be attacked scientifically and not as a series of piecemeal adjustments'. O and M techniques and knowledge, it said, should be upgraded and directed at 'planning the structure and machinery of Government' rather than merely 'attending to its plumbing and maintenance'. 'It is clear that insufficient thought has been given to adapting the machinery of Government to its new tasks', the MPs continued, with the result that 'the administration is strained almost to breaking point'. 'Little is to be gained by tinkering with a problem of such fundamental importance', they warned.[60]

The committee got nowhere. The insiders' commitment to a process of internal review and adaptation was too deeply entrenched to be shaken by a mere select committee report. Bridges and the Treasury simply ignored the recommendation that the recently established Government Organisation Committee of permanent secretaries – dealing with machinery of government and efficiency questions – should be 'strengthened where necessary by employing experts on administration from outside the Service'. And the MPs' alternative suggestion that a 'specially constituted body of a few highly placed and experienced persons might be set up to inquire into . . . the whole administrative system in order to consider the reorganisation necessary to carry out its new and old functions' – a new Haldane Committee – was a non-starter. The key figures on the Cabinet's MG committee – Cripps and Morrison – were at one with the Treasury in rejecting the idea of a complete overhaul of the whole pattern of the government machine to be drawn up by an external inquiry.[61]

Among Whitehall's parliamentary critics in these years, the most persistent gadfly was Labour MP Geoffrey Cooper. With a background in business management and as a wartime RAF Wing Commander, he had seemed a very promising member of the 1945 intake. His loud and frequent complaints about the excessive size of the civil service and about inefficiency and red tape in government hindering private industry won him few friends on the Labour benches, however. This might seem strange given that he was often making points like those that other socialists had made in the early years of the government, but his exaggerated language did not help his cause. Another factor was that he kept up his attacks during the government's troubled middle years, alienating loyalists, and then continued even when these issues were becoming more politicized in a partisan sense. After one of Cooper's exchanges with Attlee at question time, for instance, Tory MP Tufton Beamish shouted to him, 'Come over to this side'. And after listening to a catalogue of complaints in an adjournment debate on the civil service that Cooper had secured, Financial Secretary to the Treasury Glenvil Hall retorted that he obviously did 'not think much of this Government'. By mid-1949, with attention beginning to be focused on the forthcoming election, the size of the civil service and allegations about bureaucratic incompetence (particularly after the Sidney Stanley affair and the groundnuts fiasco) had become partisan issues. Socialist criticism of the efficiency of the civil service machine had largely faded away by the end of 1947 and thus interventions like Cooper's could increasingly seem to be doing the Conservatives' work for them.[62]

Although he expressed concern about the 'ever-increasing power and influence on the part of bureaucracy',[63] Cooper's main criticisms reflected what can best be labelled 'business efficiency' thinking. He called for a massive 20 per cent cut in the size of the civil service: 'It does seem . . . as if more and more people [are] doing less and less effective work'.[64] He maintained that up to 50 per cent of civil service recruits did not make first-class administrators as judged by the standards of industry and was doubtful of the benefits of recruiting through CSSB straight from university, as opposed to recruits spending some period 'in the ranks' in a 'purely executive post'.[65] Business and industrial methods should be adopted to stimulate higher standards of efficiency in the civil service, he argued, and officials should be properly trained in business techniques.[66] Red tape and Whitehall's ignorance of private business were in his view major obstacles to industrial recovery and the export trade.[67] And he repeatedly argued that the civil service could not reform itself: there should be a select committee appointed, or a Beveridge-type figure let loose to mount a searching investigation, or a Haldane-style inquiry; at the very least the Government Organisation Committee (GOC) of permanent secretaries should be expanded to include MPs and other outsiders with industrial and management qualifications and experience, and its reports should be published.[68] In many respects, Cooper was his own worst enemy. He tried the patience of other MPs with his over-long and anecdotal speeches. Fresh allegations about the use of 'contact men' outraged Labour ministers and MPs in the aftermath of the Sidney Stanley affair and the report of the Lynskey Tribunal. 'A lot of irresponsible and unsubstantiated tittle-tattle . . . a totally false picture', protested other Labour backbenchers.[69] It was not surprising that interest in the PLP Civil Service Group that Cooper set up soon flagged: forty to fifty MPs had shown an active interest at the start, he claimed, pinning the blame for the falling off of backbench interest on the government for frustrating reformers' efforts.[70] In private meetings with ministers, he got little more than tea and a polite hearing. The ministerial line put to him was that the Cabinet's MG committee was looking into the whole question of the machinery of government and its adaptation to new tasks; detailed official inquiries were continuing; and while results could not be achieved overnight, much had already been done. Civil-service internal memoranda reveal a barely-disguised contempt for Cooper. 'When it came to giving examples of the alleged inefficiency of the [civil service] machine the cases produced were not over convincing', minuted one official after a meeting between Cooper and the Financial Secretary to the Treasury. And after it had been arranged for Cooper to meet staff engaged in O and M work, another official noted: 'I gather that he appeared somewhat impressed by the people we are using on this work (many of them with good business experience of their own), but that the feeling was not reciprocated. He is not much of a listener anyhow'.[71]

It was not just an awkward customer like Geoffrey Cooper who was held at bay by the insiders, however. When a Fabian Society group produced (in August 1947) a thorough and unsensational pamphlet on *The Reform of the Higher Civil Service*, the civil service reaction was also defensive, if not dismissive. The group was a sub-committee of the Fabian Political and Local Government Research Committee. Bosworth Monck, its chairman, had been a wartime 'temporary', and the group was able to draw upon the experiences of a number of other people who had worked in wartime Whitehall and even got some informal assistance from serving career officials. Many of its proposals were based on ideas which had been put forward in Fabian and socialist circles since the 1930s, and in important respects the group was also in line with contemporary Whitehall thinking. Really radical ideas floated at some of the group's meetings, such as for the large-scale introduction of political appointees into the civil service, made little headway and were not included in the published report.[72] But despite its genesis and its studied moderation, the Fabian group's report had as little impact as the outspoken interventions of Geoffrey Cooper. Whitehall blandly resisted *all* outside influences in the Attlee years and even Fabian semi-insiders were kept at arm's length.

The Fabian report was certainly not a blueprint for a massive overhaul of what it described as 'probably the best Civil Service in the world'. Whitehall had to adapt to new tasks and its size and efficiency had justifiably come under the searchlight, but change within the existing framework was all that was needed. The report warned against 'ignorant and ill-directed' criticism: 'It must be remembered that the Civil Service could only achieve a speed [of work] comparable to efficient private business by the sacrifice both of democratic control (questions in Parliament, etc.) and of the principle of uniform treatment for all citizens'.

The bulk of the report, in fact, was concerned with detailed personnel and organizational questions (even generously addressing the subject of entertainment allowances!). The CSSB 'house-parties' were applauded as a modern and effective recruitment method. The familiar Laski–Cole–Robson proposals concerning promotions from the lower into the higher classes of the service and the need for more interchange between Whitehall and outside organizations (including private business) were repeated. An 'inbred' civil service staff college was rejected; the 'Brahminical aloofness' of the higher civil service had to be broken down, not reinforced. Establishment work – so crucial for the efficiency of the service – had to be given a higher priority. More far-reaching proposals were to fill a proportion of middle-level administrative class posts by public advertisement and open competition, and to introduce a system of centralized promotion for appointments to Assistant Secretary and above, together with a system of 'promotion age zones' and compulsory retirement – designed to bring on the best people to senior posts at comparatively early ages and to weed out the 'duds' and 'older plodders'. The 'last word on the formulation of policy' must remain with administrators, the Fabian group insisted, but specialists and technical experts should be brought more into policy-making at the early stages, and moreover they should be equal to administrators in status and pay, receive training in administration and be eligible for promotion to senior administrative posts. The group's final major proposal – in classic Fabian style – was for better provision to 'think and plan ahead'. Within departments and at the centre of government there should be established planning groups of 'brains trusters', working within the framework of a better organized ministerial and official level planning system, operating on 'Joint Staff' lines.

The reaction of senior Treasury mandarins to the Fabian's efforts can only be described as patronizing. Treasury officials did not have a high opinion of Bosworth Monck's other writings on the civil service and when Geoffrey Cooper (of all people!) wrote to Cripps in February 1948, asking him to see Monck, one or two of his co-authors and one or two MPs, Bridges was sent a most emphatic note by Padmore: 'The idea of the Chancellor's being asked to waste his time in this way appals me. . . . Neither Mr Monck nor his co-authors are the kind of people who are to be expected to be allowed to waste the time of Ministers . . . '[73] William Robson, chairman of the Fabian Political and Local Government Research Committee, had better luck, being allowed an interview with Sir Edward Bridges, but only after officials had gone to extraordinary lengths to study the Fabian report and prepare briefs for what was ostensibly an informal meeting at which Bridges gave little away.

The Fabians' recommendations were described by officials as falling into three main groups: first, ideas which had already been accepted and adopted (e.g. on training); second, ideas which the departmental Treasury considered sound but which had not yet been put up to ministers for decision (e.g. premature retirement and things in the pipeline on Whitley); and third, ideas which, although having much to commend them, went beyond anything the Treasury thought practicable at that stage (e.g. centralized promotion). A preliminary draft of a memorandum to be sent by Bridges to the Financial Secretary before the meeting with Robson is nicely revealing of civil service attitudes:

> I am afraid that in general the Report is a little disappointing. The Fabians have got on to a number of very sound ideas but so did the Civil Service Working Parties and in fact there is very little in the Fabian proposals which had not already been thought of by these Working Parties. That is not to say that we do not welcome this confirmation by the Fabians of the ideas which we had already worked out on our own.

Perhaps this was felt to be too smug; it was certainly cut from the final version of the note, in which the report was described as 'practical and level-headed' but also as containing 'nothing very startling' and much that represented lines of thought on which the civil service had been working for some time.

Bridges' note after his meeting with Robson says a good deal about the mandarins' attitudes towards outsiders and towards publicity about the workings of the government machine:

> I am sure it is worthwhile by means of these informal contacts to establish a degree of understanding with people of Professor Robson's position whose critical and constructive work is much more likely to be helpful to us if we take a little trouble to tell him what we are doing and to keep in touch with him.

For his part, Robson remained convinced that 'considerable reforms are needed in personnel policy and public administration generally; and while some of these are at least partly in sight, others are at present entirely beyond the horizon of those in high places who decide these matters'.[74]

By that time, however, this was more a plaintive complaint than a clarion call. On the Labour backbenches, Geoffrey Cooper would continue his one-man campaign throughout 1948 and 1949, but the tide had turned. The socialist critique of Whitehall in the Laski-Fabian-*New Statesman* vein we have traced from the 1930s onwards may still have been heard during the first two or three years of the Attlee government, but thereafter it faded away. Judged from this perspective, though, what happened after 1945 was essentially the non-reform of the civil service. Thus, echoing Robson, Peter Hennessy's view is that 'the [Attlee] government was not seriously interested in Civil Service reform'.[75] But measuring the changes in Attlee's Whitehall against benchmarks set by outside critics and would-be reformers of the civil service may be to approach the problem in a misleading way.

'It would not have occurred to [Sir Edward] Bridges or [Sir Norman] Brook that there was anything fundamentally wrong with the service over which they presided', Hennessy has written of postwar Whitehall's 'higher divinities'.[76] The same could equally be said of the leading Labour ministers in the 1945 government. Their time in the wartime coalition had made them into pragmatic insiders. After 1945 they experienced none of the bureaucratic resistance or sabotage that Laski and others had predicted and that might have spurred a major programme of reform. To them, the civil service machine was a serviceable instrument for a socialist government – quite simply, it did not need *fundamental* reform.

Inside the government there was confidence that Whitehall was successfully adapting to post-war requirements. Hence Durbin's view in 1946 that 'there is a good story to tell. A great deal has already been achieved', and Cripps' favourable assessment of the work of the civil service working parties (see above). Reform of selection procedures (CSSB), rationalization of the scientific civil service, Bridges' working parties and the GOC, the continuing work of the machinery of government committee – the government's was a piecemeal approach owing much to the development of a consensus at the official level (during the wartime coalition and after) about the nature of the changes needed. To ministers and to their official advisers – if not to outsiders – this was all the 'reform' the civil service needed. Root-and-branch reorganization according to some external blueprint (or red- or pinkprint) was unnecessary, there would be few political returns, and in any case other substantive policy problems were much more pressing. Outsiders urging a 'heroic' rather than a 'humdrum' approach to reform of the Whitehall machine thus seemed meddlesome and ill-informed to both ministers and mandarins in the Attlee government.

Twenty years later, in the 1960s, however, the 'heroic' model of sweeping reform of the civil service from the outside was to become fashionable once again, as the Laski-Fabian critique resurfaced. In a re-run of the events of the Attlee period, Whitehall's outside critics were again to complain that their efforts were thwarted by bureaucratic vested interests.

4 Labour and the Fulton Report

'The last great Fabian public document', is how Labour MP John Garrett has described the 1968 report of the Fulton Committee on the Civil Service, commissioned by Harold Wilson's Labour government. It might be historically more accurate to pin that label on the 1970 White Paper *The Reorganisation of Central Government*, produced by Edward Heath's Conservative government, but nevertheless Fulton's Fabian provenance is difficult to dispute. 'As regards the main body of the Fulton Report you might as well say "It's all in Laski" ', Geoffrey Fry has written. '[In] many respects it took up long-standing Fabian advocacy of particular reforms, even if this tended to be obscured by layers of later management theorising'.[1]

The Fulton Report is undoubtedly a landmark in the development of the British civil service. Rightly or wrongly, much of the debate over the last twenty-five years or so about the reform of the civil service has been organized around it. Developments in Whitehall have tended to be discussed in terms of whether or how far they measure up to Fulton's proposals. The report has indeed often been treated as something like the public administration equivalent of the Bible: 'Adherence to its recommendations, no matter how unwise, . . . has become the test of civil service reformism'.[2] Rather than conducting an audit of the implementation or non-implementation of the Fulton recommendations, however, this chapter seeks to understand the report by locating it in its political and intellectual context and then to look at its legacy in terms of its influence over thinking in Labour circles in the 1970s about the problems of administrative reform.

THE BUILD-UP TO FULTON

A small number of well-placed socialist intellectuals played a key role in the early 1960s, in shaping opinion inside (and outside) the Labour Party about the need for civil service reform. In the mid-1950s, W. A. Robson had continued to criticize civil service recruitment and training and Robin Marris had published a Fabian pamphlet discussing the requirements of economic planning in which he called for an influx of 'trained economist-cum-administrators' into Whitehall.³ But the reform debate was really triggered off by Thomas Balogh in 1959 with a blistering attack on civil service amateurism and inefficiency in his famous essay 'The Apotheosis of the Dilettante'. On Labour Party policy committees, in Fabian Society pamphlets and other writings, and in the advice he gave to Harold Wilson, Balogh repeatedly argued that radical overhaul of the civil service and of the policy-making machinery was essential for the success of a Labour government's economic planning.⁴

As Balogh saw it, the 'myth of a perfectly working government machine' was one of the major obstacles to solving Britain's problems. His review of post-war economic policy led him to the conclusion that 'a Civil Service reform as fundamental as that undertaken by Northcote and Trevelyan is long overdue, even if Britain did not adopt a basically new policy. A Labour break-through would be impossible without it'. The mid-Victorian reformers had been spectacularly successful in fashioning an administrative system suitable for a nightwatchman state, but 'while its very virtues prevent thorough reform, the change in the essence of economic life has made it unfit to deal with any of the new problems'. Squarely in Balogh's sights were the familiar Fabian reformers' targets: civil service complacency and lack of imagination and initiative, the neglect of expert knowledge in policy-making, recruitment biases, and the baleful influence of the Treasury.

Balogh planned to blitz the 'Establishment of Mandarins' – this 'ignorantly dilettante bureaucracy' – with a far-reaching programme of short-term and long-term reforms. 'It is no use to imagine that, in the short run, much more can be done than to bring in a number of experts and undertake certain reorganisation in the higher Civil Service structure', he wrote sixteen months before Labour entered office. 'Only this could assure adequate consideration and positive elaboration of policies from the *point of view of the government of the day*' (emphasis in original). These short-term measures included arming ministers in charge of large departments with private offices and expert advisers brought in from outside and dependent on the minister, recruiting from outside Whitehall trained economists to work in the economic departments of government and opening up to them the road to the senior levels of the service, and creating in each ministry an expert planning staff.

In the long-term what was needed was major change in the selection and training of civil servants. Balogh was bitter in his denunciation of the way in which the CSSB interview system favoured 'the smooth, extrovert conformist with good connections and no knowledge of modern problems'. It was essential to restore the importance of purely competitive examination. He backed the creation of a staff college, modelled on the French *ENA*, giving new recruits two years of high-powered training, with final admission to the civil service only after a second competitive examination in relevant subjects, including economics and public administration. Careers should then be built, as a rule, within each of the large departments of state or related departments. The influence of the Treasury in promotions should be reduced because its outlook had permeated the civil service in an undesirable way. Balogh's proposals to put the Headship of the Civil Service into commission and to split off from it a separate Ministry of Expansion or Planning and Production were designed to strike a deadly blow at the Treasury's hegemony in Whitehall.

'Civil Service reform alone will not restore [*sic*] parliamentary democracy or Cabinet responsibility in Britain', Balogh ringingly declared at the end of his famous 1959 essay. 'It cannot by itself create the basis for a successful Socialist Government. It is, however, one of the most essential and fundamental preconditions of both. . . . It is a challenge to Labour to achieve this and it dare not fail'. While his views were not particularly novel – obviously drawing on a long tradition of Fabian socialist work and also reflecting developing opinion outside Labour circles[5] – Balogh's access to the Labour leadership gave his ideas a special importance.

The current of reform opinion was further strengthened and focused by the 1964 Fabian report *The Administrators*, important both because of the influential membership of the group which produced it and because its approach and proposals prefigured those of the Fulton Committee. The Fabian team which met from the summer of 1962 was indeed 'a pretty star-studded collection',[6] bringing together Robert Neild (in the chair) and Thomas Balogh from the Labour opposition's network of advisers (both of whom were to move into special adviser posts at the centre of the Wilson government, and Neild was later to sit on the Fulton Committee), Labour politicians Tony Crosland and the up-and-coming Shirley Williams (then Secretary of the Fabians, soon to enter Parliament and briefly a member of the Fulton Committee before taking ministerial office), and several serving civil servants, including two future Permanent Secretaries (whose involvement with the group was, however, short-lived – both dropped out feeling that Neild and Balogh had strong preconceived ideas about what the group's report should say; neither had any hand in writing *The Administrators*, for which they had no great regard).[7]

Neild, who drafted the report, was a convinced reformer of the Balogh school, critical of the 'Oxbridge jack-of-all-trades'. 'It is no good going on with the present dilettante tradition, based on the 18th century view that an educated gentleman is omniscient and that specialists, such as economists, should be treated like plumbers', as he put it in a memorandum to Labour's Finance and Economic Policy Committee in early 1962. No revamping of the economic planning machinery by a Labour government would work without 'a reform of the recruiting, training and specialisation of the permanent staff' and without taking steps to prevent the regulars from regarding economists brought in from outside as 'a foreign body to be regurgitated after another election and humoured in the meantime'.[8]

The premiss of *The Administrators*[9] was that an overhaul of the higher civil service 'may be a pre-requisite to enabling a Labour Government – or any other government – to carry through the modernisation of the country'. The Whitehall system was obsolete: the civil service was 'plainly out of touch with the times, being unfitted to more positive government'. The mandarinate had proved itself adaptable to the job of creating the welfare state after 1945, but not so adaptable to 'the more novel tasks of forward economic planning and the modernisation of the national economy and industry'.

Based as they were in part on insiders' experience, the report's criticisms of Whitehall society were damning. It condemned civil service 'amateurism' as represented by the tradition of the 'omniscient all-rounder' and the bureaucracy's 'negative' approach: 'concentrating on procedure and on day to day dispatch of paper rather than on the substance of problems, and being too ready to seek compromises'. The segregation and the inferior status of specialists dangerously devalued the contribution of expert knowledge to policy-making. The administrative hierarchy was inbred and exclusive, 'as closed and protected as a monastic order', its members drawn from too narrow a range of universities and academic disciplines and its training inadequate. The mandarin's closed shop meant that there was virtually no movement of new blood inwards or of old blood outwards and that civil servants lived in isolation from industry, local government and the rest of the society they helped to run. The Treasury was too powerful and not well-fitted for the task of managing the civil service.

The group's proposals were designed to make the higher civil service 'more professional, more adaptable to new methods and more creative in fulfilling new tasks'. By a more 'professional' civil service, the group meant one trained in administrative and planning techniques (including quantitative analysis) and with specialized knowledge of the subjects it was dealing with. The personnel management function (Establishments) should be removed from the Treasury and undertaken by an expanded and reformed Civil Service Commission. The new Commission should launch an enquiry into recruitment with a view to widening the net and drawing more administrators from universities other than Oxford and Cambridge and from subjects outside the liberal arts. The civil service should be a more open career, with freer movement in and out and more secondment of staff to local government, nationalized industries and (with safeguards) private business. Influenced by the French *ENA*, the group proposed a greatly expanded programme of training and the establishment of a School of Administrative Studies. There should be 'better articulation of careers' so that officials acquired a progressively widening range of experience and were not jumped about between unrelated jobs. 'Class' distinctions between generalist administrators and specialists should be ironed out, with the formation of a new Senior Civil Service from the level of Assistant Secretary (and its equivalents) upwards, allowing better use of staff and more equal competition for the top jobs. More specialists should be recruited, including more economists and statisticians for the key economic ministries. Finally, there should be explicit provision for two types of political appointment – expert advisers in particular subjects brought in from outside and political assistants in the minister's private office.

The emphasis on expertise, professionalism and planning could produce, the report acknowledged, a new breed of technocrats, 'impatient of Parliamentary procedures and arrogant in their attitude to the world outside'. However, the group did not believe that 'because people are better trained and more familiar with the substance of their work they are less susceptible to democratic control. . . . Constitutional devices can be found for checking the arrogance of the executive; but no such device can remedy amateurism'. Greater openness and an end to excessive secrecy in policy-making would be one such check. Another was reform of Parliament, with committees backed by expert staff exploring policy issues in depth.

Although a powerful contribution to the reform debate, *The Administrators* had its limitations. Its focus was on the character of the top levels of the civil service and on the policy-making work of the bureaucracy. The pamphlet made only one brief reference to the need for a review of the three-class structure between Administrative, Executive and Clerical ranks, pointing out that there was already a lot of overlap, much promotion from one class to another and that graduate recruitment into the Executive Class seemed likely to increase, though the preservation of the system seemed to do little other than foster feelings of inferiority and superiority. There were no strong 'democratic' criticisms of Whitehall's three-class system and nor did the report explore the idea of 'unified grading' below the senior ranks, which was later taken up by Fulton, even though one of the papers circulated to the group had referred to the civil service class system as 'essentially a reflection of a social assumption which should be outmoded', and called for its replacement by a system of ranks from top to bottom, allowing for recruitment at a number of different levels and applying to all skills.

A second and related criticism was that, like the administrators it so heavily criticized, the report concentrated on the policy-making work of the civil service and not on the management of services and programmes, about which it seemed rather complacent. However, in a radio talk soon after the report was published, the group's chairman Robert Neild did go on to elevate management to rank alongside planning as the important problems in Whitehall, noting how the pressure of parliamentary business could lead to a preoccupation with petty issues. There was a need to 'look downwards within the service and be concerned with good management'. The Ferranti affair appeared to be the important factor behind this new concern. Neild complained:

At the same time as comparatively junior civil servants were approving estimates entailing over-expenditure of £4,000,000 or £5,000,000, under secretaries or assistant secretaries could almost certainly have been found elsewhere, working over the exact wording of answers to minor parliamentary questions.[10]

Labour's frontbench leadership soon began to take up the new reform thinking. Douglas Jay, for instance, looking back on the organization of economic planning in the Attlee government, thought that the main lesson was that 'more competent and experienced outside personnel should be introduced into the official machine and particularly into the Treasury'. Richard Crossman had been interested in these questions since the mid-1950s, when he had argued that the next Labour government should expand 'the miserably small body of economists and statisticians at present available', create a 'Brains Trust' (including outside expert advisers) in each department and set up a 'Central Fact-finding Bureau', independent of the civil service and of the Treasury, to act as the Cabinet's eyes and ears. In a 1963 Fabian lecture he criticized the generalist character of the higher civil service, its 'anti-scientific attitude' and its limited use of outside experts. A Labour government would have to remedy these defects by ensuring that professional scientific advice was available throughout Whitehall and, as a matter of long-term policy, that a steadily increasing proportion of senior administrative posts were held by civil servants with a scientific as opposed to an exclusively arts background. For Crossman, the wartime practice of introducing an army of outsiders into Whitehall was the model that should be copied for Labour's New Britain. Echoing the language of Harold Wilson's 1963 Scarborough conference speech, he declared:

> In the technological revolution to which we are now committed, we shall be in a state of permanent emergency in which we shall permanently need the marriage of established civil service and outside expertise that we developed as a temporary expedient in World War I and perfected in World War II.[11]

More important still, in the run-up to the 1964 election administrative and government reform received the backing of the new party leader, Harold Wilson. 'We are living in the jet age but we are governed by an Edwardian establishment mentality', he declared. The connection between administrative modernization and Wilson's wider political strategy has been well put by Jones and Keating:

> A more dynamic and efficient Civil Service could assist Labour's plans for growth and scientific advance, upon which its welfare

proposals rested. At the same time, Labour's political fortunes
could be helped by a successful appeal to the growing body of
scientists, administrators, and professional people including the
white-collar salariat produced by the Welfare State . . . [12]

According to a perceptive contemporary observer, Wilson had
'bolder notions of civil service reform than his predecessors as prime
minister – though still tempered by his instinctive caution'. Thomas
Balogh prepared a major document on Whitehall reform (including
plans to split the Treasury) for him in the spring of 1963. Along
with George Brown and James Callaghan, Wilson had apparently
been consulted in the preparation of the 1964 Fabian report. In a
BBC interview with Norman Hunt, the Leader of the Opposition
gave an indication of his thinking and his plans. He made it clear
that he did not want to bring in a large number of outsiders.
Whitehall should be combed for specialists such as economists and
scientists already serving in the civil service who should be moved
into the right jobs. More specialists should be recruited and there
should be greater use of short-term (three- to five-year) postings and
of exchanges and secondments with local government, nationalized
industries and the private sector. In its new departments – Produc-
tion/Economic Planning, Technology/Science, Overseas Development – a Labour government would probably bring in rather more
outside experts in the relevant subjects. Wilson said he was sceptical
about the idea of ministerial *cabinets*, but he was worried about
what he felt was 'the amateurism of the central direction of Government' and proposed to build up the resources of the Cabinet Secretariat (to include advisers from outside).[13]

The party's modernizing and reforming appeal was reflected in
its 1964 election manifesto. The Conservative's 'philosophy of the
past' was rejected as outdated, nostalgic and backward-looking. In
industry, technicians, technologists and engineers were being held
back by 'the social prejudices and anti-scientific bias of the old boy
network'. Labour pledged itself to 'make government itself more
efficient. As the tasks of government grow more numerous and
more complex, the machinery of government must be modernized.
New techniques, new kinds of skill and experience are needed if
government is to govern effectively'.[14]

THE WILSON GOVERNMENT AND THE FULTON COMMITTEE

'The Fulton Committee was very much a product of its time. Its time was the brief period of Harold Wilson's technological revolution, 1964–7', John Garrett has observed. The 1964 election narrowly won, Harold Wilson started his premiership with a flurry of machinery-of-government changes, creating a fistful of new departments: DEA, Overseas Development, Ministry of Technology (MinTech), a Welsh Office and a Ministry of Land and Natural Resources. The new Labour ministers brought in a relatively small number of experts and advisers from outside. But there was no immediate shake-up in the civil service and it was to be almost a year and a half before the Prime Minister announced the appointment of the Fulton Committee inquiry. Why the delay? In Opposition, while the party's advisers had called for certain immediate steps to be taken, such as recruiting more economists, they had generally recommended that a formal inquiry would be needed to secure full-scale change. Thomas Balogh had suggested 'a well chosen Royal Commission, avoiding the dominance of the conventional wisdom which sees no need for any reform whatever'. *The Administrators*, in contrast, was rather more impatient, claiming to detect an emerging all-party consensus in favour of civil service modernization and arguing that there was no need to set up a Royal Commission or committee to tread the ground again.[15]

It seems likely that the chiefs of the civil service were privately advising the new Labour ministers to take a cautious approach. To some extent, the outside critics had been shooting at a moving target. Officials could point to a number of developments in the service, such as experiments in training at the Treasury's Centre for Administrative Studies (set up in 1963) and plans for direct entry recruitment of a limited number of outsiders into the Administrative Class, which could be interpreted as the first steps towards a wider reform. (Robert Neild, however, was troubled whether these were anything more than 'some minor and somewhat defensive modifications to the existing system which will leave its traditions and practices largely intact'.) The view of the Head of the Civil Service, Sir Lawrence Helsby, was that if there was to be an inquiry, the government should not rush into it. As he told the Commons Estimates Committee in May 1965, he would prefer to wait at least a year,

simply for the reason that late in 1964 the Civil Service, and the machinery of government generally, underwent a series of rapid changes greater than has been experienced in peacetime and probably ever before, and I would like to see how we settle down, what new patterns for the future emerge, before embarking on a full-scale review of a sort whose results we would expect to be valid for a good many years to come.[16]

Perhaps, too, the mandarins were waiting to see what would happen to the Labour government, which had only a very small majority and would soon have to face the electorate again.

In August 1965, however, the House of Commons Estimates Committee kept up the pressure with a critical report on recruitment to the civil service. The committee, chaired by Labour MP Jeremy Bray, found it 'hard to accept that the task of Government justifies the unique significance attaching to the Administrative Class, and that only a select few are fitted to undertake this work'. It recommended a full inquiry into the structure, recruitment and management of the civil service in two stages: there should be first a Plowden-style review conducted by a committee of civil servants aided by outsiders, and the government should then report to Parliament the action it proposed to take, if necessary going on to appoint a Royal Commission.[17]

In the event, the Prime Minister decided to telescope the two stages into one and announced the setting up of a committee of inquiry in February 1966. The timing was significant. Wilson had privately settled on the end of March as the election date. The civil service review was part of a pattern of inquiries – into the public schools, the trade unions, the social services and local government – which the government could point to as inaugurating the modernization drive it had promised in 1964. Indeed, machinery-of-government reform 'to meet the needs of a modern society' was highlighted again in the 1966 manifesto. 'The truth is that for many of the tasks that they must perform, our institutions are badly organised and ill-equipped'. The government's appointment of the Fulton Committee to 'overhaul' the civil service was noted, and Whitehall efficiency would be further improved, the manifesto promised, by reorganizing and streamlining the structure of departments and by upgrading the government's information and statistical services. Given this context, there seems some justification for Richard Chapman's remark that 'the Fulton exercise may well appear, to a sceptical observer, as a political expedient for a government seeking to create a reformist image'.[18]

That Fulton was a departmental committee rather than a Royal Commission made some critics of the civil service suspect a Whitehall plot to downgrade the status and importance of the inquiry even before it had started. Certainly, Sir Lawrence Helsby had told the Estimates Committee that while a Royal Commission might have more weight than any other body, it would have the disadvantage that, by convention, no civil servants could be members even though their inside experience of the government machine would be a great asset to an inquiry team. On the other hand, a departmental committee could be expected to work more quickly than a Royal Commission and might learn more from witnesses (such as serving civil servants) able to give their evidence in private rather than in the public hearings characteristic of a Royal Commission. *If* there was a civil service 'plot' about this – which is virtually impossible to prove or disprove – it does seem not to have handicapped the committee's work and report to any significant degree.[19]

It was the committee's membership and its terms of reference which had the major predetermining influence on its approach and on its report. Harold Wilson had worked alongside the chairman, Lord Fulton (Vice-Chancellor of Sussex University), when they were both temporary civil servants in the war, and they had both apparently then believed that the traditional mandarin class had its defects.[20] The three academic members were all known to be Labour supporters: Robert Neild (who had chaired the 1962–4 Fabian group producing *The Administrators* and who was an economic adviser to the Treasury), Lord Simey and Norman Hunt (who had links with Wilson). There were two MPs: Robert Sheldon for Labour (who replaced Shirley Williams when she became a junior minister after the first meeting) and Sir Edward Boyle, widely known to be a very liberal Tory. Two leading industrialists, a trade unionist and three senior civil servants (including two permanent secretaries) completed the group. Given its make-up, Fulton could reasonably be expected by the government to produce a satisfyingly reformist report. Moreover, appointing such a committee rather than simply implementing a package of party-determined reforms – as the Fabians had suggested in 1964 – would perhaps make the changes proposed more acceptable to and within the civil service and, additionally, allow a wide range of outside opinion to be mobilized behind the reforms as a result of the public debate engendered by the committee process. Seen in this light, the Fulton inquiry was something more than a political gesture.

The committee's investigation was to be somewhat narrower than the 'fundamental and wide-ranging review' that Wilson promised, for its terms of reference were limited to the 'structure, recruitment and management, including training, of the Home Civil Service'. For a start, its remit excluded the Diplomatic Service and the Foreign Office, which went through a separate process of review and reorganization in the 1960s. Most damaging of all, however, two areas of crucial constitutional and administrative importance were corralled off from the Fulton inquiry: relations between ministers and officials and the machinery of government. Wilson explained in Parliament that

> the Government's willingness to consider changes in the Civil Service does not imply any intention on their part to alter the basic relationship between Ministers and civil servants. Civil servants, however eminent, remain the confidential advisers of Ministers, who alone are answerable to Parliament for policy; and we do not envisage any change in this fundamental feature of our parliamentary system of democracy.

Lord Crowther-Hunt, a key figure on Fulton, maintained that these exclusions from the terms of reference were 'badly wanted by the mandarins' in a classic *Yes, Minister* manoeuvre to first steer the committee away from fundamental and perhaps uncomfortable questions about the structure and functions of government and the balance of power between politicians and bureaucrats and then, once the committee had reported, to undermine its recommendations by arguing that they took no account of the wider issues.[21]

Factors other than a possible bureaucratic conspiracy are also important here. First, if Fulton was a 'one-dimensional inquiry', as Hennessy argues, the same could be said of its important Fabian precursor, *The Administrators*, which also did not deal with machinery-of-government questions (except for Establishments) or take up in detail the issue of civil service power. Although papers on the organization of central economic ministries and on political appointments did go to the Fabian group, the focus of its report was on the *personnel* of the higher civil service, which was to be largely the case with the Fulton report four years later. Second, in reaffirming his government's adherence to the principle of ministerial responsibility, Wilson was expressing a constitutional orthodoxy which was both part of Labour's tradition and politically convenient for socialist ministers. And third, on the machinery of government, Wilson was quite clear that so much depended on circumstances, personalities and political factors that 'it is impossible to refer this subject to outside inquiry'.[22] Even within the government itself, these matters were kept within a very tight circle.

Fulton sat for two years, sifting through a mass of memoranda, holding private evidence sessions with ministers and senior officials, commissioning exhaustive statistical surveys of the civil service, and launching a management consultants' review (led by Norman Hunt and including on the team John Garrett, later a Labour MP). Wilson apparently wanted the committee to report as quickly as possible so that the government could be publicly seen to be doing something about reforming the bureaucracy. Lord Fulton and Norman Hunt met from time to time with the Prime Minister, probably not so much to get instructions from him as to keep him in the picture and brief him about the committee's thinking – such 'busy-body' meetings were very much a feature of Wilson's style (as seen in the Crossman, Castle and Benn diaries), though it is not clear in this case how much they influenced the committee's findings and report.[23]

Wilson and other leading ministers do not appear to have had much of a hand, if any, in the preparation of the Labour Party's own formal evidence to the committee. In May 1966 the NEC's Home Policy Committee decided that the party should begin the preparation of evidence and in July it approved a short paper outlining the issues that might be covered. A rough draft was drawn up in the Research Department which was circulated for comment to a number of people in the party and in the Fabian Society (including civil servants). The final 16,000-word document was discussed and approved by the Home Policy Committee in November but it apparently went straight through the NEC in December 1966. Although both bodies had a sizeable ministerial contingent, when some of its contents hit the headlines government sources were quick to point out that ministers had not been closely involved in drawing up the submission. As *The Economist* saw it, the party's evidence was best interpreted as reflecting the disappointments and frustration of the Transport House staff who since 1964 had had much less effect on the actions of the government than they had originally hoped: 'It is not a blue-print of the dread things that the Labour Government is likely to do to Whitehall, however Fulton eventually reports'.[24]

In fact, Labour's evidence was not particularly original or radical. Controversy was aroused only by the claim that some ministers were tools of their departments a good deal of the time because of the amount of information withheld from them and because they were undermined by inter-departmental committees of officials, a view firmly rejected by Wilson, who in a television interview went out of his way to snub the party's evidence. For the most part, the party's memorandum followed closely on the 1964 Fabian report and on the fashionable reform thinking of the 1960s (reflected, for instance, in a book by Peter Shore, head of the party's Research Department before 1964 and Wilson's PPS 1964–6, published in early 1966, *Entitled To Know*). As the party's evidence admitted, 'To an extent we are merely putting the weight of the Labour Party behind familiar proposals', observing that many current suggestions for reform could be traced back to Laski. Not surprisingly, this prompted the left-wing journal *Tribune* to comment tartly that, 'What is lamentable is that the Government should not have *acted* upon some of these recommendations long ago'.[25]

The Civil Service was now 'in the business of managing a highly complex techno-industrial society', the party argued, and it had not adapted iself quickly enough to this job, which called for different and more technical skills and a more positive approach than had its traditional functions. The briefest recitation of the party's arguments and proposals shows how derivative they were: the day of the generalist administrative superman was over; the divisions between the Executive, Administrative and Professional Classes had to go; more specialists should be recruited and they should be given wider administrative responsibilities; there should be much greater movement in and out of the service at all levels and on both a temporary and permanent basis; in graduate recruitment, there should be a more determined effort to end the Oxbridge/arts degree monopoly; the Treasury should lose its personnel management functions to a strengthened Civil Service Commission; ministers should be reinforced by politically committed expert advisers brought in from outside and by a small group of personal assistants forming a *cabinet*; there should be a major expansion in training, with a graduate school of government laying on a two-year course for an increased graduate entry into the service. Rather more original ideas were to encourage mobility and break down the isolation of the service by advertising specific senior posts both inside and outside Whitehall, and (taking up a proposal floated by Balogh in 1959) to divide ministries into bureaux, to end the concentration of power in a single permanent secretary and to allow a closer identity between staff and policy. And although it was outside Fulton's terms of reference, the party's evidence also questioned whether the distinction between the Home Civil Service and the

Diplomatic Service was not a largely artificial one which inhibited exchanges of staff.

Throughout, there was an emphasis on better equipping the civil service to cope with the problems of modern government. The central problem was seen to be that 'a Government which is going to take initiatives, which is going to manage the economy and run the social services needs a more dynamic Civil Service'. Accordingly, 'steps should be taken to develop a more forceful concept of public service, and a Civil Servant who is more professional, adaptive and creative'. But here there was in the party's evidence, as later in the Fulton Report itself and in much of the contemporary reformist thinking, 'a fundamental ambiguity on the question of elitism'. To be sure the Oxbridge stranglehold on the traditional Administrative Class was condemned, but the stress on the need for greater professionalism and expertise and above all the envious eyes cast at the French *ENA* 'implied elitism of a different sort', as Jones and Keating have commented. The party did say that it would not like to duplicate the social biases of *ENA*'s recruitment – 'it is not the whole [French] system that must be adopted, but some of the Gallic polish and thoroughness must be grafted onto our own' – but the main thrust of its evidence suggested a move towards a more meritocratic elite and not an egalitarian remodelling of the civil service (see Chapter 5).[26]

With *The Administrators* so recently published and Robert Neild sitting on Fulton, and with the Labour Party effectively repeating so much of the 1964 report, another comprehensive Fabian Society blueprint would have been otiose. Instead, the Society's evidence to the Fulton Committee was a short memorandum mainly concerned with drawing lessons from the experience of the 'irregulars' brought into Whitehall since October 1964. It complained about the absence of a systematic approach in the government's recruitment of 'irregulars' and that their number had been allowed to shrink. 'The unplanned recruitment of 1964–66 must now develop into a planned permanent infusion of talents', using modern methods of 'executive search' to head-hunt outsiders with the right skills and experience. 'Irregulars' must be properly fitted into the administrative hierarchy, and it was probably best to have a mixed team of career officials and 'irregulars' co-operating fully rather than a self-consciously segregated ministerial *cabinet*: 'Information is best shared between people who are working together'. More generally, the Society suggested, there should be an attempt to beef-up long-term thinking in departments, both on future policy problems and on executive methods. Splitting the post of permanent secretary and having a departmental board of separate and equal senior officials responsible for policy advice, management, financial control and research might be a way forward.[27]

Of course the memoranda from the Labour Party and the Fabian Society were just two out of a total of 153 written submissions from government departments, outside organizations and private individuals. And the secretary to the Fulton Committee has testified that it paid little attention to the evidence that was put before it. In his words, the committee produced 'a composite report, which was like a kind of sandwich with a piece of Fabian rye bread on top and a piece of managerial white bread underneath'. There was a strong 'Fabian input' to its thinking and recommendations, he recalled, and the management consultants' report had a major impact, particularly on the parts of the report dealing with management and organization. According to Lord Crowther-Hunt, the management consultants' report was also decisive in the committee's condemnation of the cult of the generalist, though, as we have seen, this had been a Fabian target too. The Fulton Report may also have represented something of an internal committee compromise in the sense that it has been suggested that its more conservative element, including the two permanent secretaries Sir James Dunnett and Sir Philip Allen, agreed to and toned down a unanimous report (with a dissenting note from Lord Simey) because they feared that if the committee split a more extreme majority report might be implemented by the Labour government if it won the next election, which it seemed likely to do at the time.[28]

Fulton's findings and proposals are well-known and need only be briefly noted here. The civil service, it argued, was in need of 'fundamental change'. Its structures and practices had not kept up with its changing tasks and there were six main defects: (1) the service was still essentially based on the obsolete philosophy of the generalist; (2) the horizontal and vertical divisions of its system of classes seriously impeded its work; (3) the role permitted to specialists and their career opportunities were far too limited; (4) too few civil servants were skilled managers; (5) Whitehall was too isolated from the rest of the community because of its closed career system and its narrow social and educational base; (6) personnel management and career planning were inadequate. Its proposals for reshaping the bureaucracy, like these criticisms, echoed both current reformist opinion and long-standing Fabian themes. The core recommendations concerned changes in recruitment procedures and training, the introduction of a unified grading structure and the abolition of classes, securing greater mobility in and out of the civil service, and recasting the central management of the service. In addition, the committee wanted Whitehall efficiency improved with the adoption of systems of accountable management and of management by objectives and by an exploration of the idea of 'hiving off' areas of civil service work to non-departmental bodies.[29]

On the day the report was published the Prime Minister announced that the government broadly accepted Fulton's analysis and that it had decided to accept its main recommendations: a new Civil Service Department to take over the management of the civil service from the Treasury, the creation of a Civil Service College, and the abolition of classes. We now know that this was not a foregone conclusion. The Fulton Report had hardly been rapturously received by the Cabinet. Members of the committee had apparently carried out a great deal of high-level lobbying of ministers, senior officials and civil service unions trying to sell their recommendations. Wilson wanted a quick response to the report and immediate acceptance of the three central proposals. But Roy Jenkins, the Chancellor, furious at not having been consulted by Wilson over the removal of the management of the service from his bailiwick, and pointedly excluded from the committee's pre-publication lobbying, argued for delay and a cautious response. Only Tony Benn and Peter Shore supported Wilson at the first Cabinet meeting on the report, a mixture of apathy, counter-lobbying from the civil service, personal and political rivalries and antipathies, and ministerial logrolling on quite different items of business thwarting the Prime Minister. It took a second meeting before Wilson could successfully manage the Cabinet to get the decision he wanted so that he could, as Crossman put it, 'improve his image as a great modernizer'.[30]

Wilson may have got the publicity he desired but that the report was a modernizer's charter was not beyond dispute. Retired senior civil servants Lord Helsby and F. A. Bishop argued, not unfairly, that the headline-catching criticisms of its first chapter diverted attention from what were far from radical proposals which actually assisted, encouraged and accelerated developments already underway.[31]

Some socialist critics of the civil service enthusiastically welcomed the report: others dismissed it. For Roger Opie, Fulton went 'far to meet the criticisms of many socialist critics'. Its proposals amounted to 'a programme for dragging . . . the British civil service kicking and screaming into the 20th century'. He gleefully anticipated 'howls of outrage from the civil service and its spokesmen'. The veteran Fabian reformer William Robson, however, arguing that in the 1960s the civil service had been made into a scapegoat for real and imaginary national ills, castigated Fulton for painting a distorted picture, for taking little account of recent developments in Whitehall, and for not properly thinking through its recommendations, some of which were in any case old hat. According to others on the left, Fulton did not deal with the real problems. Eric Hobsbawm wrote it off as 'a compendium of the commonplaces of the 1960s' and full of cloudy thinking. 'It does not so much as glance at the major problems of bureaucracy today, which are those of its social and political control rather than those of its efficiency', he complained. John Griffith, reviewing the report in *Socialist Commentary*, was equally scathing. 'What has all this to do with socialism?' he asked:

> Very little indeed. It is all sub-machinery with the super-structure of policy decisions, Departmental 'views', strong and weak civil servants, annual changes of Departments for Ministers, and all the other major determinants of power, remaining unchanged. . . . These reforms will not matter much. They will probably strengthen and make more effective the working of the civil service. Whether this is more or less likely to bring socialism any nearer is an open and a marginal question.

Thomas Balogh felt vindicated by the report, which he saw as marking 'the beginning of a new, vigorous period of change'. Fulton was for him only the first step: 'the need for a further basic reform of the government machine has clearly been established'. The problem was that this raised the sort of issues that had been ruled out of bounds to Fulton, as when Balogh voiced his concern that the new-type civil service, more professional and expert, could be in an even stronger power position relative to ministers and when he called for Whitehall's mechanisms for inter-departmental co-ordination to be investigated to find ways of combining continuity of policy and long-term planning at the official level with proper ministerial control.[32]

In other respects, too, the Fulton inquiry could be said to have raised but not resolved some tricky questions which the Labour government itself showed no sign of being able to or even wanting to answer. The ambiguity on the question of elitism has been noted above. Greater interchange between the civil service and private industry and business was a sensitive subject not just for those on the Labour left who were suspicious of what they saw as the already close and sympathetic relations between the bureaucracy and business interests. Calls for a 'new Haldane'[33] made a link between the machinery and the tasks of government on the one hand, and the nature of the civil service on the other, but the government wanted to keep these issues separate and, as we have seen, the idea of an outside review was anathema to Wilson, whose approach to the machinery of government (in contrast to Heath's) showed no evidence of strategic purpose or design. A closely related question was how far the proposed new management techniques and forms of organization could be reconciled with the constitutional conventions governing the relations of ministers, civil servants and Parliament. Fulton can fairly be criticized for neglecting the constraints imposed by the political and parliamentary environment on the organization and working of the civil service, but the government had effectively ruled out from the beginning the sort of wide-ranging review that could have properly addressed these matters.

A truly radical reform of the civil service could hardly be expected to result from the restricted and shallow inquiry Fulton was permitted to mount and with such a 'confusion of purpose' on the part of both the committee and the Labour government.[34] The report's leading champions, however, were more inclined to blame the limited and disappointing results of the reform process on civil service sabotage. Few could doubt whom Roger Opie had in mind when he warned on Fulton's publication that 'the termites are no doubt already at work on the proposals . . . the reforms cannot start too soon'. A decade later, reviewing what he saw as the patchy and half-hearted implementation of the report's main proposals, Lord Crowther-Hunt argued that they had been ignored, distorted or watered down as the mandarins chose which recommendations to carry out and which to ditch or fudge in order to protect and even strengthen their power and position. 'How Armstrong Defeated Fulton', a chapter heading in the book he co-authored with Peter Kellner, graphically identified the then Head of the Civil Service, Sir William Armstrong, as the chief villain. In fact, it was not just Armstrong's scepticism but also the vested interests of the main civil service unions (except for the Institution of Professional Civil Servants, representing specialists) that ensured that unified grading was not extended below the top three grades. John Garrett also saw the Fulton reforms as 'hindered by the opposition of the higher Civil Service to new ideas', but argued that most importantly 'they were thwarted by the lack of political interest in fundamental change. Ministers would not devote the time and effort to what most of them see as peripheral and boringly technical questions'.[35]

Harold Wilson has testified that, prompted by his principal private secretary Michael Halls, he 'maintained a very close interest in the progress of the reforms in the civil service'. But Fulton's agenda was not always the Prime Minister's: it was Wilson, not 'obstructive' bureaucrats, who vetoed the report's proposal for 'preference for relevance' in direct entry recruitment. Wilson has admitted, though, that while there was an immediate burst of activity after Fulton reported, 'by about 1969 it was tailing off a bit . . . the thing was losing steam'. The problem was that other issues were pressing in on the Labour government, absorbing high-level political attention and taking priority over implementing Fulton, including House of Lords reform, the government's prices and incomes policy, and the controversy over the *In Place of Strife* proposals. 'With so many urgent problems at that time', Wilson recalled, 'I was not able to give my mind to it [Fulton] sufficiently.'[36] Quite simply, with ministers' short-term political horizons and with *detailed* involvement in civil service reform (as opposed to the creation of a general modernizing image) offering only limited political returns, the outcome was virtually inevitable: a process of piecemeal adaptation and of reforms being implemented in a way entailing less fundamental change than Whitehall's outside critics had hoped.

LABOUR, THE FULTONITES AND THE CIVIL SERVICE IN THE 1970s

In the late 1960s Labour's interest in the reform of the civil service largely faded away after Fulton had reported. Looking back on changes in the organization of government and in the civil service during the 1964–70 government, Thomas Balogh argued after the 1970 electoral defeat that 'complete success for the next Labour government demands, in my opinion, further reform'. He criticized Fulton's terms of reference for 'excluding from its purview the question of government machinery, despite the fact that the policies to be pursued would seem to determine both the organisation and training of the civil service'. But if the implication was that Labour should learn from this mistake and from Edward Heath's approach to the machinery of government, which did seem to start from first principles relating to the scope and purposes of government, and which had been based on extensive preparations in Opposition, the lesson went unheeded. For instance, Tony Benn and the left in the party made the running in the development of an interventionist industrial policy, but, while they supported the introduction of ministerial *cabinets*, they never really got to grips with the problem of devising effective Whitehall machinery for a Labour government's economic planning and industrial policy-making which would counter the power of the Treasury.[37]

While Labour was in Opposition after 1970, the only serious and sustained thinking about the civil service that took place was in fact done by the party's Fultonites but was not linked to the formal process of party policy-making. Labour's shadow spokesman on the civil service (and also on Treasury matters), Robert Sheldon, had of course been a member of the Fulton Committee. Norman Hunt – who had been a driving force on Fulton and who was a friend of Harold Wilson – was diverted away from civil service matters into broader questions about the constitution and devolution as a member of the Royal Commission on the Constitution, 1969–73. John Garrett emerged as a key figure in this period. A member of the management consultancy group that had advised the Fulton Committee, Garrett had well-developed 'managerialist' views about the reform of government but – unlike some proponents of business methods – was well aware that the special tasks and the political environment of the civil service meant that private-sector techniques could not be simply transplanted into government but had to be substantially adapted. He had been involved in Fabian Society discussions about the machinery of government in the late 1960s, and became a Labour parliamentary candidate in the early 1970s.

Garrett published a major book on *The Management of Government* in 1972 in which he made it clear that he was not an uncritical admirer of the Fulton Report.[38] Fulton did bear out 'most of the accusations levelled at the higher Civil Service by its critics in the preceding thirty years'; it had spotted 'most of the cracks, pressure points and distortions which had appeared in the management systems of the Civil Service'; and it had given an 'initial impetus to a number of over-due reforms'. At the same time, however, it had presented its analysis and its recommendations in 'a self-defeating way'. It had neglected the extent to which the characteristics and attitudes of the higher civil service were shaped by constitutional conventions and by the practices of Cabinet and parliamentary government. Its tone and style had alienated the very officials who would have to implement the report. And its proposals for change were not clearly and precisely enough specified.[39]

In 1973 he joined forces with Robert Sheldon to write a Fabian pamphlet setting out what the next steps in administrative reform should be.[40] 'Our concern is not only with administrative efficiency and effectiveness', they declared, 'but also with the need in a democracy to make the activities of central administration as open as possible to public debate'. Accordingly, the very first reform they proposed was legislation establishing the principle of the public's 'right to know'. They backed the familiar proposal that ministers should have personal *cabinets* of expert advisers but also made the more novel suggestion that there should be established a Prime Minister's Department. 'Concerned with carrying out studies of major strategic policy issues and with the highest level of efficiency studies within the Civil Service', this should absorb the Central Policy Review Staff (CPRS) think-tank and the management services divisions of the Civil Service Department (CSD), which would then have greater clout (CSD would become a Department of Personnel). They also favoured the then highly fashionable idea of 'programme budgeting', and argued that it should be introduced to reform the existing public expenditure planning system inside government and Parliament's antiquated supply arrangements by linking the objectives of spending programmes, the structures of managerial authority and accountability, and measures of programme effectiveness and managerial efficiency. Accompanying these changes, parliamentary select committees should be strengthened and the system of state audit massively improved.

Garrett and Sheldon took Fulton's thinking about 'accountable units' a stage further and suggested that there could be benefits from a move towards a system of 'departmental agencies'. Whitehall departments could be broken down into units 'whose justification and performance can be scrutinised and whose organisational forms and systems can be more accurately tailored to the needs of the task and of the community they serve'. An agency should have autonomy in staffing matters, substantial delegated spending authority and its head should be answerable to the Public Accounts Committee. The widespread application of this concept could produce a pattern of 'generally small administrative branches' and 'generally large executive scientific and technical divisions constituted as departmental agencies'.

As far as the civil service itself was concerned, they endorsed the Fulton 'preference for relevance' proposal for graduate recruitment;

wanted a resumption of progress towards a unified grading structure 'all the way down to junior management levels'; and argued that Whitehall's personnel management had to be improved and recognized as a key function, departmentally and at the centre of government.

All in all, this was a pretty coherent and a potentially far-reaching programme. It was also a programme that had no impact on the 1974–9 Labour government. As Garrett was later to recall:

> During the period of the Labour Government, 1974–9, there was little progress on Civil Service reform. There were some improvements in the presentation of expenditure plans and work on accountable management proceeded but the development of personnel management was virtually halted by public expenditure cuts and labour relation problems. . . . [An] attempt by the [House of Commons] Expenditure Committee to get the Civil Service to re-start the Fulton programme was unenthusiastically received by the government, which had clearly lost interest in the matter.[41]

Ironically, it was the Thatcher government which, after 1979, made substantial progress with the Fultonites' agenda, extending unified grading, for instance, and, with the 1988 Next Steps project, launching a major drive towards the introduction of the sort of departmental agencies Garrett and Sheldon had sketched out in 1973. Garrett was, however, to be extremely critical of the Conservative government's management initiatives, both on matters of detail and because of their underlying objectives (see Chapter 7).

In contrast to the technocratic and modernizing attitudes of the 1960s, which had inspired the appointment of the Fulton Committee and led the then Labour government to accept its main recommendations in 1968, Labour ministers in the 1970s appeared for the most part to be firm supporters of the Whitehall status quo. The 1974–9 government had to its credit the establishment of the Number 10 Policy Unit advising the Prime Minister, and the extension and institutionalization of the practice of ministers bringing advisers from outside the civil service into their departments (see Chapter 2), but its record in other respects was disappointing and served only to fuel criticism inside and outside the party. The government resisted growing parliamentary demands for a comprehensive set of departmental select committees to monitor Whitehall administration and policy-making. Its record on open government reform infuriated freedom-of-information campaigners inside and outside the party (see Chapter 6). Little headway was made in developing institutions and techniques to improve management efficiency and policy analysis in government. Deeply suspicious of anything connected with former Conservative Prime Minister Heath – despite the affinities between the Fabian/managerialist approach of the Fultonites and the principles informing his reorganization of the machinery of government in 1970 – Programme Analysis and Review (PAR) was allowed to wither away and the role of the CPRS more narrowly defined under Labour.[42]

When not actually conservative, the 1974–9 government was at least evasive and non-committal in its response to pressure for civil service reform which was coming from a number of directions. The champions of the Fulton Report continued to evangelize on its behalf. But although they were well-placed (Norman Hunt had been given a life peerage in 1973 and as Lord Crowther-Hunt became the Prime Minister's Constitutional Adviser in 1974 to work on devolution and then was appointed a junior minister at Education; Robert Sheldon held ministerial posts in the CSD March–October 1974 and then in the Treasury; and John Garrett entered Parliament in 1974 and was Sheldon's PPS at the CSD), Labour's Fultonites failed in the 1970s to rekindle the reformist impulse of the mid-1960s. When in 1976–7 the Commons Expenditure Committee reviewed progress since Fulton in civil service recruitment, training, organization and management, the government's response was notably cautious and defensive, promising action only on minor recommendations. On the Labour left, critics of Whitehall's secrecy and social elitism and of (alleged) civil service obstruction of socialist ministers were able to use the Machinery of Government Study Group established by the NEC's Home Policy Committee in 1976, and chaired by Eric Heffer, to bring forward a draft freedom of information bill and proposals for civil service reform. But while these were endorsed by the 1978 party conference, they were ignored by the government. And as far as the Foreign Office and diplomatic service were concerned, a wide-ranging CPRS study, the *Review of Overseas Representation* (*ROR*), engendered massive controversy but only marginal change.[43]

Comparing the Labour governments of 1964–70 and 1974–9, a crucial difference was in attitudes at the very top towards the reform of the machinery of government and the civil service. Wilson in 1974 had none of the modernizing zeal of 1964. His approach to the machinery of government had become much more low key. Callaghan, too, shared the caution and scepticism prevailing in the mid-1970s among senior politicians of both main parties and among the topmost officials as regards the likely benefits of structural redesign in central government. Wilson dismembered the giant Department of Trade and Industry – largely for reasons of Cabinet management and political balancing between Labour's factions – and Callaghan carved out a separate Department of Transport out of the Department of the Environment, but the era of large-scale departmental reorganizations was over.[44] The change in mood did not just put classic 'MG' questions onto the backburner but also meant that another round of civil service reform, Fulton-style, was never on the government's agenda either.

Garrett and Crowther-Hunt (who left the government in 1976) used both the Expenditure Committee investigation and the Labour Party's own Machinery of Government Study Group to press their views. Garrett sat on the Expenditure Committee's general sub-committee (chaired by Labour MP Michael English) which conducted the parliamentary inquiry; he and Crowther-Hunt each submitted detailed memoranda, and Crowther-Hunt also gave oral evidence. They were both members of Labour's Machinery of Government Study Group. In their analysis and prescriptions, they were naturally Fulton-like, though Crowther-Hunt was now much more concerned about the problem of civil service power and Garrett, along with virtually all the other Labour MPs on the Expenditure Committee, voted for Brian Sedgemore's alternative first chapter, with its biting attacks on the attitudes and power of the civil service.

'The power of the Civil Service has increased, is increasing, and ought to be diminished. At the same time its efficiency and humanity leaves very much to be desired', Crowther-Hunt argued in a paper to Labour's Machinery of Government Study Group.

> Thus, I assume that the changes we wish to advocate should have two objectives. First, we must make the Civil Service much more efficient and its efficiency should have a human face. Secondly, the Civil Service must be firmly under the control of Ministers and Parliament.

Ministerial *cabinets* would help meet this second aim. As for the first, the message was clear: 'Implement the neglected parts of Fulton. In particular, we must abolish all classes and have a unified grading structure. There are many other neglected Fulton recommendations which need to be implemented'. In their memoranda for the Expenditure Committee, Garrett and Crowther-Hunt developed this theme in more detail, cataloguing the limited progress made on the Fulton reforms and the continuing defects of the civil service in terms of recruitment, training, grading, personnel management, the position of the generalist, planning units, the problems of the CSD, and so on.[45]

In the event, the Expenditure Committee's report, issued in July 1977, was very much a Fultonite document except that where Crowther-Hunt's disappointment with the performance of the CSD led him to want to see it strengthened, the committee wanted its responsibilities for efficiency and manpower control transferred back to the Treasury, making CSD much more a personnel department and giving more power to the civil service reformers' longtime *bête noire*. (The question of the organization of the centre of government was at this time a live issue, with Prime Minister Callaghan apparently contemplating splitting the Treasury to make a Ministry of Finance and a Bureau of the Budget – which would absorb the CSD – though the Chancellor's opposition scotched these tentative plans.)[46]

The report of the party's own Machinery of Government Study Group came out a year after the Commons' report, but the parts dealing with recruitment and the internal structure of the civil service added nothing to the post-Fulton reform debate. More than half of the main eleven-page report dealt in fact with the question of civil service power and with the party's proposals for *cabinets* and a closer political control over top appointments (see Chapter 2). And as far as the structure of the civil service was concerned, the report merely reiterated conventional Fultonite arguments in favour of a unified grading structure, greater opportunities for specialists, more interchange between the civil service, local government, commerce and industry (public and private), improved management training and a system of accountable units, providing very little in the way of analysis to back up these points. The 1978 party conference backed these proposals but no one could seriously think that that was going to make any difference with the government. In its reply to the Expenditure Committee's report, published in March 1978, the Callaghan government had in any case already made it very clear that it was just not interested in this sort of prospectus.[47]

The government's unwillingness to contemplate a major shakeup of the Whitehall machine and of the mandarinate was also seen in the case of the Foreign Office and the Diplomatic Service. The Labour government in the 1960s had appointed the Duncan Committee, but in George Brown's view its 1969 report had been 'possibly the most missed opportunity of quite several decades to bring about a genuine reform of the Foreign Service'. The Duncan Committee had made Fulton-like noises about 'the cult of the amateur' and the need for greater familiarity with the social sciences (including modern management and marketing techniques), but thought that diplomats should remain generalists. Its central analysis of the basic nature of Britain's diplomatic interests – involving a distinction between an 'area of concentration' and the rest of the world – and of the consequent division between 'comprehensive' and 'selective' missions in different countries, together with its emphasis on the overriding importance of commercial work and export promotion, were not, however, well received and the report was more or less pigeon-holed.[48]

In Opposition in the early 1970s, a Fabian Society working party discussed the problems of foreign policy-making but there was no sign of anything radically new in Labour thinking about the relationship between the Foreign Office and a Labour government. Proposals that the Foreign Secretary should bring in his own political advisers and complaints about the narrow social basis of Diplomatic Service recruitment – found in the Fabian tract that grew out of these discussions – were hardly original.[49]

Ironically for an institution regarded with some suspicion by Harold Wilson in 1974 as a 'Tory Trojan horse' and attacked by Tony Benn as a tool of a conspiratorial bureaucracy, it was the CPRS's 1976–7 *ROR* exercise which was to canvass the most radical surgery and to call into question the continued survival of the Diplomatic Service in its existing form. It was only to be expected that the Foreign Office would be vehemently opposed to a report which criticized its social tone, complained about over-manning, urged the need for greater specialization (even repeating the Fulton recommendation for 'preference for relevance' in recruitment), and which envisaged the abolition of a separate Diplomatic Service, which it proposed should be merged with the Home Civil Service, with a Foreign Service Group being formed within the new combined service. Indeed, the think-tank's recommendations regarding the BBC external services and the British Council helped to ensure a devastating Establishment counter-attack. The CPRS group's membership was a particular subject of criticism, with dark mutterings about youngish female sociologists from the LSE . . . (in fact review team member Tessa Blackstone was to become an active Labour peer in the late 1980s!).

Not surprisingly, the Callaghan government ditched the *ROR*'s main recommendations. Foreign Secretary David Owen had his own ideas about the need to promote able staff much earlier and to weed out 'duds'. And the government would have no truck with the abolition of a distinct Diplomatic Service, simply bringing forward proposals for more interchange with the rest of Whitehall, some modest staff economies and further reviews of detailed subjects.[50]

'It is as if Labour in office has now lost all stomach for administrative reform', declared John Garrett in a parliamentary debate on the civil service held in the dying months of the Callaghan government. He was right. By 1979 it certainly looked as if the great civil service reform movement sparked off twenty years earlier by Thomas Balogh had fizzled out, leaving unfulfilled – as in the 1930s and 1940s – the high expectations of Whitehall's outside critics and self-styled modernizers. In a book published a year after Labour had lost office Garrett complained:

> in general the Civil Service of 1980 is not much different from the Civil Service of 1968. . . . The top management of our large and technically complex departments of state is still dominated by generalist arts graduates from public schools and Oxbridge.

Whitehall had not been static, of course, but 'there has not been any sense of pushing through the great strategy for development which Fulton envisaged. After 1969 no politician with sufficient weight cared sufficiently to understand the strategy or to see the importance of reform'.[51]

That was to change after 1979, when Mrs Thatcher was to provide the political clout necessary to make progress with the sort of management reforms Garrett favoured. This put the Fultonites in a difficult position, of course, not least because the Conservative government elected in 1979 had most unFabian views about the merits of a big civil service. But the Thatcher premiership was also to generate wider controversies over alleged 'politicization' in Whitehall and over official secrecy and civil service ethics that were to put the future of the civil service back on to the agenda with a vengeance.

5 Efficiency or democracy? Labour and civil service recruitment

Mr Wareing [Labour MP for Liverpool West Derby] has concluded that the Foreign Office system for selecting its 'fast stream' candidates has a built-in 'reactionary' bias. . . . [He] said yesterday: ' . . . The unstated qualification seems to be that you come from the top drawer of society.'

The Independent

If I was giving a son advice . . . on how to get into the modern Civil Service today, I would say, 'Be born in Social Classes 1 or 2, go to a public school, read classics at Oxford . . . and you have on that basis the best chance of getting to the top of the Civil Service.' I submit to you that that is not the sort of advice that one ought to give for getting into the modern Civil Service.

Lord Crowther-Hunt

There is a risk of over-dramatising the case or of oversimplifying the lessons to be drawn from complicated statistics, but how does one explain to an undergraduate at a redbrick university or a polytechnic why it is that in 1985 a fair and unbiased selection procedure for [Administration Trainees] attracted 309 Oxbridge applications, 42 of whom (14 per cent) eventually passed the Final Selection Board, compared with 24 out of 1,814 (1.32 per cent) of those from other universities and polytechnics? Readers might usefully look at the more detailed statistics for themselves . . . and try to devise a plausible (and, if possible, reassuring) explanation.

Gavin Drewry and Tony Butcher

To Harold Laski, the class basis of recruitment to the higher civil service very largely explained its character and political philosophy. Because of the officials' class backgrounds and elite public school and Oxbridge education, 'the predominant temper and outlook of the administrative class represent too narrow an area of public opinion. . . . The major assumptions of the important officials are roughly those of the ruling class', he wrote in 1942. Laski argued that the narrow class range from which the top civil servants were drawn, when combined with the traditions of departmental thinking, meant that in the 1930s Whitehall failed to respond imaginatively to the country's serious economic and social problems:

> At the top of the hierarchy, the civil servant hardly knows – no doubt there are exceptions – at first hand what unemployment does, what the Means Test implies, the effect on an able boy of a decision to economize on the number of free places in the secondary schools.

Herbert Finer's study of top civil servants in Britain in the 1930s had suggested to him that,

> If their composition included the memory of misery, hunger, squalor, bureaucratic oppression, and economic insecurity, perhaps a quality would be added to their work in the highest situations which could not fail to impress the Minister at a loss for a policy or an argument.

Laski agreed, maintaining that inter-class promotions of able civil servants from the lower grades into the higher would go far to remedy this deficiency. It was even possible, Laski speculated, that civil service class bias would handicap the chances of success of any 'wholesale experimentation with the postulates of a new social order', such as attempted, for instance, by a Labour government elected on a socialist platform:

> A Civil Service such as ours might easily fail because it did not believe in the experiment it was asked to attempt. And were that to be the case, I believe that the source of the failure would largely be due to the fact that most of those responsible for the administrative measures necessary to implement it would be at least sceptical and at worst intellectually hostile to the purposes of those measures. And this in its turn, would be due to the fact that the main personnel in the service is too narrowly class-conditioned in the social experience it represents.[1]

One of Laski's students, J. Donald Kingsley, in a celebrated book, introduced the concept of *Representative Bureaucracy* (1944). Primarily concerned with the historical development of the British civil service, Kingsley, too, believed that the social arithmetic of higher civil service recruitment raised 'the fundamental problem of whether socialism could be achieved with the aid of a Civil Service dominated by representatives of the ruling commercial classes'. The secret of the success of the civil service after the mid-Victorian reforms was that it mirrored the dominant forces in society. Its representative character was important because 'the essence of responsibility is psychological rather than mechanical . . . it is a matter of sentiment and understanding rather than of institutional forms'. Kingsley's view was that 'the Civil Service as now constituted would be much less representative of a State in which Labour wielded power than it has been of a State in which that prerogative belonged to the upper middle classes'. This unrepresentativeness, he conjectured, might be a source of difficulty, for, as bureaucracies are responsible and responsive to political leadership only to the extent that they are broadly representative, the social background and experiences of members of the Administrative Class would not suggest that 'as a group they would be able to participate creatively in the development of a Labour program'.[2]

These academic arguments found practical expression in 1946 and 1947 when at the Labour Party conference there were rank-and-file criticisms of the unrepresentative, class character of the Foreign Office and the Diplomatic Service. Such allegations were not new, of course. Laski had criticized Foreign Office recruitment as being based on the assumption that 65 per cent of the country's natural diplomatic talent was to be found in eleven leading public schools. A 1930 Fabian pamphlet had provided critics with chapter and verse on the backgrounds of diplomatic personnel since the mid-nineteenth century. The issue now became a useful stick with which opponents of his foreign policy could beat Bevin. A writer in *Socialist Commentary* in 1946 argued that 'Government has changed from the hands of the aristocracy and upper middle classes to those of the lower middle classes and the workers. Accordingly, future diplomats should be chosen from these latter groups in preference to, though not exclusive of, the others'. A Foreign Office staff 'perfectly representative of the class which was, until a year ago, the ruling class in this country' was not a suitable instrument for a Labour government. *Tribune* in 1947 joined in the attack with lengthy articles on the 'charmed circle' and the social and educational exclusiveness of the Foreign Service.[3]

At the party's 1946 conference, a resolution was moved calling for a 'drastic revision' of methods of recruitment for the Foreign

Service, for the appointment of officials fully in sympathy with a
socialist foreign policy, and for the retirement of out-of-touch or
obstructive diplomats: 'They should not be men who were brought
up in the old narrow ruling circles of Eton and Harrow and Rugby,
followed by Oxford and Cambridge. These men are quite incapable
of representing us'. A 1947 resolution proposed that 'the Diplomatic
Corps should be broadened' by the appointment of staff 'more in
touch with the aspirations of the common people of the world'.
Bevin, who had during the war appeared to support the democratization of Foreign Office recruitment (see pp. 147–8), as Foreign
Secretary firmly rejected suggestions of class bias in Foreign Office
personnel or policy. 'I am not one of those who decry Eton and
Harrow. I was very glad of them in the Battle of Britain. Those
fellows paid the price in the Royal Air Force on those fateful days',
he retorted at the 1946 conference. 'If the Universities are to be
criticized, well put up a vote of censure on Harold Laski, because
it is the product of the Universities I have got to accept'.[4]

What took the steam out of the 'representative bureaucracy'
argument was that it was Bevin's views, not Laski's, which reflected
mainstream party opinion and that, in the Foreign Office as elsewhere in Whitehall, the post-war Attlee Labour government did
not experience the sort of class-inspired bureaucratic resistance
anticipated before 1945. In the cruel words of an American writer
on this subject: 'On the simplest level of political prophecy, the
Kingsley–Laski predictions seem today remotely archaic and even
a bit fatuous'.[5]

In the 1960s the spotlight was on Whitehall efficiency rather than
on the social make-up of the civil service. Nevertheless, seeking to
explain the failures of the 1964–70 Labour government, Marcia
Williams, returning to the Laski–Kingsley thesis, argued that 'a
glance at the Service, and particularly recruitment at higher levels,
makes it quite impossible to accept the neutrality argument'. Maintaining that it was socially and geographically unrepresentative in
its origins, she alleged that the Administrative Class was politically
inclined more to the right than to the left. The civil service is
'undemocratic, particularly at the top; exclusive; and with a strange
personality of its own, half reminiscent of the Army, half of a
masonic society. Certainly many members of the Administrative
Class seem unrelated to the outside world'. 'Without reform at the
roots the vicious social circle will preserve the *status quo*', argued
Mrs Williams. Public school and Oxbridge education, together with
parents' social background, 'will stand for more than ability', while

'the clever ones from ordinary schools, ordinary universities, and from ordinary backgrounds will be continually put off from applying to become members of this elite group of people'.[6]

Left-wing critics of the civil service in the 1970s also in part based their arguments on a class analysis. For instance, the 'minority report' prepared by Labour MPs on the 1976–7 Expenditure Committee referred to 'a bias of class, caste and cast of mind' in higher civil service recruitment. The mandarins sought to 'govern the country according to their own well-defined interests, tastes, education and background'. Manipulating or supplanting ministers, 'they act in what they conceive to be the public good. Some would say they perceive that good in the interest of their own class: others that they see it in terms of the tenets and taboos of their caste'. And Rodney Fielding, the author of a Fabian pamphlet on the making of Labour's foreign policy, explicitly identified the class basis of Foreign Office recruitment as a problem for a socialist government.

> The homogeneous social base of the Foreign Office indirectly affects the formulation of Labour's foreign policy. The restricted social outlook and social contact of the personnel of the [Diplomatic] Service means that they are far removed from any basic understanding of the working of the Labour Party, and of its members. . . . There exists little real knowledge and understanding within the Foreign Office of the political aspirations of the average working class Labour Party member operating at the grass roots, who is expecting results from a Labour Government.

A Labour government should take 'positive steps' to encourage more recruits from varied social backgrounds into the Diplomatic Service, he argued. Broadening the bases of recruitment was necessary to make the Foreign Office more responsive to the demands of radical change in foreign policy, for at present 'the social base of the Foreign Office is such as to make it at the worst antithetical, and at the least indifferent, to the aspirations of Labour'.[7]

To the extent that criticisms such as these rest on an association between civil servants' class backgrounds and Oxbridge education and political views supposedly hostile to Labour, they can be dismissed as bad sociology. Geoffrey Fry has caustically noted that 'it does seem strange how social critics and Labour leaders avoid behaving similarly, given that their origins are often much the same unlike the impeccable working-class credentials of, say, Ramsay MacDonald'. He points out that the Laski–Kingsley-type view 'tends to be expressed in a sufficiently generalized form to be incapable of substantiation – or refutation'. In any case, Whitehall's political views or policy stances are not monolithic. Contrary to Laski's view, one senior civil service 'insider', H. E. Dale, judged that 'the general temper of mind and character' of interwar Whitehall was 'Left Centre'. His estimate was that 'in their political principles, not always expressed by their votes, about one-fourth of the Higher Civil Service are Conservative, one-half or slightly more are Liberal, and the remainder Labour of one shade or another'. On an individual level, mandarins with progressive or socialist views have worked closely with Labour (and Conservative) ministers: in the Attlee period, Robert Hall and 'Otto' Clarke at the Treasury and Andrew Cohen (who hoped to find a Labour seat in the 1950s) at the Colonial Office stand out; Sir William Nield, a senior official in the DEA and the Cabinet Office in the 1960s, had worked in Labour's Research and Policy Department in the late 1930s; and Sir Leo Pliatzky, a key figure at the Treasury in the 1970s, never made any secret of his active Fabian background. A survey conducted (in what was admittedly one of Labour's best years – 1966) for the Fulton Committee found that among the small group of Principals who had joined the civil service in 1956, Labour voters outnumbered Conservatives by almost two to one, although many of these young officials, when their political attitudes were probed, claimed to be floating voters. Despite Labour's traditional suspicions of the Foreign Office, one former career diplomat wrote (just before the SDP split) that 'it was common knowledge that two-thirds of the Foreign Office and Service voted Labour nowadays'.[8] Although impressionistic, such 'insider' evidence does not support the crude demonology found in some Labour circles.

The links between social class origins, educational background, political views and administrative behaviour are a matter of some dispute. It is at least arguable that more emphasis should be placed on post-entry socialization into the culture of Whitehall than on pre-entry (family and educational) socialization. 'There is not really very much reason to suppose that the son of working class parents, whether he enters the Administrative Class by open competition or promotion, will necessarily have greater regard to the interests of the workers than the child of middle or upper class parents', wrote one critic of the Laski–Kingsley view. It is not clear that those who climbed up through the ranks from the bottom of the civil service hierarchy, such as Sir Horace Wilson in the inter-war period, did inject into Whitehall thinking, as he thought that they would, what

Laski saw as the missing qualities of originality and humanity. As Thomas Balogh, a vituperative Labour critic of the traditional mandarin caste, complained: 'The promoted warrant officers and privates have mostly outdone each other in imitating the worst characteristics of the public school educated graduates of the old universities'.[9]

THE FABIAN TRADITION

Candace Hetzner has shown that questions of class equality or of elitism in Whitehall recruitment have not been central to the debate within the Labour Party about the working and reform of the higher civil service. Nor has the social composition of the topmost ranks of the mandarinate been an important issue. In general, Hetzner argues, criticism has focused not on unrepresentativeness but on efficiency and/or 'power pure and simple' rather than on 'class power'. Making the higher bureaucracy more representative of the community as a whole or of the working class has seldom featured as an important part of reform schemes prepared within or by the party.[10] Only a handful of rank-and-file resolutions to the party conference have ever proposed the democratization of higher civil service recruitment. The party's parliamentary leadership has shown barely a flicker of interest in this issue.

One of Keir Hardie's parliamentary reports to the ILP included the passage:

> Our short experience has been sufficient to teach us that it is important to democratise our administrative departments as it is to democratise our Statute Book. We have found that the doors to the higher offices in Whitehall are closed to everyone who has not had a middle-class or aristocratic education, and recent changes have placed our Civil Service more completely in the hands of the wealthy classes.

In a similar vein, Arthur Henderson, setting out *The Aims of Labour* in 1918, stated: 'We want to see the Civil Service democratised' and hit out at the Diplomatic Service as an 'aristocratic preserve'. And Ernest Bevin, in a speech to the TUC conference in 1940, also brought up the issue of Foreign Office recruitment:

> There must be an absolute broadening of the [entrance exam] curriculum, and of the right of entry into the Diplomatic Service. If the boys from the Secondary schools can save us in the Spit-

fires, the same brains can be turned to produce a new world. Democracy does not seem to me a mere question of voting at elections. Democracy seems to me a complete broadening, right down to the humblest house, of every opportunity in a democratic State. Neither can there be any limitation to a narrow class from which servants of the community can be drawn.

[The reader will have noted that by the time of Bevin's 1946 Labour Party conference speech, quoted on p. 144, these RAF pilots had become public schoolboys.]

In the event, however, Hardie did not bring forward concrete proposals designed to open up recruitment to the higher civil service, and the only practical suggestion Henderson made – the abolition of the requirement that budding diplomats had a private income of at least £400 a year – had already been suggested by two Royal Commissions and led to virtually no democratization worth noticing when it was removed in 1919 (as *Tribune* complained in 1947). Bevin's own contribution to the reform of the Foreign Service had in practice little impact on its social base.[11]

The Fabian themes of *efficiency* and *meritocracy* have more often been at the forefront of Labour Party thinking on civil service recruitment than democratic or egalitarian arguments for a 'representative bureaucracy'. Sidney Webb – from a lower-middle-class family and winning a place in the civil service through a brilliant examination performance – virtually personified the Fabian ideal of the meritocratic recruitment of the new administrative elite. The Webbs wanted a new elite of talent to supplant the old elite of birth. They believed strongly in equality of opportunity and the right of individuals to better themselves, anticipating that the spread of democracy and of education would allow upwardly mobile scholarship boys from ordinary backgrounds to enter the highest administrative ranks, but their emphasis was always on expertise and meritocratic achievement rather than on class as such.[12]

There are many examples of this Fabian line of thinking about higher civil service recruitment. For example, the view of the Labour Party's International Advisory Committee, considering the reorganization of the foreign services in the mid-1920s, was that, 'An officialdom capable of expressing and executing the principles and procedures of Labour in foreign relations can best be got, not by "democratising" the services from outside, but by developing them as democracies from within'. The committee's target was the inferior social status and professional prospects of the Consular

Service and the Second Division. It wanted to open the diplomatic career to those who could not afford the education necessary for entry as a First Class Clerk. A 'better class of candidate' would be attracted to Consular and Second Division posts if they had the possibility of promotion to diplomatic appointments:

> For the day is past when this three class system corresponded to social conditions at home and abroad. The Foreign Services of a Democracy can no longer be run in first, second and third class compartments, without communicating corridors or third class admission to the dining car.

Significantly, the committee was clear that 'this reform must be recognised as one that merely makes for efficiency and economy, and not as one that will render official character and capabilities more democratic.' Two additional proposals made by the IAC were to open the Foreign Service as a profession to women (a measure eventually introduced in 1945 by Bevin) and to break up the unified Foreign Service into specialized regional services to meet the changed conditions of the post-1918 international scene. Obliterating the old horizontal distinctions of political/diplomatic, commercial/consular, and clerical functions and staff, with first, second and third class careers respectively, the new set of vertical divisions into regional services would allow 'a career open to the talents from top to bottom'. The regional services would link with the universities, where candidates for entry would prepare by postgraduate studies, while non-graduates, entering at clerical level, might win promotion to higher posts by distinguishing themselves in regional studies, perhaps undertaken at the schools of regional studies in the University of London.[13]

Similarly, Harold Laski's proposals for the reform of civil service recruitment and promotion practices were very much in this Fabian vein. From the 1920s, he had urged the promotion of talented younger officials from the lower grades of the civil service into responsible administrative posts to allow Whitehall to tap energy, initiative and social experiences otherwise overlooked or wasted. He wrote:

> I see no reason why, up to some such age as thirty, a young official who has taken a good university degree, or qualified himself with distinction for the Bar, or done, as some have done, an interesting piece of social investigation, should not be given

a temporary 'acting' appointment in a higher grade to see whether he cannot justify exceptional promotion.

What Laski clearly had in mind as the avenue to promotion was further education, undertaken in the evening at institutions like his own LSE; indeed, he claimed to have taught able young Higher Clerical and Executive Officers of the sort deserving promotion. Junior officials who had demonstrated ability as representatives on a Whitley Council also ought to be talent-spotted and tried out for administrative work in probationary posts. In relation to the scale and the nature of the problem Laski diagnosed, however (see above), this strategy for changing the social composition and outlook of the higher civil service seems somewhat problematic and certainly unlikely to have a large-scale, direct or short-term impact. There could be no guarantees that such internal promotees would come from the working class, for in the 1930s the opportunity to compete for appointment even to the civil service Clerical Class was restricted to about 10 per cent of the nation's youths (the Administrative Class graduate entrants being drawn from less than 1 per cent).[14]

G. D. H. Cole set out his views on this subject in these words:

> As a believer in the value of higher education I do not carry democracy to the point of believing that, in general, those who enter the Civil Service from school are likely to be the equals of university graduates with first-class degrees. . . . Accordingly, I cannot regard it as wrong that most of the top positions in the Civil Service go to men of high educational qualifications. . . . But the more confident I feel of the advantages of higher education, the more must I insist on the need for giving everyone who can be benefited by it a fair chance, even if he proves his quality after, and not before, he has begun on the business of earning his living.

Like Laski, he wanted to break down the barriers hindering inter-class promotions in the civil service, and advocated provision of bursaries and fellowships to allow promising lower-grade staff to attend universities. As he put it, the 'diffusion of educational opportunity, cultural as well as vocational, is the right way of making more extensive promotion from grade to grade so work as to increase the efficiency, as well as the democratic character, of the Service'. Cole hoped and believed that 'first-class honours in one of the great cultural schools of Oxford or Cambridge' would continue to have a high value as a preparation for a career in the top ranks of the civil service, but felt that in a reconstructed post-war civil service more recruits would have to be drawn from a wider range of academic degree subjects, particularly sciences and social sciences, and perhaps from relevant postgraduate courses.[15] But, as with Laski's proposals, these ideas of Cole's would only partly and indirectly democratize the social base of the higher civil service. They were chiefly addressed to the problem of efficiency not class power.

Labour concern about class inequalities in civil service recruitment was often displaced on to the education system and inequalities in the wider society. As Laski put it on one occasion: 'The truth is that the democratisation of the Foreign Service depends upon the democratisation of British society; the one will be achieved in proportion to the other'. The underlying problem was that 'British society remains [a] . . . curious mixture of aristocratic remnants, plutocratic influence, and a popular base from which occasional elements, judged sound, are permitted to stray upwards'. Only by a multiplication of opportunities in education could a democratic civil service be recruited. 'Recruitment from the universities for the highest public positions is indispensable on grounds of efficiency', argued W. A. Robson in 1936, 'but it is consistent with political democracy only if access to the universities is really open to every child of sufficient ability, instead of, as at present, to an infinitesimal fraction of the educationally submerged masses'.[16] As Ernest Bevin had put it in 1946 (see p. 144), any complaint must be made against the undemocratic nature of university recruitment.

The Fabian assumption that the highest administrative posts should still be the preserve of an exclusive elite, but that the social base of that elite should be gradually enlarged and diversified through a rigorously selective and hierarchically organized education system, had a powerful influence. In a revealing memorandum, the party's Advisory Committee on Education argued in 1920 that classics ought not to be required for entrance to university or to the civil service because that would discriminate against non-public-school candidates. However, the committee continued,

If the State is going to insist upon a classical training as a preliminary to entering the higher branches of the Civil Service, the Labour Movement considers that every public school in the country specialising in classical subjects should be open to all children of ability, irrespective of the social position of their parents.

Labour's attitude towards elitism was thus fundamentally ambiguous: its aim could be seen as to substitute a meritocratic elite for an ascriptive elite. The problem was that meritocratic selection criteria continued to work to the advantage of the upper-middle and middle classes and did little to advance those from working-class backgrounds. The glacial pace of change prompted one commentator to ask in 1951, 'Must the working-class boy or girl wait until the educational millennium for an equal chance with middle-class children to become administrators of policies initiated by a working-class movement?'[17]

POST-WAR CONCERN

Much of the post-war thinking in and around the Labour Party about civil service recruitment continued to be concerned with the widening of recruitment to the Administrative Class: not on egalitarian grounds, but in order to promote bureaucratic efficiency. Bosworth Monck's Fabian committee on reform of the higher civil service proposed greater provision for promotion from lower Classes into the Administrative Class and that a certain proportion of Whitehall posts should be filled by bringing in outsiders, with the aim of leavening the Administrative Class with people from different backgrounds and disciplines and with experience in fields outside the civil service. The more critical Fabian pamphlet of 1964, *The Administrators*, lambasting civil service amateurism and calling for more movement in and out of Whitehall and for wider opportunities for specialists (though silent on the civil service Class divisions hindering promotion from the lower ranks), advanced the argument that

if civil servants are to be broadly representative of the public they serve they must be drawn from as wide a range of universities as possible and include natural scientists as well as social scientists, the products of the newest as well as the oldest universities.

The group's proposals would, however, first and foremost broaden the *educational* base of the higher civil service and only to a lesser extent its *social* base, given that, despite the post-war expansion of educational opportunities, the proportion of male university students from working-class backgrounds was broadly the same in the 1960s as before the war.[18]

The Labour Party's evidence to the Fulton Committee was also very much of a piece with the whole thrust of this Fabian analysis, as we saw in the previous chapter. It, too, wanted to bring in more talent from the lower and the specialist grades, and more graduates from universities other than Oxford and Cambridge and with degrees in non-arts subjects. Improved training should be available for suitable non-graduates to fit them for the highest posts. But the class composition of the higher bureaucracy was not explicitly addressed in the party's evidence save for a tangential reference that it would not like to see Whitehall's graduate entry as restricted or socially biased as that of the French *ENA*.

In turn, the Fulton Committee itself paid relatively little attention to the social and educational composition of the civil service, though its background and research papers presented a mass of evidence on this question and on the issue of recruitment. Fulton deplored the fact that 'direct recruitment to the Administrative Class since the war has not produced the widening of its social and educational base that might have been expected',[19] but went on to place the emphasis on the need to recruit from a wider range of universities and degree subjects, including a 'preference for relevance', on the abolition of Class divisions holding back specialists and promotees from inside the service, and on opening up the career structure of Whitehall by encouraging late entrants, temporary appointments, and secondments in and out. Joining the well-established Fabian tradition with 1960s managerialism, it was perhaps hardly surprising that Fulton's modernizing analysis and prescriptions did not emphasize social unrepresentativeness or class inequalities in recruitment as such. The evidence from Fulton's research surveys of Whitehall's social composition and recruitment patterns, however, added fuel to arguments that had been rumbling on since the 1930s about the apparent upper- and middle-class, public school and Oxbridge bias in the selection procedures themselves.

In the inter-war period, Laski and W. A. Robson had maintained that the weightage attached to different subjects in the exams for entry to the higher civil service very seriously handicapped students from London and the provincial universities, and by being so closely aligned with Oxbridge degree schemes tended to introduce something like a class bias. The oral interview added to the procedures after the First World War reinforced this bias and prejudiced the chances of working-class and non-Oxbridge candidates, in the view of Kelsall. This method of entry was supplemented after the Second World War by the system of aptitude tests and extended interviews of the Civil Service Selection Board, the two routes becoming known as Method I and Method II respectively. Although some senior Labour ministers in the 1945–51 government, such as Dalton, had doubts about CSSB, the great majority of Labour MPs apparently supported it as a modern and progressive selection process. The 1947 Fabian committee also defended what it called the 'house-party' procedure (CSSB was originally held at a country house) as 'in conformity with modern psychological doctrine and method' and as not giving an unfair advantage to the 'public school type' or the 'socialite'. Thomas Balogh, however, in a blistering attack on CSSB, argued that the recruitment system was indeed class-prejudiced. His view was that the interview had assumed a greater importance in the 1930s to counteract the consequences of the democratization of educational opportunities. Interview panels dominated by the Establishment and by conformists weakened the safeguards against class prejudice and nepotism established by anonymous examinations. After 1945, according to Balogh, the civil service had used the opportunity presented by a complacent and gullible Labour government to go further in that direction. The CSSB tests, he said, favoured the 'grasshopper mind and the exhibitionist . . . the smooth, extrovert conformist with good connexions and no knowledge of modern problems'.[20]

By the mid-1960s, Method II/CSSB provided virtually all of the successful candidates for entry to Assistant Principal posts; Method I was withering on the vine. At the same time, as Fulton's researchers demonstrated, the intellectual calibre of recruits, as measured by class of degree taken, was falling and the new graduate intake was becoming more middle-class in background. Applicants from state grammar schools and working-class backgrounds had a better chance of success via Method I than Method II/CSSB. Fulton was divided on the future of Method I, but recommended an inquiry into the recruitment methods to consider 'possible ways of making the process of selection more objective in character'.[21] The Davies Committee was set up by the then Labour government to investigate Method II and concluded that there was 'no evidence of bias in Method II itself, either in the procedures or on the part of the assessors' and that Method II was 'a selection system to which the Public Service can point with pride'. Its recommendation that Method I be abolished was accepted by the government. Lord Crowther-Hunt subsequently denounced that Davies Committee's 'white-washing conclusion' as running counter to the committee's own statistical evidence, while Thomas Balogh saw the appointment of the Assistant to the Governor of the Bank of England (and, we should add, a former secretary of the Cambridge University Appointments Board) to lead the inquiry as a characteristic civil service and Establishment 'fix':

> How could an employee of the Old Lady, sitting in the innermost nook of the old boy network, impartially adjudicate whether an interview (with the old boy network) would or would not yield the happiest of results? By condemning it, he would condemn himself.[22]

Labour's renewed critical interest in the civil service from the mid-1970s – despite evidence of continuing social and educational inequalities and biases in recruitment[23] – still did not take the form of a clear class analysis of 'unrepresentative bureaucracy'. Jones and Keating have pointed out that, despite the strong language of class bias of the 'minority report' of Brian Sedgemore and his Labour colleagues on the Expenditure Committee (see p. 145),

> they do not *explicitly* accuse the Civil Service of right-wing bias caused by its social composition. Their task might have been easier if they had gone all the way with such an analysis, for then changing the pattern of recruitment would naturally follow as the means for making the service more socially representative *and* a better policy instrument.

The party's Machinery of Government Study Group also shied away from overtly linking civil service recruitment biases and unrepresentativeness with lack of responsiveness to Labour policies. A paper prepared in the research department was circulated around the group arguing that,

> Since Oxbridge, public schools and a middle-class background still continue to dominate the elite of the civil service and since it is indisputable that this closely moulds the class relations of top civil servants towards the wider society, recruitment procedures to Whitehall should be reviewed. . . . The class preferences of interview boards should be minimised by first-preference quotas embodying a target percentage for working class applicants.

Thomas (Lord) Balogh responded sharply – if a little inconsistently with some of his earlier views:

I do not agree that the Selection Boards favour Oxbridge. They try to favour the red-brick and plateglass universities whenever possible. It is the weakness of these universities hurriedly staffed with second rate teachers which is the trouble. Nor do I think that it is Oxbridge which imparts a conservative liberal bias to the Service. The most obnoxiously reactionary and snobbish civil servants in my experience were those who came from the Executive class because they wanted to be accepted by the capitalist plutocratic establishment.

And even Tony Benn's left-wing special adviser Frances Morrell preferred the less-strident language of seeking 'a cross-section of the educated population'.[24]

In its report, while concluding that 'the present recruitment procedures lead to a dominance in the civil service by a particular elite drawn from a very narrow section of the community', the group proposed nothing more specific than that 'New selection procedures should be introduced to provide equal opportunities for all', otherwise repeating Fulton-style demands for greater opportunities for specialists and more interchange between Whitehall and industry, as we saw in chapter 4. The Callaghan government was also put under pressure by the report of the Commons Expenditure Committee, calling for the post-Fulton Administration Trainee scheme to be scrapped and replaced by uniform entry arrangements for all graduates and for better-organized promotion procedures for those already in the service – proposals which could be expected to have some indirect effect upon the class and educational elitism of the higher grades of the civil service. Its response, however, was to defend the AT selection procedures in its observations on the committee's report, and to set up another 'insider's' review of the scheme – a committee consisting of eleven administrators and two outsiders – which, unsurprisingly, rejected charges of bias in selection.[25]

Finally, we should note here that while *Labour's Programme 1982* routinely repeated the 1978 NEC proposal to introduce 'new selection procedures in order to reflect the wide range of experience in our community', and while a 1982 Fabian group believed that 'civil service appointments should give weight to the need to appoint from minority and under-privileged groups and from people who have experienced life beyond New Malden', after 1979 other issues – particularly those of civil service power, politicization and secrecy

– took up more of the (limited) attention paid within the party to the civil service (see chapter 7).[26]

Labour has thus never adopted a Jacksonian position on higher civil service recruitment. Hetzner has identified the shared backgrounds and culture of Labour's intellectual elite and the leading mandarins as the crucial factor in explaining why the party has never developed a strong egalitarian or democratic critique of Whitehall elitism or pushed for large-scale democratization of recruitment to fashion a 'representative bureaucracy':

> An implicit or explicit assumption among [Labour's Fabian intellectuals] has been that those civil servants in positions of leadership ought to be there as these top bureaucrats are some of the most able individuals available in society. If these civil servants are overwhelmingly middle class and Oxbridge, and if the education system is still not democratized, no matter, democratic socialism must, nonetheless, be driven by a superior engine. . . . To whom should bureaucratic power and authority go? – to people like the intellectual Labour leadership, well educated, civilized, restrained, and dedicated to provision of the public good.[27]

The social class, educational and geographic biases of the leaders and membership of the Fabian Society itself should perhaps be borne in mind here. In addition, two other factors, one historical and the other sociological, may be relevant in trying to understand Labour's thinking about Whitehall recruitment. The experience of the 1945–51 government was clearly important in allaying Laski- and Kingsley-style fears that a socially exclusive mandarin caste would obstruct a Labour administration's socialist programme. And perhaps too the embourgeoisement of Labour's parliamentary party after 1945, with growing numbers of white-collar, university-educated and middle-class MPs, reinforced the tendency to see any problem of bureaucratic recruitment in terms of efficiency, for a thoroughgoing assault on 'class power' could have led to uncomfortable questions being asked about the backgrounds of socialist parliamentarians and ministers and not just top civil servants.

6 Labour, parliamentary accountability and open government

Far too many Socialists regard it as reactionary (or at least as no part of a Socialist's duty) to take up the cudgels for the individual citizen who feels that his rights have been violated by a Department of State, a public board or a semi-public authority. That kind of political activity, they think, should be left to Tories or Liberals.

So wrote Richard Crossman in 1956 in his controversial Fabian pamphlet *Socialism and the New Despotism*, identifying the control of the concentration of power in the state bureaucracy as one of the main, and neglected, tasks of socialism.[1] Although some in the Labour Party, in the anti-bureaucratic, radical-liberal tradition, have been suspicious of executive power, there has also been the contrary tradition of support for strong government, dominating Parliament and pushing through the party's electorally legitimated programme. Labour's approach to the problems involved in securing the democratic accountability of the civil service machine, including the relationship between Parliament and the executive and the issue of official secrecy, illustrates the tensions between these views. In office, Labour has accepted the culture of secrecy and done little to advance the cause of open government; Labour ministers' attitudes towards select committees and the parliamentary ombudsman have been defensive, if not hostile. Over the years though, many in the party have advocated measures designed to subject ministers and the civil service to greater democratic oversight and accountability, albeit with only limited success.

Labour governments have always accepted the constitutional conventions of individual ministerial responsibility and collective Cabinet responsibility, and this has meant that they have had rather conservative views on issues such as civil service anonymity, Whitehall secrecy and the scope and techniques of parliamentary control. To this constitutional orthodoxy have been added the pressures of an adversarial political system. As James Callaghan candidly told the Franks Committee:

> Now I fully agree with the critics . . . who say there is an unnecessary air of secrecy about Government Departments, and I think there is a lot in that, but of course it is inevitable, is it not, when you consider that at any one time only half the country is in favour of the Government, and the other half wants to get rid of them tomorrow. So a Government is not like an ordinary institution, it is not like a cricket club where on the whole all the members belonging to the club want it to go on, provided it wins games, and are not so concerned, whereas frankly half the people in this country are concerned to find things that will redound to the discredit of the Government, every day. It is inevitable in this case that a Government is going to have some defensive reaction and say 'We are not going to tell you anything more than we can about what is going to discredit us.'[2]

Labour governments have not wanted to create rods for their own backs, and help their competitors in the struggle for office, by releasing more information or by greatly improving Parliament's capacity for effective scrutiny and control, even if such steps would help Labour itself when in Opposition. In fact, leading Labour figures, such as Ramsay MacDonald and Herbert Morrison, have expressed satisfaction about the effectiveness of the traditional methods of parliamentary accountability in keeping governments responsible and as a check on administration, although this has not been the view of the party's anti-bureaucratic liberals.

'The mind recoils with something like terror from conceptions of a state run and ruled by officials, terminating in officials, with an official as its highest expression', H. G. Wells famously wrote in *New Worlds for Old* (1908), voicing fears of a Webbian bureaucratic leviathan. The Guild Socialists, too, rejected the state-socialist traditions of Fabian collectivism. In G. D. H. Cole's words,

> The idea that the State is not only supreme in the last resort, but also a capable jack of all trades, offers to the bureaucrat a wide field of petty tyranny. In the State of today, in which democratic control through Parliament is little better than a farce, the Collectivist State would be an Earthly Paradise of bureaucracy.

Often (unfairly) attacked in this way as illiberal 'administrative socialists', the Webbs actually believed that the existing methods of parliamentary supervision of the administration were inadequate – a 'sham'. The increasing functions of government had led, they thought, to 'the gradual establishment of a largely unselfconscious bureaucratic conspiracy against Parliamentary interference or control'. For the future socialist commonwealth they proposed a complex structure of Social and Political Parliaments, functional parliamentary committees, 'control departments', and decentralization, for 'if the present powers of the Crown, the Cabinet, the House of Commons and the Civil Service were to be applied to the ownership and administration of industrial capital, the individual might well find himself practically helpless'. The personal liberty of the individual was always in danger 'in the densely peopled, highly organized modern community'.

> Socialists are at least as anxious as Liberals or Conservatives to protect individual liberty against the enthusiasms of a Social Parliament, which might be carried away by its absorption in improving the mental and material environment of the present generation, or in making provisions for future generations; and likewise against the zeal of administrative bodies, eager to surmount difficulties, or tempted to 'make people better by Act of Parliament'.[3]

This libertarian tradition resurfaced after 1945 with the extension of state activities and the growth of far-reaching government controls (imposed during wartime and its aftermath) appearing – to some socialists as well as to Labour's political opponents – to create a problem of 'bureaucracy'. But the Attlee government did nothing to strengthen the existing channels of accountability or to create new ones, apart from clearing up what had long been denounced as a legal anomaly and, under the 1947 Crown Proceedings Act, allowing citizens the right to sue the Crown if harmed by a government department, a measure which was a far cry from the strengthened judicial controls and the creation of an administrative court proposed in the 1930s by W. A. Robson and Ivor Jennings. Out of office in the 1950s and early 1960s, the party was more receptive to liberal ideas as it sought to shake off the image of bureaucratic socialism pinned on it in the 1945–51 period and to broaden its electoral appeal in a changing society. 'The growth of a vast, centralised State bureaucracy constitutes a grave potential threat to social democracy', argued Richard Crossman, one of the most prominent and influential of the party's liberal reformers at this time. 'The idea that we are being disloyal to our Socialist principles if we attack its excesses or defend the individual against its incipient despotism is a fallacy'. Crossman believed that constitutional reform – including parliamentary committees and the reform of the judiciary – was at least as important as the extension of public ownership or the redistribution of wealth. Socialist extensions of state power should be matched and counter-balanced by new socialist defences for individual freedom:

> Certainly a Socialist will want to be sure that the next Labour Government will have sufficient power to carry through its programme speedily, and that requires a strong political leadership and a disciplined Party at Westminster and in the country to back it up. But the next Labour Government will not only need to nationalise: an almost equally important task will be to democratise the vast institutions already theoretically responsible to it.[4]

In the 1960s, although the Labour government created an ombudsman to guard against maladministration and sponsored a range of specialized Commons select committees, reformers were disappointed by its constitutional conservatism. The commitment of the new 'natural party of government' to the values of openness and democratic accountability seemed too flimsy, too much like the Whitehall-centred approach of its predecessors (Conservative and Labour) to meet the (perhaps exaggerated) hopes of the reform movement. The policy failures and 'betrayals' of the 1964–70 period, and later of the 1974–9 administration too, gave a new emphasis to this debate as the Labour left came in the 1970s to support Freedom of Information legislation and parliamentary investigative committees as tools for checking the concentration of power in Whitehall and so helping a Labour government to meet its election pledges. The failure of the 1974–9 government to redeem its 1974 manifesto promise to reform the Official Secrets Act came to symbolize the disjunction between the party leadership's governing perspective and the 'outsider's' perspective of the parliamentary left and the constituency activists. But whereas liberal, pluralistic and technocratic values had inspired the commitment to reform in the 1950s and 1960s, a model of 'party government' lay behind the left's championing of constitutional changes in the 1970s, introducing tensions and contradictions into their position which were not properly worked out.

LABOUR AND THE HOUSE OF COMMONS

'Love of the House of Commons' was Herbert Morrison's revealing definition of one of the chief qualifications necessary for an MP to become an effective parliamentarian or minister. *Government and Parliament* remains one of the most conservative and complacent accounts of the working of the British system of government, but its reverence for the traditions of parliamentary politics reflected mainstream Labour Party views. From the beginning, most Labour MPs were 'content – indeed anxious – to play the parliamentary game by the parliamentary rules', as Marquand put it. Although perhaps more ready than the Conservative and Liberal parties to criticize those cumbersome features of parliamentary procedure that might hold up its programme, Labour has held back from root-and-branch reorganization of Parliament. A. H. Hanson explained the party's reasoning in these terms:

> To moderate and 'middle-of-the-road' Socialists, who have never ceased to dominate the party's counsels, schemes for radical reform of parliamentary government seemed both unnecessary and dangerous. Unnecessary because it was difficult to prove that a traditionally-patterned House would manufacture Socialist legislation less effectively than Liberal or Conservative; dangerous because any suggestion that Labour might lay impious hands on the ark of the Constitution would inevitably be exploited by political opponents to alienate those sensitive marginal voters in whose hands lay the key to parliamentary majorities.[5]

The municipalization of Parliament, as advocated by Fred Jowett, was adopted as ILP policy before the First World War and again in the mid-1920s, but never commanded serious support in the Labour Party at large, being rejected at the 1930 party conference. Tapping the discontent within the ILP at Labour's support of the Liberal government before 1914 and later with MacDonald's leadership and the record of the 1924 Labour government, Jowett's targets were the bottle-neck of antiquated procedure holding up rapid legislation, and the way in which strict party discipline and collective Cabinet responsibility combined to exclude the ordinary backbencher from any share in administration and to make him a mere voting machine, registering in the lobbies the decisions of his leaders. The remedy was the introduction of a system of committee government on local government lines. Each government department should be placed under an all-party committee. With access to all information and to departmental officials, all committee members could take part in the work of administration and the determination of policy, the committee taking over the powers of the minister, who would become its chairman. Also following the local government analogy, the committees would have a major legislative role, subject to the final approval of the House of Commons as a whole. On each issue, backbenchers would be free to vote on the merits of the question and according to their own convictions, the abolition of ministerial responsibility meaning that they would not be jeopardizing the government's existence or risking a dissolution. The balance of power between the party leadership and its rank-and-file parliamentary supporters would thus shift in favour of the latter, the Cabinet becoming simply a co-ordinating General Purposes Committee under the Prime Minister.[6]

Jowett's model was a fundamental challenge to the conventional forms of parliamentary government accepted by Labour, but his opponents in the party's leadership and among its intellectuals easily had the best of the argument. Legislation and administration would be delayed and the Opposition's opportunities to obstruct greatly increased; a minority Labour government would be completely paralysed by departmental committees with anti-Labour majorities. The scheme would fracture party unity and make more difficult the Cabinet's co-ordination of government policy. Accountability to the electorate would be blurred. The House of Commons, they argued, was properly a forum for the debate between parties; bipartisanship and the immersion of committees in administrative details would damage its broader educative function. There was nothing specifically 'socialist' about these arguments, of course. They merely demonstrated the depth of Labour's constitutional conformity. Jowett's opponents on the ILP's committee on parliamentary reform (1925), however, in a report drafted by Laski, also argued that the Cabinet system could be justified not only on these (cross-party or non-party) grounds, but because it was 'essential under Class War'. Jowett and his supporters hoped that the committee plan would strengthen (left-wing) backbenchers in holding the (right-wing) leadership to party policy, but there could be no guarantee that this would be its effect. Committee government would encourage a consensus style and the making of concessions between parties. While this approach might be practicable in a classless society, in a class-divided society, marked by basic political differences between the main parties, the 'driving force' of a Cabinet backed up by a disciplined party was necessary to ensure 'a forward Socialist policy'. A future Labour government should not disarm itself at its moment of greatest opportunity. The leadership's critics were thus outflanked by the argument, accepted in the party at large, that the conventions of Cabinet government in a parliamentary system were not only no hindrance, but were actually *essential* to the furthering of the socialist cause.[7]

Jowett's plan had some (ILP) political steam behind it, unlike the controversial proposals of the Webbs for a divided Parliament, put forward in *A Constitution for the Socialist Commonwealth of Great Britain*. Distinguishing the functions of 'political government' or 'police power' from social and industrial administration, or 'house-keeping', they envisaged the division of the House of Commons into two co-equal assemblies. The Political Parliament and its Executive would deal with foreign affairs and defence, law and order, and the administration of justice. The Webbs' plan retained both Cabinet government and full ministerial responsibility to the Political Parliament, which would establish a system of committees to scrutinize the work of each ministry and provide a check on policy implementation. To the Social Parliament would fall the control and direction of the nation's economic and social activities, the administration of public services and the power of taxation. Its work would be based on the municipal model of the London County Council, with Standing Committees supervising each department and electing their own chairmen, who would not be bound by any doctrine of collective responsibility. In this sphere, there would be a clear separation of policy – the concern of the Social Parliament and its Committees – from current administration. As an additional safeguard against bureaucratic power and a spur to greater efficiency, 'control departments', staffed by 'independent and disinterested experts', would furnish the Social Parliament with statistics, audits and reports on the performance of public services and nationalized industries.

It was easy for Labour-supporting constitutional theorists of the calibre of Laski and Jennings to show that the Webbs' plan would be unworkable. The functions of government could not be compartmentalized in the way proposed – foreign policy, for instance, had close connections with trade policy. Where policies overlapped, the two Parliaments could be deadlocked and the Webbs' suggestion of Joint Committees or Conferences to resolve disputed issues would be unwieldy. The dangers of inconsistent policies would be compounded if the two chambers had, as was possible, different political complexions. The Webbs' plan was unattractive to both left and right in the party. It could be dismissed as unrealistic and academic, a 'fireside construction' in MacDonald's mocking phrase. More importantly, in terms of Labour's political strategy the Webbs' scheme came unstuck in the same way as Jowett's. Both advocates of 'socialism in our time' and the party's Fabian and trade-union gradualists saw their goal as a Labour majority in the House of Commons, supporting a government with a coherent programme. Dismembering Parliament as the instrument of strong party government simply made no sense to those struggling to capture control of it.[8]

Radical reconstruction of Parliament was thus ruled out, but proposals for reform within the existing constitutional framework also failed to make much headway in this period. The most significant of these was probably Laski's plan for a system of all-party Commons committees to monitor the work of each department, which formed the major positive proposal of the second (Laski-drafted) report of the ILP's parliamentary reform committee in 1925, in opposition to Jowett's municipally-inspired first report.[9] These committees would not take over the ministerial function of policy-making, but would have a consultative role, considering proposed legislation, estimates, delegated legislation and general administrative policy. They would have access to all but the most confidential papers and would be able to summon civil servants before them to give evidence. Ministers would be able to discuss new policies with them in confidence, assessing the political reaction and giving committee members an input at the early stages of policy-making. A committee system on these lines would ensure that parliamentary debates would be better informed and would also have the useful function of better preparing MPs for ministerial office. The advantage of these *advisory* committees, as opposed to Jowett-style *executive* committees, was in not weakening the 'driving force' of the Cabinet. The government would become more responsive to the views of the House of Commons, but could not be stymied by Opposition obstruction, although the Opposition would have access to more information, which could benefit Labour when out of office.

In the event, it was Jowett's plan and not Laski's which became ILP policy at its 1926 conference, but the role and powers intended for the Commons Foreign Affairs Committee proposed by Labour's International Advisory Committee in 1926 were clearly influenced by Laski's scheme (as well as having UDC roots). Such a committee, the IAC argued, would allow the government 'to take confidentially the sense of the parties in the House on points unsuitable for public debate', including the general principles of policy at the formative stage and even the course of diplomatic negotiations. It would not weaken a Labour Foreign Secretary, but 'during a reaction, it would stabilise the policy and might even stop secret commitments'. When Labour returned to office in 1929, however, this recommendation – like others the IAC made (see chapters 2 and 3) – was ignored. The government was understandably preoccupied with the economic crisis. MacDonald professed to having an open mind on 'Advisory Committees', but parliamentary reform was not a priority and his executive-oriented approach was demonstrated when, abandoning his pre-war view that 'the guillotine really kills Parliament', he argued as Prime Minister that all government bills should be subject to guillotines (time-allocation motions).[10]

PARLIAMENT AND THE TRANSITION TO SOCIALISM

The events of 1931 abruptly altered the terms of the debate in the Labour Party on the reform of Parliament. The central issue became whether a Labour government could carry through a socialist programme with the existing parliamentary machinery, and in conditions of crisis, capitalist resistance and extra-parliamentary sabotage. Cripps, Laski, Cole and the left-wing intellectuals of the Socialist League, with their loose talk of 'constitutional revolution' and 'democracy or dictatorship', and given an accidental prominence by the scale of Labour's defeat, were transformed into not very convincing bogeymen by the party's opponents.However, such was the mood in the party that even a cautious constitutional lawyer like Ivor Jennings could argue that a socialist government 'would be justified in taking powers to prevent sabotage by an interested minority'. Labour's left, it must be emphasized, remained strongly parliamentarian, seeking to make the institutions of parliamentary government into more effective instruments for, rather than obstacles to, the achievement of socialism. The most controversial aspect of the debate within the party was the argument that a Labour government, needing to move rapidly, flexibly and decisively to deal with a financial panic, would have to take sweeping emergency powers. This was an issue on which the main parliamentary leadership and the chief union bosses, such as Bevin, were anxious that the party's constitutionally-respectable image should not be tarnished. The NEC's 1934 report on 'Parliamentary Problems and Procedure' was thus a cautious document, emphasizing the temporary and limited nature of any emergency powers that might be sought from Parliament.[11]

The storm over the issue of 'executive dictatorship' (and over the future of the House of Lords) tended to distract attention from proposals designed to provide more effective democratic checks on the government. The idea of backbench advisory committees of the type proposed by Laski in the 1920s was recycled: they would permit closer scrutiny over the greatly extended powers of government departments. At times, Laski himself seemed to envisage that these committees would be composed of Labour MPs only, to ensure a close relationship between the Cabinet and the parliamentary party, the absence of which he thought was a weakness in the MacDonald governments (Dalton backed this idea too). But other versions were clearly all-party in character, with Cripps stressing the desirability of a bipartisan atmosphere in committees.[12] In neither form, though, did these committees feature in the NEC's 1934 report on Parliament or become party policy.

As it was, the predictions of the 1930s seemed to be proved false by the experiences of the Labour government elected in 1945. Morrison, Labour's Leader of the House of Commons, proudly recalled that 'Parliament carried a heavy post-war legislative burden without resort to any drastic schemes involving a basic change in its procedure and a departure from its tradition of gradual development'. Rather than fundamentally changing the character of the legislative process by introducing an Enabling Act, the government relied upon greater use of standing committees, following a scheme worked out by ministers in the coalition. In place of the advisory committees recommended by Laski and others, the PLP established back-bench policy groups, encouraged by Morrison who hoped that they would allow MPs to develop specialized interests and maintain links with ministers, or at least keep them occupied. The results were mixed. 'Those Members of Parliament who expected that the Groups would give them a chance to take part actively in policy-making . . . had their hopes rudely dashed', observed an American commentator. 'From the start Ministers made it clear that they did not look on the Groups in this light'. The party's factional politics and ministers' reluctance to share information and power were the chief problems. Morrison was clear that meetings of backbench MPs could not be given detailed and secret information about departmental and Cabinet policy issues, not least because of the danger of leaks. 'It would be unconstitutional, injurious to good government, and likely to lead to ill-thought-out decisions being foisted upon the Government to admit the right of the party to instruct Ministers or to receive premature details in advance of Cabinet decisions', he thundered. Dalton's Finance Group apparently worked well, but Bevin's Foreign Affairs Group, filled with cranks and fellow-travellers, was treated with contempt by the Foreign Secretary. The success of the Attlee administration in implementing its programme kept most Labour backbenchers satisfied, however, and made the processes of parliamentary government a non-issue in the party in the 1940s and 1950s. Symbolically, Laski's *Reflections on the Constitution*, lectures delivered just before his death in 1950, in which he rebutted most of the then current suggestions for the reform of Parliament, was almost Morrisonian in its conservatism.[13]

THE REFORM OF PARLIAMENT

Parliamentary reform once again became an issue in the early 1960s as part of the 'what's wrong with Britain?' debate on national modernization. Much of the running was made by Labour-supporting academics who, together with officers of both Houses of Parliament, set up the Study of Parliament Group in 1964 which pressed for reforms, including investigative specialized select committees. Harold Wilson, when he became party leader, was quick to associate himself with this current of opinion, though, apart from a commitment to appoint an ombudsman (see p. 172), the Labour government of 1964 did not enter office with any carefully worked-out scheme for parliamentary reform. New intakes of Labour MPs in 1964 and 1966, many of them young, university-educated and with professional backgrounds, were unwilling to accept the role of lobby-fodder and provided the political pressure for reform. A Select Committee on Procedure, set up in December 1964, helped to keep up the momentum with a series of reports, but the changes in parliamentary procedure and the development of select committees after 1966 depended to a large degree on government improvisation, Labour's Leader of the House 1966–8, Richard Crossman, favouring reform but not apparently having a detailed blueprint.[14] The party's 1966 manifesto promised changes to 'improve procedure and the work of committees', and the government recognized that it had to at least appear to balance measures helping it get its business through (by simplifying and streamlining financial and legislative procedures) against reforms improving the Commons' capacity for effective scrutiny. If the reformers were disillusioned by 1970 it was because these changes had not fundamentally altered the imbalanced relationship between Parliament and the executive, an entirely predictable outcome in a system of strong party government which was itself not questioned by them.

Reformers diagnosed the problems of Parliament as deriving from the development of strong party loyalties and the growth in the scale and complexity of government functions, removing the Commons' ability to defeat a government and making the traditional techniques of question time and debate increasingly ineffective as checks on the conduct of administration. The remedy was a system of specialized select committees which would make more information available and open up the process of policy-making, strengthening the House of Commons without compromising the constitutional authority of the government. The supporters of select committees thought that they would function best if they avoided policy issues which were controversial between the major parties and operated in a consensual manner. The first modest step came with the appearance of specialized sub-committees of the Estimates Committee, as recommended by the Procedure Committee, in the 1965–6 and 1966–7 sessions. Following the 1966 election and Crossman's appointment as Leader of the House, two 'experimental' specialist committees were set up, on agriculture and on science and technology, a move which to reformers seemed to herald a major break-through in the campaign to revive the influence of Parliament. In fact, the experience of the 'Crossman committees' was chequered. The Agriculture Committee was closed down by the government after two years' work and after bitter wrangles with ministers and officials in the Ministry of Agriculture and the Foreign Office. Other committees were established – Education and Science (1967), Race Relations and Immigration (1968), Overseas Aid and Development (1969), Scottish Affairs (1969) – but there was no comprehensive committee system, and no committees appointed to tackle the important and sensitive subjects of economic policy, defence or foreign policy.[15]

By 1969 it was clear that the government had lost any enthusiasm for the select committee experiment. 'Most ministers wished to continue their work unfettered by any such scrutiny', complained John Mackintosh. Only a handful of Cabinet ministers – including Crossman, Benn and Crosland – were supporters of specialist committees. Others reflected the view of their departments, which were hostile. Some, Mackintosh claimed, had objections in principle:

They argue that a Labour government, dedicated to major social changes is bound to have all the principalities and powers arrayed against it. Anything, they say, that encourages Labour M.P.s to think of themselves as parliamentarians, as checks on the executive rather than as supporters of their own frontbench, is wrong and is merely playing into the hands of the Tories.

According to Richard Crossman, Michael Stewart said at a Cabinet meeting that

> he couldn't understand how any socialist could propose to limit the powers of the Government by creating Specialist Committees to poach on their preserves. My [Crossman's] proposal would split colleagues and disrupt the unity of the Government and make Parliament inefficient.[16]

On the Labour backbenches, parliamentary reform soon became the hobbyhorse of only a small group of 'ideological democrats', as John Mackintosh called them. Some Labour MPs, particularly on the left, opposed select committees as a threat to the adversary confrontation in the chamber of the House of Commons. John Mendelson denounced 'committee mania', which he saw as tending to create two classes of MP, with committee-members – 'the club within the club' – moving closer to the government (colonization), and as leading to bipartisan government and consensus politics. Michael Foot believed that 'the proliferation of parliamentary Committees is not a cure but part of the disease'. 'Anybody with any experience of committees upstairs knows that the cosier the atmosphere the less the clash between the parties', Foot declared.

> I am in favour of the clash between the parties and the debates within the parties being in the open, because the public has a right to hear them. The clash at elections should be reflected in the House of Commons.

Other backbenchers were apathetic, coming to the view that the committees were politically irrelevant. The lure of even junior ministerial office remained strong, and the cause of parliamentary reform became unpopular after conflicts in the Labour Party over discipline and as the next election loomed, with the emphasis turning to inter-party conflict.[17]

The parliamentary reformers can be criticized for evading the issue of power. As John Mackintosh saw, 'the House of Commons, whatever its views, cannot reform itself'. But the reformers put the onus for change on the government. The contradictions of this approach soon became obvious. With the government determining the shape of the committee system and the whips deciding who would and would not be members, the committees could not be expected to be very effective checks on the executive. Moreover, Labour as a party of government remained committed to working through the existing system of executive-dominated, strong party government. As Jones and Keating have noted, it was not clear how select committees fitted in to this political strategy:

> Under a Labour government, should they be seen as a means of permitting opposition to the government, including dissent from Labour back-benchers? This could be justified on a liberal, pluralist interpretation of Labour's traditions. Should they be used as a means whereby Labour could mobilize support for its programme, confident that factual enquiry could only strengthen its case? Few argued this. Were they, then, to be used to achieve bipartisan political consensus or find solutions beyond the range of ideology? On the loyalist Right of the party was a fear of the former and on the Left a fear of the latter.[18]

Not for the first time, the apparent congruence between the party's political interests and the institutional interests of the government in relation to Parliament inhibited major reform.

The creation of the ombudsman or Parliamentary Commissioner for Administration also illustrates Labour's constitutional conservatism and what Jones and Keating have called its 'ambivalence about state power and its control'. Disquiet about the growth of administrative power and about the limitations of established methods of control fuelled an interest in the Scandinavian ombudsmen in academic and legal circles from the late 1950s, culminating in the *Justice* organization's recommendation of the establishment of a Parliamentary Commissioner in an influential report in 1961. The anti-bureaucratic libertarian tradition within the Labour Party partly explains its receptivity to this proposal. Some key figures in the party leadership and among Labour lawyers, including Richard Crossman, Gerald (Lord) Gardiner QC (Lord Chancellor 1964–70), Elwyn Jones QC (Attorney-General 1964–70), and Peter Shore (head of the party's research department 1959–64), favoured an ombudsman. Other senior Labour politicians were to latch on to the idea primarily for electoral reasons, seeing the ombudsman concept as a useful symbol of the party's 'modern' approach (especially as the Conservative government had rejected it) and as a way of defusing concern about other party proposals involving increased government intervention.[19]

A joint working party of the NEC's Home Policy Committee and of the PLP was set up to examine the subject. Some members were not convinced by the case for a Parliamentary Commissioner. Douglas Houghton, for instance, argued that the existing means of obtaining redress against the bureaucracy were working 'very effectively', and that even raising the issue could undermine citizens' confidence in public administration and rebound against the party:

> And need I ask, especially if Labour Ministers are going to do better than Tory Ministers, why not give them a chance? Or are we to convey the impression that Labour means more bureaucracy, more controls and more restrictions, and that there must be a man to protect the citizen against maladministration?[20]

However, in June 1964 the NEC endorsed in principle the ombudsman idea and a month later Harold Wilson announced that a future Labour government would appoint a Parliamentary Commissioner, to be supported by a parliamentary select committee. Labour's 1964 manifesto declared, in sweeping terms, that the party had resolved 'to humanise the whole administration of the state' and to establish a Parliamentary Commissioner 'with the right and duty to investigate and expose any misuse of government power as it effects the citizen'.

Once in office, a sub-committee of the Cabinet's Home Affairs Committee was set up, chaired by Douglas Houghton(!), to prepare proposals. A White Paper appeared in October 1965, legislation was passed by March 1966, and the Parliamentary Commissioner for Administration took office on 1 April 1967. Richard Crossman called the creation of the Parliamentary Commissioner 'a complete constitutional innovation', yet critics argued that the office was so hedged about with restrictions that it was more properly an 'ombudsmouse'. In the first place, citizens would not be able to approach the Commissioner direct, but route their complaints through an MP. The Labour Party's working group had envisaged direct access to the ombudsman, but Wilson and Houghton were sensitive to the fears of Labour back-benchers that that might damage their role as constituency welfare spokesmen. Second, whereas the party's working group proposed the scope of the Commissioner's work as covering complaints and disputes arising from decisions taken by central government departments, local authorities and 'other public bodies', the government's scheme confined him to central government administration, excluding local government, the National Health Service and the police. (In 1969, though, the Labour government announced that the ombudsman system would be extended to local government and the NHS, Commissioners being established in 1974 and 1977.) The Commissioner's role was to investigate 'maladministration', not questions of policy or the merits of discretionary decisions taken legally. He had no powers to give orders to the bureaucracy or to compel departments to provide remedies for aggrieved citizens.[21]

According to Crossman, the Parliamentary Commissioner's role was 'to get behind the facade of Ministerial responsibility to Parliament to see how decisions are really taken in a Department'. That was precisely the reason why some of his Cabinet colleagues, taking the traditional view of the constitutional convention of ministerial responsibility, opposed the creation of an ombudsman. The view taken by Labour's Foreign Secretary, George Brown, in the Sachsenhausen case was 'if something goes wrong, you shoot the Minister'. Brown argued that if the introduction of the Parliamentary Commissioner were to lead to changing this constitutional convention, so that civil servants were attacked and not ministers, then the accountability of ministers to Parliament would be undermined. Yet as Sir Elwyn Jones, the Attorney-General, admitted, 'to let this independent official go through the files behind the Minster's back and talk to Tom, Dick or Harry in his department is a tremendous encroachment upon his responsibility'. In establishing the Commissioner, he thought, Parliament had intended to undermine the convention of ministerial responsibility 'up to a point'.[22] Constitutional theory was here lagging behind political and administrative realities, but Labour ministers seemed prepared to uphold orthodox doctrine, not least because it was a convenient shield against more effective parliamentary interference in the detailed working of their departments.

HOLDING OUT AGAINST PARLIAMENTARY REFORM 1974–9

The debate about parliamentary reform rumbled on in the 1970s, but the reformers had lost much of the *élan* of the 1960s and the Labour Party leadership did not throw its weight behind their campaign. In fact, the 1974–9 government was involved in several skirmishes with the existing Commons committees. Harold Wilson refused to allow Harold Lever, Chancellor of the Duchy of Lancaster, to give evidence to a select committee on the Chrysler rescue in 1976 on the grounds that he was not the responsible departmental minister. The Treasury refused to provide the Expenditure Committee with key details of the assumptions about economic trends underlying public expenditure plans. There was a row between the Nationalised Industries Select Committee and the British Steel Corporation over the release of information. But to the government's discomfort, parliamentary demands for greater select committee scrutiny increased. In 1977 the Expenditure Committee, in its report on the civil service, called for a comprehensive set of departmental select committees. Nearly 400 MPs signed a motion calling for a foreign affairs select committee. And a Select Committee on Procedure, appointed in 1976, reported in 1978 recommending the establishment of twelve specialist departmentally-related select committees.[23] Michael Foot, Leader of the House 1976–9, would have no truck with such ideas, but he was forced by pressure from the Conservative frontbench and Labour and Conservative back-benchers to concede a debate on the proposals and then to promise the House an opportunity to vote on the recommendations. The 1979 election intervened before Foot could suffer what promised to be an embarrassing rebuff in such a vote, and (ironically) it fell to the Thatcher government to set up the sort of select committee system that the Labour-inclined reformers and founders of the Study of Parliament Group had called for in the 1960s and which Harold Laski had first proposed in the 1920s.

Labour's Machinery of Government Study Group was working on its own proposals for House of Commons reform in the late 1970s. It recommended changes in the legislative process, including the replacement of the existing standing committees with new 'legislative committees' to discuss and amend bills, which could call witnesses to give evidence on points raised by the legislation before them. Influenced by John Garrett, the Group's report included the Fabian-managerialist call for a strengthened system of state audit to examine the management, efficiency and effectiveness of all public bodies and spenders of state funds. Investigatory committees, with 'more powers' than present select committees, should be established to cover the work of each government department and also areas of policy crossing departmental boundaries. 'Since we see no future in consensus government by all-party committees, these investigatory committees would, in addition to being supported by the necessary secretariat, be staffed and advised by specialists and on party political lines', declared the Study Group. 'Effectively, the establishment of such committees would disperse power in Parliament and out of it to the political parties, and to those groups and individuals who support political parties'. As Jones and Keating have noted, this rationale was quite different from the norms of cross-party consensus and impartial investigation inspiring the mainstream reform of Parliament/select committee movement.[24]

The Study Group argued that its proposals steered a middle course between those seeing Parliament 'primarily as the servant of the executive and a place where the only function of back-bench members is to support the leadership of their parliamentary party' and those believing 'that we should move firmly in the 19th century direction of the separation of powers and in the process take the purse strings away from the executive, put policy firmly in the hands of back-bench Members, weaken the party political debate and with it the whole ethos of Cabinet government'. The House of Commons should be reformed in such a way that 'democracy can be enhanced and extended through the party political debate and struggle' and 'the executive, by which we mean the Cabinet and the Civil Service, can be made properly accountable'. Here was an unresolved tension. If government backbenchers were to 'check the executive' and to 'undertake a constructive and critical role' on legislative and investigatory committees, it was difficult to see how far they could simultaneously 'help the executive push its policies through against opposition in Parliament, against outside and vested interests and maybe against the opposition of the civil service'.

These proposals (endorsed by the NEC and by party conference) had a mixed reception at a meeting of the Parliamentary Labour Party. Some backbenchers supported the document. Others argued that the proposed legislative committees would lead to delay and a 'paralysis of government'. George Strauss, a long-time opponent of select committees, thought that 'the constant "checking up" would frustrate the work of a Department' and that 'if the checks on the Executive went too far, the machinery of government would come to a halt'. Michael Stewart, Foreign Secretary in the 1960s, objected to the phrase 'disperse power in Parliament'. He could not accept any committee system which brought conflict with the government: 'Power to govern must rest with the Government'. The TUC–Labour Party Liaison Committee was concerned that the proposals would make it 'virtually impossible' for a Labour government to carry through legislation promised in its manifesto in the first and second sessions of a new Parliament. As Jones and Keating tartly noted:

This, of course, was not the objective of the proposals which were intended to keep a Labour government to the programme; but the critics were undoubtedly right to see the implications of limiting the prerogative of the executive and that such limitations could not be expected to work in one direction only. Strengthened parliamentary control over the executive could not constitutionally be limited to left-wing control over right-wing governments.[25]

In the 1980s, the left's thinking about the role and power of select committees remained muddled (see chapter 7). The Callaghan government, though, had set its face against parliamentary reform and the fact that the source of these particular ideas was the party machine and the left-wing NEC was for it just an extra point against them. What seemed to be a Canute-like attitude on this issue demoralized even its middle-of-the-road supporters, however, and put the government on the defensive. A cynical view would be that as executive power has not been fundamentally challenged by the select committee system established in 1979, the Labour government need not have been so concerned about this issue – it simply lacked the wits to handle it properly, and its problems were probably compounded by having such a fervent opponent of select committees (Foot) in the key ministerial position (Leader of the House), though it would appear that most Labour ministers had views as negative as those of their counterparts ten years earlier.

LABOUR AND THE POLITICS OF SECRECY

Writing in 1909, Ramsay MacDonald expressed disquiet at the 'immunity from criticism' which some government departments 'claim and receive':

The argument that the work of these offices is so delicate that it cannot stand the east winds of public opinion is a pure fiction. But it tends to become true, because the methods of secrecy create their own justification. They establish a bureaucracy which hides itself from the public gaze and protects itself from public control by fictions regarding the marvellous work of the expert and the miraculous omniscience of the permanent official. It is just upon these offices which transact delicate business that the winds of public opinion should blow most freely. The withdrawal of foreign policy into the secret places of Whitehall is altogether deplorable. Party discipline has aided the withdrawal, and is used to protect the seclusion.

Eight Labour members, including Keir Hardie, Arthur Henderson, George Lansbury, Ramsay MacDonald and Philip Snowden, together with two Liberals, were the only MPs to vote against the Official Secrets Act when it was rushed through Parliament in August 1911. The 'secret diplomacy' that led up to the First World War was frequently denounced by Labour opponents of the conflict. However, when Labour entered office for the first time in 1924, Whitehall's barriers of secrecy were not dismantled and the 'winds of public opinion' were not allowed to blow freely. The 1924 government made the modest innovation of issuing a press communiqué after each Cabinet meeting, listing the ministers present and the subjects discussed, a practice disliked by Hankey, the Cabinet Secretary, who on its fall persuaded Baldwin to release to the press only a list of names of those present. In 1929, MacDonald did not attempt to reintroduce the (marginally) more detailed briefings. Like all prime ministers, he reacted to leaks by appealing to ministers for 'the gravest discretion'. Outlining the need for the careful rationing of information within Whitehall on a 'need-to-know' basis, he emphasized in a paper circulated to ministers 'the particular importance of secrecy in regard to Cabinet proceedings'. Harold Laski, at the start of the 1920s, had argued that all official publications should bear the name of the officials who wrote them, but he did not fully think through the constitutional implications of lifting the veil of civil service anonymity in this way and the Mac-Donald governments made no radical gestures in this direction.[26]

Early champions of the public's 'right to know' included the Webbs and George Lansbury. In *A Constitution for the Socialist Commonwealth of Great Britain* the Webbs attacked the 'disease' of official secrecy and described the 'searchlight' of publicity as indispensable for securing effective democratic control over and increased efficiency in government. After 1931, Lansbury criticized the way in which secrecy facilitated manipulative power-play inside government. 'This secrecy business is quite impossible', he complained. 'I often heard more about Cabinet and Government business outside the Cabinet than inside. In fact, pressmen often told me of happenings before I heard of them in the Cabinet room or read of them in documents: this was especially true of foreign and dominion affairs.' In a democratic state, argued Lansbury, Cabinet Minutes should be public property, and 'with extremely few possible exceptions' a full record should be published immediately after Cabinet meetings:

> In a Socialist Government all this make-believe of secrecy would be abolished. Nothing that happened in the Labour Government in its dealings with the unemployed and the proposed cuts in 1931 could injure the well-being of the nation if revealed. The publication of the bare Minutes of proceedings in the Labour Cabinet during the four or five days before we broke up might make me and others appear in an invidious position. Even so, I would be quite content to have the whole published . . .

It would be a mistake to think that these sentiments were widely shared among the Labour leadership, however. In a revealing incident, when Compton Mackenzie was prosecuted in 1932 over his wartime memoirs about his time in military intelligence he was unable to get prominent members of the Labour Shadow Cabinet interested in the subject of official secrets reform. Arthur Henderson actually told him: 'You see, we might want to use the Act ourselves when we get back into power'.[27]

When Labour again formed a government in 1945 its leaders accepted without question the traditions of 'closed government'. 'The method adopted by Ministers for discussion among themselves of questions of policy is essentially a domestic matter and is no concern of Parliament or the public', Attlee observed in a Cabinet paper he circulated in August 1945. That November, he warned his colleagues about the danger of leaks: 'If our intentions are disclosed before policies have been finally formulated, we lose the initiative and criticism outruns our exposition of our plans. . . . No Government can be successful which cannot keep its secrets'. Secrecy was thus regarded not as a problem but as an essential feature of good government. Attlee was content to keep most of the Cabinet, let alone Parliament and the public, in the dark about Britain's atomic weapons programme. There was no serious pressure for 'freedom of information' or 'open government'. The left-wing back-benchers of the 'Keep Left' group talked about the need to ensure that sufficient information was available 'to enable the ordinary citizen to discuss government policy *before* and not after the decision is taken'. And Labour MP Geoffrey Cooper asked the Prime Minister to publish a list of Cabinet committees, but he was such a maverick figure (see chapter 3) that his intervention could easily be brushed off.'[28]

Secrecy was put on to the reform agenda in the 1960s as part of the Fabian–Fulton critique of the civil service. The Fabian authors of *The Administrators* argued that 'secrecy is an obstacle to good policy-making when it prevents the tapping of a sufficiently wide range of expert advice and when it narrows public discussion of policy issues'. Greater openness was both possible and desirable, to allow more informed public discussion and outside research and analysis at an earlier stage in policy-making. The Fulton Committee believed that 'the administrative process is surrounded by too much secrecy. The public interest would be better served if there were a greater amount of openness'. They recognized that 'there must always be an element of secrecy (not simply on grounds of national security) in administration and policy-making', but while the policy discussions of ministers and officials cannot become public knowledge, more of the factual and analytical material on which those discussions were based should be made available to the public at the formative stages of policy-making. The Committee suggested that the government should set up an inquiry to make recommendations 'for getting rid of unnecessary secrecy in this country'. The Official Secrets Act would need to be included in such a review.[29]

The Wilson government reduced from fifty to thirty years the time-limit placed on the opening of government records – in the face of opposition within the Cabinet and in Whitehall – but that was hardly a massive move in the direction of greater access to information. In 1969 it issued a White Paper, *Information and the Public Interest*, which explained that more factual and statistical information was being published, including economic and budgetary forecasts and consultative documents such as Green Papers (the first of these appearing in 1967). The White Paper insisted that, to maintain relations of trust between ministers, and between ministers and their civil servants, secrecy was necessary at the policy-making levels of government. A criminal sanction, as provided by the Official Secrets Act, was needed to protect some official information. It was the government's view, however, that the Official Secrets Acts in themselves were not a barrier to greater openness since they were concerned only with the 'unauthorized' release of information – the government proposed where possible to expand the range of 'authorized' disclosures. The self-congratulatory benevolence of this White Paper was in sharp contrast to the actions of the Labour Attorney-General who initiated the *Sunday Telegraph* secrets trial, concerning information embarrassing to the Wilson government, and which led (in February 1971) to the acquittal of the defendants and the judge declaring that section 2 of the Official Secrets Act should be 'pensioned off'.[30]

In Opposition from 1970 to 1974, although the Franks Committee, appointed by the Conservative government, produced a hard-hitting and influential report on reform of section 2, the Labour Party paid little attention to the issues of official secrecy and open government. Labour welcomed the main proposals of Franks to narrow and define the area of information protected by criminal sanctions. But Arthur Davidson, a Labour back-bencher, attacked his party's conservatism:

> I do not suppose it will, but I would like the Labour Party leadership to come out with a firm commitment to what the [Conservative] Government are not prepared to make a commitment – that there is a right, in the public, of access to information and that if that information is refused there should be a duty upon those refusing to say exactly why they are refusing and why it is in the public interest to refuse it.

Tony Benn was willing to take up a radical position on this issue, however. In 1970 he called for 'a frontal assault on secrecy in decision making':

> most of the current business of Government could easily be made more generally known to those who were interested in it. There could certainly be a full description of the Cabinet Committee structure together with all its sub-committees, Ministerial and official, including a full list of their membership.

He noted how the justifications given for secrecy usually equated the national interest with the political convenience of ministers and the desire of civil servants for the protection of anonymity. At this stage, Benn thought that a policy decision in favour of a progressive relaxation of secrecy, rather than amending legislation, would be enough to produce more open government. He wanted the balance of the argument shifted so that continued secrecy rather than openness had to be justified. To be fair to Benn, this was not a sudden Road to Damascus conversion or some opportunistic Opposition posturing, for while still a Cabinet minister in 1968 he had put forward similar views. In an article in *The Times* in 1973 he went even further, though, saying that the public should know more about what was going on inside government, 'even to the point of knowing when ministers disagree on important issues coming up for decision'.[31]

Benn's plugging away at the secrecy and openness issue paid off in the end. Labour's February 1974 manifesto did not mention the subject, but its October 1974 manifesto included an explicit commitment to 'replace the Official Secrets Act by a measure to put the burden on the public authorities to justify withholding information'. This proposal had its origins in a report on 'People and the Media', prepared by a party study group (of which Benn was a member) in June 1974, which had suggested Freedom of Information legislation to provide a public right of access to official information. As James Michael has commented, few in the party understood the full implications of such a pledge:

> The proposal was probably not the subject of any debate, or perhaps even of any discussion, when the 1974 autumn election manifesto was hammered out between the National Executive of the Labour Party and the leadership of the Parliamentary Labour Party. If it had been even partly understood by most of them it almost certainly would have been toned down or even dropped. It was a stick that the open government campaigners would use again and again on the shoulders of Labour Home Secretaries and Prime Ministers until 1979.[32]

GOING THROUGH THE MOTIONS: SECRETS REFORM 1974-9

In September 1978, Tony Benn, then Secretary of State for Energy, gave a lecture to the British Association for the Advancement of Science on 'The Right to Know'. In his view, the 'growing demand for open government' was being held back by various arguments, each of them understandable but which, taken together, constituted 'an entrenchment of secrecy at a level which is becoming increasingly unacceptable'. Thus the defenders of secrecy put forward arguments relating to national security, the protection of financial and commercial interests and of individual privacy, and arguments based on administrative convenience. He concluded that the real reason why open government was so strongly resisted was that

> disclosure weakens the prerogative of Ministers and the role of officials who enjoy their greatest power when they alone know what is up for decision, what the choices are and what are the relevant facts. Then their advice is hard to challenge.

The Labour Party's Machinery of Government Study Group, introducing its draft Freedom of Information bill in 1978, saw, contemptuously, secrecy as a weapon suiting 'weak ministers . . . and strong bureaucracies'. The 1974–9 government was also vulnerable to similar attacks from its Conservative opponents. Leon Brittan, for instance, calling section 2 of the Official Secrets Act 'indefensible', argued in 1978 that 'it is still there, inspite of the Government's assurances, because they have not had the courage to fight and overcome the strenuous rearguard action mounted in the more obscurantist corners of Whitehall'.[33]

From his vantage point as Head of the Number 10 Policy Unit, Bernard Donoughue was disappointed to see 'how many Ministers took a reactionary position on this issue. After Roy Jenkins had resigned in 1976 there was no senior Minister who took a radical stand'. Peter Shore, for instance, who had trenchantly dissected the disadvantages of secret government in his polemic *Entitled to Know* (1966), had now, as a Cabinet Minister, apparently come to the conclusion that the public was not entitled to know. ('You cannot discuss things openly', Tony Benn quotes him as insisting at a Cabinet meeting on official secrets reform.) Donoughue wrote:

> It was clear that most people in central government saw only potential embarrassment in revealing to the electorate more about their activities on behalf of the general public. . . . I was shocked by the elitism and reactionary assumptions behind many of the assertions made against change.

It seems that Chancellor Denis Healey and the Treasury had the most liberal and relaxed views on reform, being willing to rely on the civil service discipline code rather than criminal sanctions to protect against the disclosure of economic information.[34]

A Cabinet committee on open government – MISC 89 – chaired by Home Secretary Roy Jenkins was set up by Harold Wilson. A Freedom of Information Act along US lines was ruled out after Jenkins returned from a visit to Washington DC saying that it would be 'costly, cumbersome and legalistic'. The government played for time, the 1975 Queen's Speech announcing that 'proposals will be prepared to amend the Official Secrets Act and to liberalise the practice relating to official information', a promise of a White or Green Paper rather than a bill, but little had been done under either heading when Callaghan succeeded Wilson as Prime Minister in April 1976. 'I see no reason why one should just alter things for the sake of it', Callaghan had told the Franks Committee. 'I sometimes think we almost make it impossible for a Government to govern here'. Unsympathetic to Secrets Act reform, he was however galvanized into action by the *New Society*/child benefit scheme leak in June 1976, telling the Commons that he had changed his mind – he now wanted its coverage 'both more limited and more effective'. The Cabinet committee working on proposals, restyled GEN 29, was now chaired by the Prime Minister himself.[35]

In November 1976, Merlyn Rees (who had succeeded Jenkins as Home Secretary that September) made a statement to the Commons outlining the government's intentions on reform of section 2. The government had concluded that it should be replaced by an Official Information Act on the broad lines recommended by Franks, but with certain changes in the categories of protected information. Legislation was promised, but it could not be introduced during the 1976–7 session, though there would be a White Paper. Rees's menacing remark that the 'blunderbuss' of section 2 would be replaced by an 'Armalite rifle' showed that the plan was to modernize and strengthen the defences of government secrecy, not dismantle them. Not surprisingly, the government's proposals, published in a White Paper in July 1978, failed to satisfy Labour backbench supporters of open government. The Machinery of Government Study Group and the party's NEC dismissed them as 'quite inadequate'. Tony Benn, in the lecture quoted above, in effect publicly dissociated himself from the government's proposed blanket protection of all information relating to security and intelligence matters, whether or not it was classified (a more restrictive view than that of Franks). Explicitly stepping back from the October 1974 manifesto, the government said that it had come to no conclusion on Freedom of Information legislation and had 'an open mind'. But the White Paper very pointedly raised the potential resource costs of such legislation as a drawback, and questioned the relevance of foreign (Swedish and American) experience for the British system in which 'the policies and decisions of the executive are under constant and vigilant scrutiny by Parliament and Ministers are directly answerable to Parliament'. Merlyn Rees's retort to Labour MP Robert Kilroy-Silk that there probably were not more than two or three people in his constituency who were concerned about it suggested that the government was determined to resist pressure for open government legislation.[36]

Callaghan hoped to appease the government's critics by a policy of more voluntary disclosure of information, promising the Commons in November 1976 that:

When the Government make major policy studies, it will be our policy to publish as much as possible of the factual and analytical material which is used as the background to these studies . . . unless . . . there is some good reason, of which I fear we must be the judge, to the contrary.

It was not until July 1977 that Whitehall moved to give effect to the Prime Minister's announcement, when the Head of the Civil Service, Sir Douglas Allen (later Lord Croham), sent a letter to permanent secretaries saying that in the past it had normally been assumed that background material for policy decisions would not be published, but that henceforth the working assumption should be that such material should be published once ministers had reached their conclusions on it unless they decided that it should not be. Briefing papers should be written in such a way that factual material could easily be separated from advice on policy options, with the first being released and the second element remaining confidential. Sir Douglas admitted that it was a 'modest step', but warned his fellow mandarins in revealing terms that:

There are many who would have wanted the Government to go much further (on the lines of the formidably burdensome Freedom of Information Act in the USA). Our prospects of being able to avoid such an expensive development here could well depend on whether we can show that the Prime Minister's statement had reality and results.'[37]

Ironically, the Croham Directive (as it became known) became public knowledge only after it was leaked to the press. *The Times* monitored the flow of documents from departments, which was rather uneven. Tony Benn's Energy Department releasd a great deal of material; in other parts of Whitehall the exercise simply became part of the normal public relations machine. When Labour MPs and Peter Hennessy, Whitehall correspondent of *The Times*, asked to see the background papers for the 1978 White Paper, they were told that no civil service briefs could be published and were referred to the Franks Report as the analytical paper for the government's secrets law reform. The *New Statesman* publication of a leaked Callaghan memorandum to ministers explaining that all details of the Cabinet committee system should remain secret, not least because disclosing any information 'would be more likely to whet appetites than to satisfy them', confirmed that the government was determined to allow 'open government' only on its own terms.[38]

Pressure on the government mounted during 1978 and 1979, both inside the Labour Party and outside. The party's Machinery of Government Study Group drafted a Freedom of Information bill which was approved by the NEC and carried at the 1978 conference. The introduction to the draft bill declared:

> It is nothing short of absurd and conducive only to bad government that the general public should have less access to information than favoured individuals and groups to argue their case, who in turn have less access to information than junior ministers, who in turn have less access to information than their Cabinet colleagues, who in turn have less access to information than certain civil servants.

The Study Group was convinced that the principles of its proposals were sound and workable and 'necessary to the proper working of a socialist democracy'. The bill, its clauses based on the relevant US and Swedish statutes, would require public authorities (defined to include Whitehall departments, nationalized industries, Quangos, local and police authorities) to make available to the public broad categories of information, subject to specified exemptions. Cabinet and Cabinet committee papers would normally be published after two years. An Official Information Panel, appointed by the House of Commons and supported by a select committee, would police the provisions of the bill, with the possibility of actions in the courts to enforce it (and award damages to aggrieved citizens). In any prosecution under section 2 of the Official Secrets Act, it would be a defence that the information in question ought to have been disclosed under the Freedom of Information Act.

It goes without saying that had draft legislation on these lines been prepared by the party *before* Labour took office in 1974, then the government would probably have found it much harder to stonewall on this issue. As it was, the government paid no serious attention to the party's proposals, though it made the gesture of allowing Liberal MP Clement Freud's private members' Official Information bill an unopposed second reading in January 1979 – a measure supported by the NEC's Home Policy Committee, further emphasizing the divisions between the party and the government.[39]

In its last days the government published a Green Paper on Open Government and the background Civil Service Department report reviewing overseas practice.[40] A statutory right of access was rejected as a constitutional novelty incompatible with the accountability of ministers to Parliament. The government reaffirmed its belief in the desirability of an evolutionary approach, suggesting a 'Code of Practice' on open government and a ministerial 'statement of intent' on the release of information. Once again seeking to defer the subject, the details of such a Code and the machinery for monitoring it were held to need further detailed examination through a parliamentary select committee.

Labour's 1979 manifesto declared that the party would 'introduce a Freedom of Information Bill to provide a system of open government, and enact the proposals made by the Government in its White Paper to reform section 2 of the Official Secrets Act'. This promise, marrying the proposals of the government and its critics, had to be pressed on Callaghan.[41] It must be a matter for conjecture as to what would have happened to the commitment if Labour had won the 1979 election, given that the outgoing Labour administration had just ruled out a Freedom of Information Act in its Green Paper – the Conservative's victory perhaps saving Callaghan some further opprobrium on this issue.

On the left, the failure to implement the 1974 manifesto pledge was seen as one more example of the need to develop stronger democratic controls over the Whitehall bureaucracy and stronger party controls over the leaders in office, to hold them to the party's programme. With the NEC's draft Freedom of Information bill available, there could be no backsliding next time around. In their defence, Callaghan and Rees could point to the government's precarious parliamentary position, the complexity of the issues involved, and the lack of agreement on the details of secrets law reform among its advocates.[42] Labour ministers had undoubtedly needed little persuading by sceptical or hostile mandarins to set their faces against open government reform. They were clearly surprised at the extent and strength of support for Freedom of Information legislation, and their responses in the 1976–9 period served only to fuel demands for change. If the Labour Party machine can be criticized for failing to develop a clear and practicable policy in Opposition before 1974, then the Callaghan government can fairly be criticized for its failures of political management on this issue.

7 Labour, Thatcher and the future of the civil service

'I hope you're right about the way civil servants block radical ministers. It's our best protection against rampant Thatcherism.' So Peter Kellner reported the reaction of a socialist friend in mid-1980 to the book he (Kellner) had recently written with Lord Crowther-Hunt depicting the civil service as the country's real ruling class. 'Conservative governments that come unstuck in the same manner as Labour governments are those who want to change society in a radical direction', Labour MP Brian Sedgemore, had insisted back in 1977, arguing that the civil service had obstructed the radical Selsdon-man policies of the Heath government. Anticipating that history would repeat itself in that way, Tony Benn in 1980 was publicly wondering how long it would be before civil service pressure was successful in guiding Mrs Thatcher back to the well-trodden paths of the established Whitehall consensus policies followed by other recent Labour and Conservative governments after they had been driven to abandon their manifestos. These views and predictions were soon proven to be quite wrong. The experience of ministers in the Thatcher government was to make nonsense of the claim made by Marcia Williams (Lady Falkender) in 1983 that 'the battle to establish the precedence of the elected Government over a non-elected Civil Service has still to be resolved'.[1] Despite initial scepticism in some parts of Whitehall (including inside the Treasury) towards its radical programme, with numerous press 'leaks' naturally fuelling suspicions of disloyalty, all the signs were that any civil service resistance or foot-dragging that there might have been after 1979 failed to stymie the Thatcher government. An elected government with radical intentions and clear priorities *was* able to impose its will upon Whitehall.

Both left and right were to criticize the organization and ethos of Whitehall's mandarin society in the 1980s, often in strikingly

188 *The Labour Party and Whitehall*

similar terms. On the Labour left, the civil service was an obvious culprit in the post-1979 inquest into the 'failures' of the Wilson–Callaghan governments. The career bureaucracy was seen as a conservative power-bloc – a 'negative machine', peddling a corporatist consensus and sabotaging radical ministers. On the right of the political spectrum, Thatcherites rejected the style and substance of a 'failed' consensus institutionalized by Whitehall. A former Number 10 adviser to Mrs Thatcher, Sir John Hoskyns, attacked what he saw as a fossilized mandarinate and argued that only a large-scale influx of 'fresh blood' in the shape of several hundred politically committed business outsiders could ensure the radical changes needed to save the country. From both perspectives, the higher civil service seemed politically suspect – inveterate social democrats, consensualists, always trying to push governments towards the 'common ground', as one permanent secretary put it.[2]

Michael Meacher warned the Labour left that 'very radical overhaul' of what was a 'mandarin-dominated bureaucracy' with only limited democratic accountability had become 'perhaps more important than the preparation of any specific new policy departure since only if the former is tackled can the latter be expected to be achieved'.[3] No single coherent Labour Party blueprint for reform of the bureaucracy and the machinery of government emerged, however, though there was significant overlap between the packages put forward by such diverse groups as the NEC's and the Fabian Society's machinery of government study groups, both identifying Whitehall secrecy and civil service power as key problems and proposing freedom of information legislation and political reinforcement of departmental ministers (but detailed schemes differed). The vital issue of civil service management and efficiency was, however, the missing item on these left-wing and Fabian agendas for civil service reform. In fact, it would not be too unfair to say that in this area the Labour Party had neither learnt nor forgotten anything since the Fulton Report.

Party polarization gave a new twist to this debate about civil service reform by raising the question of how far Labour, as the principal Opposition party and alternative government, could go along with the changes in Whitehall introduced and occasioned by the Thatcher government. Opinions differ about just how radical the Conservative government's impact has been on the structures, procedures and personnel of the civil service and the machinery of central government, but the importance of Labour's reactions and responses cannot be underestimated, both for the party's own conception of its tasks as a potential government and for the future of the civil service.

TO PURGE OR NOT TO PURGE . . .

That Mrs Thatcher took a much closer personal interest in top-level civil service appointments than did her predecessors in Number 10 poses a special problem for an incoming Labour government. Will Labour ministers be able or willing to work on the traditional basis with the mandarin elite they will inherit, one appointed in what has become a highly personalized promotion process and in a period of greater ideological polarization? Or will they be driven to look for senior advisers with outlooks close to their own because of scepticism about how well officials could dissociate themselves from the values and policies of the Thatcher government, whatever professions of 'neutrality' might be made? One answer to these questions was provided by John Silkin in 1982, who suggested that Mrs Thatcher had tampered with the traditional political neutrality of the civil service and pledged that a Labour government would subject top officials to a 'test of impartiality'. Former Labour Premier James Callaghan, however, denied the allegation that Mrs Thatcher had politicized the higher civil service and did not think that an incoming Labour government would need to make changes at the top of Whitehall. One particularly controversial Thatcher appointment was that of (Sir) Peter Middleton to head the Treasury, but the former Labour Chancellor, Denis Healey, went out of his way to praise Middleton's abilities, implying that a Labour government could work with him. And the Labour Party leader, Neil Kinnock, in a television interview in 1985, indicated that, given loyalty and enthusiasm for a Labour government's policies, he was prepared to work on 'the conventional basis' with top mandarins. Clearly political appointees, though, such as the Chief Economic Adviser Sir Terence Burns, would obviously be replaced. The then Head of the Civil Service, Sir Robert (now Lord) Armstrong, was quick to welcome Kinnock's remarks, publicly assuring him that 'the Civil Service would serve the Government of which he was the head with no less loyalty, energy and goodwill than they have served the present Government and its predecessors'.[4]

Some senior Labour figures, however, believe that there is more of a problem here than Mr Kinnock is prepared to acknowledge. Tony Benn has declared himself totally opposed to a US-style 'spoils system', arguing that 'the civil service by being professional has a great deal to offer'. He says that he would not want a Labour permanent secretary, only one broadly sympathetic to the policies that were being pursued or committed to not obstructing a Labour minister. But Benn is prepared to contemplate retiring or transferring to other posts senior civil servants closely identified with, indeed perhaps the major architects of, the policies a new government is elected to reverse. Dr Jack Cunningham argued in early 1989 that Mrs Thatcher's 'is he one of us?' approach meant that 'there must be a number of people in Whitehall now in senior positions who are, frankly, compromised by that – and they'd have to go'. He doubted whether, if he became Labour's Environment Secretary, he could work with the DOE's permanent secretary, Sir Terence Heiser. 'Most permanent secretaries are now deeply imbued with the values of Thatcherism, even those in less overtly "political" areas', Michael Meacher told a *Tribune* conference in late 1989. He thought that Labour should seize on the Next Steps management reform programme (see p. 198) to 'break the oligarchical control of the Whitehall mandarins by an infusion of new blood from less elite walks of life. . . . Cracking the monolith would also allow us to ditch the pretence of a non-political Service, even at the highest policy levels'.[5]

Two points can be made against these views. First, it would be wrong to anticipate outright hostility in all corners of Whitehall to Labour's programme – many officials in the domestic and social policy departments may in fact welcome new Labour ministers and their spending policies. Even in the Foreign Office and the Ministry of Defence there is likely to be less tension between Labour ministers and their mandarins than seemed probable in the mid-1980s because of the party's changing positions on the European Community and on defence policy. Second, Mrs Thatcher did not appear to have applied a partisan litmus test when making top appointments, but to have preferred a decisive and energetic 'can do' style. Inasmuch as the new breed of top officials is much more adapted to pushing through ministerial policy than the old, Labour should not lightly jettison such able potential allies. Anticipating the election of a Labour government in 1987, David Lipsey thought that for these reasons a wholesale purge of the Whitehall elite would be an unnecessary blunder. 'Officials will be delighted to see the back of a government that is anti-state in general and anti-civil servant in particular', Lipsey believed. And while there was press speculation in mid-1990 about 'an almost certain rearguard action by Whitehall' in the face of Labour's plans for regional assemblies, a new second chamber, freedom of information and strengthened parliamentary scrutiny, it seems likely that the most a Labour government would do in the early 1990s would be to reshuffle the civil service top brass, not massacre it.[6]

James Callaghan could not recall that he ever as Prime Minister overruled the recommendations of the Head of the Civil Service and of Whitehall's Senior Appointments Selection Committee when making senior appointments and promotions (see chapter 2). In contrast, a more active personnel policy than even that pursued by the Thatcher government was urged by groups on both left and right of the party. The plans of the party's Machinery of Government Study Group in the late 1970s – reaffirmed as party policy in *Labour's Programme 1982* – would, it should be recalled (see chapter 2 again), give ministers on entering office the right to confirm or not confirm appointments to the top three civil service grades and to seek to transfer officials if they thought it right. And the 1982 report of the Fabian Study Group on the Machinery of Government also backed the proposal to give ministers greater influence over civil service appointments to selected posts:

> It should be normal, acceptable and in no way a reflection on individuals for governments to try to ensure that key posts are filled by people who have not only the technical skills but also the temperament to make a success of the government's policies in the sectors concerned – in other words, to pursue them with personal enthusiasm and commitment. This could include the appointment of some committed party supporters from outside Whitehall to departmental posts. . . . 'Key posts' could be quite low down the hierarchy, so as to ensure that policies were not only planned but implemented.[7]

Such powers have long been recognized as belonging formally to ministers, but it must be doubtful whether Mr Kinnock would sanction using them to the full in the way suggested, which would constitute a drastic and controversial change in the established practices and procedures. Nor has the Labour leadership taken up the idea, supported by Dr Jack Cunningham and by Clive Ponting (in a 1989 Fabian publication), that all senior posts be held on contract for fixed periods following public advertisement and open competition between civil servants and outsiders. Instead, outside experts may be brought in on short-term contracts to work on specific pieces of legislation or policy initiatives, and Kinnock plans to provide political reinforcement for Labour ministers by the introduction of a *cabinet* system. In addition, taking up the proposals of the 1982 Fabian Group, and particularly of Tessa (now Baroness) Blackstone, Kinnock plans to augment civil service advice by alternative sources of ideas and analysis, and to try to mitigate the effects of departmental fragmentation on a Labour Cabinet's collective strategy, by enlarging and strengthening the Prime Minister's Policy Unit and by reviving the CPRS, both to include politically sympathetic outside experts (though half the CPRS staff would be civil service insiders).[8]

Appointing politically committed outside experts in particular subjects and creating ministerial *cabinets* have, of course, been staple items in Labour's reform thinking for many years (see chapter 2). The party leadership has, however, never properly faced up to difficult questions about exactly what a *cabinet* system should be and how it should operate. Dr Jack Cunningham sees a *cabinet* as having three elements: a small number of political advisers; a group of experts on the department's policy areas ('one doesn't need card-carrying Labour Party members for that', he says); and a few high-flying civil servants. For his part, Kinnock seems to envisage simply an expanded network of special advisers grafted on to the private office system, with an advisory rather than an executive role ('the political intelligence function' is how he describes it). The number of advisers brought in to Whitehall would be quite small – two or three per minister – which to some critics is not enough. The view of Tessa Blackstone is that the number of ministerial political and policy advisers 'would need to be considerably greater than the token one or two appointed under the Wilson and Callaghan governments, if they are to counter effectively the over caution and conservatism of the mandarins when faced with radical policies'.[9]

An alternative model of the *cabinet* sees it as a large team of political sympathisers and activists. On the NEC's Machinery of Government Study Group in the late 1970s, Tony Banks (then special adviser to Judith Hart) had called for a 'political office' of twelve or more, depending on the size of the department and the wishes of the minister. There should be no fixed limit on numbers or on the political activities of advisers (normally classified as temporary civil servants and restricted by the strict Whitehall rules governing the political behaviour of officials), since the intention should be to provide ministers with 'a personal office with real muscle-power', performing 'wide-ranging political functions'. This sort of unit would have a major (if not wholly beneficial) impact upon Whitehall's traditional methods of working, but recruiting from Labour Party circles sufficient high-quality staff to provide ministerial aides able to make a real contribution could be problematic. Tony Benn's version of this model substitutes MPs for outside assistants. Going back to Fred Jowett's work before the First World War (see chapter 6), he proposes committees of twelve to fifteen backbenchers of the party in government assisting the minister in running the department, providing a political network to run alongside the civil service network, and having access to official papers. Although, as Benn points out, this proposal would have the advantage of allowing a political presence on the large number of official committees in Whitehall, bringing around 200 back-benchers into the government has serious implications for party discipline and for Parliament's oversight function. The Benn scheme is probably best regarded as a piece of political science fiction.[10]

Although frequently claiming to be inspired by the French system of ministerial *cabinets*, Labour reformers since Laski in the 1930s have not thought through the fundamental issues relating to the organization of departments and the structure of the civil service which need to be faced if the continental model is to be imported from across the Channel. French *cabinets* are large, are composed mostly of civil servants and, because most departments lack permanent secretaries, directly co-ordinate the numerous divisional *directeurs*. In its evidence to the Fulton Committee, the Labour Party favoured a move towards dividing departments into bureaux and the consequent emergence of a small group of officials with equal access to the minister, ending the concentration of power in the hands of the permanent secretary. Thomas Balogh had in 1959 floated the idea of putting departments under a committee of equal permanent officials who would advise the minister as a body on all major questions, a proposal he repeated in a paper to the Machinery of Government Study Group in the 1970s. But the link between these ideas and the introduction of *cabinets* was never spelt out by Balogh or in Labour's Fulton evidence. Both seemed to suggest that *cabinets* could be introduced into the existing administrative system, which could only mean that their role would be quite different from that of their French namesakes. The 1980–2 Fabian machinery of government committee apparently examined the option of abolishing the post of permanent secretary as a way of changing the balance of power between ministers and the civil service, but the idea did not survive into the group's report.[11] There is no sign that the main party leadership is currently even thinking about this question; yet, arguably, without taking up the issues involved in fundamental departmental redesign on the French pattern, any steps towards beefing up the system of special advisers – few in number and outside the administrative chain of command – can have only a marginal impact in terms of increasing ministers' grip on the policy-making process.

OPEN GOVERNMENT, THE PONTING QUESTION AND PARLIAMENTARY SCRUTINY

After 1979 there could be no doubt about the Labour Party's commitment to open government. The party's *1982 Programme* and its 1983 and 1987 manifestos promised freedom of information (FoI) legislation, and (along with the other opposition parties) Labour welcomed and supported the launch of the 1984 Campaign for Freedom of Information. Debate was about the details, not the principle, of a FoI scheme: how far should open government go? The Fabian machinery of government group was split: a minority of 'maximalists' wanting civil service policy advice to ministers published even before ministers had taken their decisions, the majority arguing that this would erode collective Cabinet responsibility and undermine the confidential relations of trust necessary between ministers and officials. The NEC's 1978 draft FoI bill – under which Cabinet papers would be published after two years, subject to defined exemptions – remained on the table, and was endorsed in the *1982 Programme*. In 1984 an NEC spokesman said it would be kept under review and changed if necessary.[12]

The most recent version of the party leadership's intentions on this subject comes from the Policy Review exercise where there is a pledge to 'establish in law "the right to know"'. Applying to local and regional as well as national government, the proposed FoI Act would be based on the familiar presumption that all information should be freely available, with exemptions (which would be appealable) to protect national security and individual privacy (the party also plans to strengthen and extend data protection legislation). There would be provision (within even the categories of protected information) for a 'public interest' defence, to be tested in the courts. Labour criticized the Conservative government's 1989 Official Secrets Act for reinforcing rather than diminishing the power of the government to suppress the publication of politically inconvenient information, and (unsuccessfully) moved amendments during its passage to incorporate a 'public interest' defence into what Tam Dalyell called 'an anti-Clive Ponting jury Bill'.[13] Given the party's repeated support for a FoI measure, a parliamentary leadership now firmly committed to its speedy introduction, the detailed work done on the issue since the late 1970s and the pressure of the all-party campaign, in the event of a Labour government taking office a repeat of the 1974–9 debacle must be considered virtually inconceivable.

The Ponting affair gave the open government debate an extra twist by raising the issue of a 'public interest' defence in secrets cases. Shirley Williams, then Labour's shadow Home Secretary, had floated this idea in 1973, but it was not a proposal taken up by the 1974–9 government. The initial reaction of Dr Oonagh McDonald, the party's then civil service spokesman, to the Note issued by the Head of the Civil Service (Sir Robert Armstrong) on *The Duties and Responsibilities of Civil Servants in Relation to Ministers* in February 1985, following Ponting's acquittal on section 2 charges, was that the memorandum's definition of the duty of civil servants as being solely to the government of the day was 'far too narrow'. She referred to the US code enjoining civil servants to 'put loyalty to the highest moral principles and to country above loyalty to persons, party or government department'. A more guarded response was the view of James Callaghan and Bernard Donoughue that the Armstrong Note was a perfectly good statement of the traditional relationship. On the Labour left, Brian Sedgemore had argued in 1980 that 'a civil servant's overriding loyalty is to the democratic process':

> we need above everything else civil servants who respect the democratic process and in so doing are prepared to answer to their consciences. . . . If civil servants knew that politicians were behaving improperly whether on the basis of some Watergate or lesser scandal, it would be their duty to expose the politicians. Doctrines of ministerial responsibility and accountability . . . cannot be a shield which allows politicians to act illegally or immorally.

But, writing after Ponting had been charged under the Official Secrets Act, Sedgemore now thought that 'it may be asking too much for governments to institutionalize, still less legalize, notions of disloyalty backed by dangerous philosophical concepts such as "the public good"'. He claimed that civil servants had leaked information to the press, seeking to damage Labour's Energy Secretary Tony Benn, and in private had said that they did it 'for the public good'.[14]

The traditionalists lost the argument inside the party, however. When the 1985 party conference debated freedom of information, Tam Dalyell (a vociferous campaigner on the Belgrano and Westland issues) called for an appeal mechanism for civil servants on matters of conscience – 'a charter for deepthroats' – which the NEC promised to take on board. In the aftermath of the Westland crisis, Dr Oonagh McDonald called upon the government to update the Armstrong code to provide an independent body to which civil servants could refer in cases of conflicts of conscience. The first report of the Policy Review Group on Democracy further developed this proposal as a way of 'reinforcing the integrity of the Civil Service'. The Thatcher government, it argued, 'has identified the civil service with the government of the day, and has punished "disloyalty" severely'. Labour

> would put a duty on civil servants – conscious of improper behaviour on the part of ministers, for example – to report such matters to the permanent secretary. The latter would then be under a duty to investigate matters and report to an all-party parliamentary select committee. There would thus be no question of such action leading to dismissal.

The group's report did not spell out what it is proper and what it is improper for ministers to do, and so the conditions under which civil service 'whistleblowing' would be justified were not defined, although they could perhaps be inferred from the 'public interest' amendments the party moved to the new Official Secrets Act which referred to 'crime, fraud, abuse of authority, neglect in the performance of official duty or other misconduct'.[15] Mysteriously, the final report of Labour's Policy Review, published in 1989, had dropped the reference to a civil service appeal mechanism, though it seems likely that a future Labour government would seek to deal with this matter in consultation with the civil service unions, perhaps in the context of a code of ethics for officials.

Labour's Policy Review argued that a FoI Act would have a significant impact on the ability of Members of Parliament to question and scrutinize all aspects of government policy, but the party further proposed to increase the openness and accountability of government by extending parliamentary scrutiny in other ways, particularly by strengthening departmental select committees. Roy Hattersley dismissed the Commons select committees introduced in 1979 as 'simply a recent example of the establishment allowing the system to bend a little in order that it should not break'. Whereas

Hattersley seemed to regret that select committees lacked the clout to really 'push and probe' the executive, Brian Sedgemore insisted that their role should not involve 'frustrating strong government' but rather was to provide 'a forum for the party political debate where outside opposition to the government's policies can be exposed as invalid . . . strengthening the spine of weak Cabinets, and in the process strengthening Cabinet government by making it more responsible to the democratic process'. Tony Benn justified his scheme for sending teams of Labour MPs into Whitehall departments in terms of them being able to 'keep an eye on the Civil Service' and 'keep a Labour Government closer to its own policies' – in other words, as strengthening *party* government – rather than as a means of improving the accountability of the executive to *Parliament*. Yet at the same time, he criticized the existing departmental select committees for being 'part of the support group for Whitehall . . . they have become a sort of fanclub or advisory group to Government.' While the committees have their limitations, the experience of Labour MPs serving on them does not bear out such a dismissive attitude. Sedgemore's and Benn's arguments have made little headway. Thus, Labour's plan, as set out in the Policy Review, is to strengthen the work of select committees by requiring them to investigate departmental expenditure programmes and by providing them with permanent research staff (the research facilities and expertise available to the House of Commons as a whole will also be increased). In addition, committees may be given the opportunity to introduce legislation based on their reports. These measures would doubtless improve the effectiveness of parliamentary scrutiny, but the party leadership's traditional government-centred perspective can also be detected in remarks in the Policy Review about the need to 'streamline' parliamentary procedures, to 'expedite' the scrutiny of bills, and to consider a specific timetable for each bill.[16]

FULTONISM, THE NEXT STEPS AND BEYOND

'I am an unreconstructed Fultonite', declared Labour MP John Garrett fully twenty years after the report of the famous committee with whose work he had been so closely involved. Maintaining that 'nobody has shown the diagnosis and the prescriptions of the Fulton Committee to be wrong', he kept up throughout the 1980s a steady stream of criticism of civil service amateurism, inefficiency and managerial incompetence. Remaining firmly with the Fabian-managerialist tradition associated with Fulton, Garrett's attacks on the generalist and his calls for changes in civil service recruitment, training and organization, and for an overhaul of Parliament's scrutiny and monitoring arrangements, represented virtually the only serious thinking in Labour circles about the problems of Whitehall management and efficiency until the late 1980s.[17] Much of the 1980s management shake-up in Whitehall could be interpreted as growing out of and developing Fulton. But the Thatcher government politicized the issue of civil service efficiency by placing the emphasis on cutting the size and spending of the public sector, and by its confrontational management style. The question for Labour then became, in effect, whether the new management techniques should be repudiated or whether they could be adapted to serve a socialist purpose.

Official opinion in Whitehall was that the sharpened managerial approach embodied in Raynerism and the Financial Management Initiative (FMI) was politically neutral and should endure across a change of government because, given resource constraints, the new techniques were as useful for politicians committed to expanding the role of the state as for those wanting to cut it back. Labour's response to these developments was rather muted but seemed to bear out the mandarins' hopes. Opposition civil service spokesman Dr Oonagh McDonald said in 1986 that the party agreed with 'the Rayner objectives of efficiency and wellbeing [*sic*] for the civil service'. A Labour MP, Jeremy Bray, had chaired the Treasury and Civil Service Committee inquiry into efficiency and effectiveness in the civil service (1982) which had praised Michael Heseltine's MINIS management information system in the DOE and urged its adoption across Whitehall – following which the government had introduced the FMI. John Garrett criticized MINIS's focus on administrative rather than programme expenditure – 'Mr Heseltine can pore over every penny spent on office carpets, but still knows nothing of the results of money being spent, say, on Toxteth' – but believed that it would not be difficult to impose 'a socialist perspective' on the FMI. In contrast to the Conservative's aim of a narrowly conceived 'value for money', Garrett thought that a Labour definition of the FMI's aims would include 'the effectiveness and the impact, as well as the efficiency of public spending'. He suggested that a system measuring the benefits to women of spending programmes would be more effective and have a greater policy impact than a Minister for Women, the party's official proposal.[18]

The government's launch of the Next Steps Initiative in 1988, involving plans to establish a range of executive agencies to manage

Whitehall's service-delivery and operational tasks, threatened to arouse much more partisan excitement. Roy Hattersley, speaking for Labour in the Commons, argued that 'the Civil Service is not the property of any one Government' and called for all-party discussions before any 'radical' changes: 'to maintain confidence in its impartiality and efficiency, changes in its organisation have to be made by consensus, not by confrontation'. The party has not, however, taken up the proposal made by some outside observers that there should be appointed a Royal Commission on the Civil Service. Giles Radice, the Labour MP chairing the rolling Treasury and Civil Service Committee inquiry into these proposals, has described the Next Steps as

> a natural progression from the Fulton Report of 1968 and I want to see it become a success . . . my view is that it is very important that services which affect millions of people are delivered in the most efficient way possible. It is not in the interests of the British left to be uninterested in efficiency. Socialism and efficiency are not mutually exclusive.[19]

In the Commons, however, Labour MPs have repeatedly questioned whether the establishment of agencies is a step towards privatization and have raised the issues of safeguards for staff and the future of national pay rates. The danger of reduced accountability to Parliament and the handling of MPs' constituency cases in sensitive areas such as social security have also been important Labour complaints.

The reaction of John Garrett, Labour's leading figure on civil service management questions, to the Next Steps has been extremely critical and negative. A strong supporter in the past of a move towards a system of agencies (see chapter 4), Garrett argues that the managerial thinking of the 1960s developed in 'an atmosphere which was broadly sympathetic to a large Civil Service'. In contrast, he says, the Next Steps proposals have been presented 'in the context of an attack on the Civil Service' – a denigration of civil servants' status, and a desire to reduce their numbers, end unified pay and conditions, and eventually privatize. He told the Treasury and Civil Service Committee:

> What begins as a fairly neutral proposal for making the Civil Service run better, and more managerial – a concept I am wholly behind – then becomes the dismemberment of the Civil Service, the reduction of Parliamentary accountability and the change in the ethos and standards of our Civil Service.

Clive Ponting, in his recent Fabian study, while also critical of the Thatcher government's plans, sees a move towards a bipartite divison between Whitehall departments and administrative agencies, together with the creation of an independent 'inspectorate of administration' to monitor the performance of agencies and police the quality of administration, as the only way to revitalize the public sector and improve its efficiency and responsiveness to its 'customers'. The fact that government in social-democratic Sweden operates through hived-off agencies (albeit in a system with more open government than in Britain and with a FoI Act and powerful ombudsmen) might be thought to be a recommendation in certain Labour quarters at any rate.[20]

There is as yet no settled party position on the Next Steps – opinion on agencies is still evolving. Peter Hennessy reports that the Whitehall view is that this process of reform could be and should be a non-party matter: 'Great upheavals in the structure of the Civil Service are clearly not worth the effort if political change is likely to stop them in mid-wrench.' Top civil servants have spoken about 'building for the state . . . not just for any particular government' and have stressed that changing the way in which agencies operate to reflect Labour's policy priorities would be a simple matter. A straw in the wind may be the remarks by Patricia Hewitt, deputy director of the socialist think-tank, the Institute for Public Policy Research, and well-connected with the Kinnock leadership. She said that 'it seems improbable that Labour will simply abolish the Next Steps agencies' and so should start thinking about how best to run them. But far from regarding it as a politically neutral framework for increasing managerial efficiency, it seems likely that Labour opinion would harden against the initiative if the privatization of key services followed on from the creation of agencies and/or if major disputes broke out with the civil service unions over pay and conditions. Much then depends on the way in which the scheme develops and how the new mechanisms of policy-making and administration work in practice in the newly established agencies. It is difficult to disagree with Hennessy's pragmatic judgement that 'the real test of the political durability of *The Next Steps* will . . . be a simple matter of whether the existing agencies are working well and showing continued promise at the time of the general elections of the 1990s if a new government takes office'.[21] In any case, there is evidence of an important new development in Labour Party thinking about administrative efficiency and management which could be of crucial importance to the future of White-hall departments and agencies in the event of a Labour government. The new thinking in the party concerns the *quality* of public services and has emerged as part of Labour's Policy Review. Most work appears to have been done on local government services, but the party's proposed 'Quality Programme' would also apply to the National Health Service and to the services delivered by central government: 'Central government must also develop a commitment to quality; Ministers and civil servants – as well as councillors, managers and employees – must embrace change through better management, more training and sharing "best practice"'. One review paper argued, 'By concentrating on quality, we outflank Tory values, move the agenda on and add another dimension. . . . Quality does not reject the notions of efficiency and economy but it takes in other factors that don't have a cash price.' Detailed proposals have been made to improve local government services and many of these ideas could be extended to apply to the civil service and central government, such as: setting and publicizing targets and standards for services so that users would know what to expect; imposing sanctions on service providers if they failed to meet targets (such as financial compensation for customers); widening the accountancy-based 'value for money' audits of services to take in 'value for people' – 'quality audits'; developing techniques to measure customer satisfaction; a major investment in training at all levels (including exposing ministers and top officials to the front-line of service provision – e.g. manning reception desks in social security offices); negotiating performance-related pay or fixed-term contracts for senior managers, linked to performance targets.[22] There would seem to be no necessary contradiction between this approach to public service management and efficiency and the Next Steps model of departments and agencies operating within a policy and resources framework that specifies clear objectives and targets and monitors performance. Labour's 'Quality Programme' could well be the means of reconciling the party to the Thatcher government's management revolution.

In the Commons Labour has criticized what it says is an emphasis on cost-cutting and financial performance rather than on quality of service in the government's approach to agencies. The party's civil service spokesman, Dr John Marek, has proposed the creation of a Civil Service Commissioner or Ombudsman 'who would have control over quality standards' and the 'power to set minimum standards of service for Civil Service agencies . . . and to look into, and recommend appropriate remedies and compensation for, complaints made by members of the public with regard to the operation of any . . . government agency or trading fund'.[23] Clearly, Labour is starting to grapple with new and interesting ideas about public-sector management. A major problem, however, is in relating this thinking to the basic constitutional principles which the party also wants to maintain. Marek's proposal, for instance, would seem to be in conflict with the doctrine of ministerial accountability to Parliament, for ministers are supposed to be responsible for setting targets and objectives (including standards for quality of service) for agencies reporting to their departments.

To the extent that the new managerialism involves a shift in emphasis from a 'producer' to a 'consumer' perspective, there is also the question of union reaction. The restoration of union rights at GCHQ would be an important symbolic move by a Labour government, but the difficult questions concern civil service pay. In 1983 Labour pledged to seek stable long-term pay arrangements based on comparisons with the private sector and the party's 1990 policy document spoke of developing 'fairer and more rational ways of settling pay and conditions for public sector employees', but the civil service unions will not forget how the last Labour government suspended pay research and imposed cash limits on public spending (limiting the scope for pay rises). Labour has complained about the drive for regional pay in the context of the Next Steps, but the party now appears to accept the idea of performance-related pay, at least for senior managers, and the whole agency approach implies a move away from national pay bargaining in the name of managerial autonomy (perhaps limited by nationally determined minimum wages). John Marek has proposed that changes in conditions of service, appointment and promotion for staff working in agencies functioning as government trading funds should be made only if supported by a majority vote in a staff ballot, which might go down well with the civil service unions but which does raise some wider constitutional questions about a government's relations with its employees (for example the difference between consultation and workers' control).[24]

Other important problems concern the development of ways of measuring the quality as well as the cost of public services (there are many difficulties even with existing performance indicators) and the relationship between measurements of 'consumer satisfaction' and decision-taking. Labour spokesmen have talked airily of feeding surveys of consumer satisfaction into the public expenditure planning process, but what if consumer preferences signal very different policy choices from those favoured by Labour ministers, MPs and activists?[25] In moving from slogans to details, the new managerialism thus has implications not just for the organization and operation of public services but for the meaning and working of democracy that may sometimes be uncomfortable for a Labour government.

CONCLUSIONS

The Labour party, as it enters the 1990s, does not possess a detailed and coherent programme for Whitehall reform. The 1978 NEC statement is now very dated and covers only a limited range of issues – its flimsiness and somewhat uneasy mixture of Fultonite managerial thinking and left-wing views on civil service power meant that it was in any case never a very convincing programme even when it was drafted. The 1982 Fabian study group report is a more substantial document but (inevitably) does not deal with the post-Ponting question of civil service ethics or with the recent management changes and proposals (FMI, Next Steps agencies). The party's 'plans' for the civil service are nowhere clearly and unambiguously set out in a single document, assembled after careful study and deliberation of all aspects of the different issues and their interconnections. Rather than bringing forward well-thought-out proposals of its own, Labour, when it has paid any attention at all, has in many respects simply been reacting to the initiatives and actions of the Conservative government, having to decide whether it could live with any changes introduced by the Conservatives if it came to power. In Britain, administrative change in the past has come about through a process of piecemeal adaptation rather than by the conscious implementation of reformers' blueprints – if it comes to office in the 1990s, Labour looks set to continue this pattern, as was the case with previous Labour governments.

In the 1980s, as in earlier periods, what ideas the party has are not necessarily original or distinctively 'socialist'. Throughout this book, we have noted that, often, the proposals of socialist intellectuals and Fabian and Labour groups have to be seen against a background of thinking and opinion that crosses party lines or is non-party. There are many examples of this: the Webbs and the campaign for 'national efficiency'; the idea of an Economic General Staff in the 1920s and 1930s; the pressure for administrative reform in the early and mid-1940s; the 'what's wrong with Britain?' mood of the early 1960s and the managerial thinking emerging in that decade; ideas over the years about improving parliamentary accountability and reducing secrecy in government. Since 1979, ministerial *cabinets* and FoI legislation, to take just two specific reform proposals, have had many supporters outside the Labour Party, and in some cases it is worth noting that other opposition parties and independent commentators and groups have put forward particular proposals for reform of the civil service and the machinery of government which are more radical than Labour's plans. Labour's caution in respect of the civil service is perhaps symptomatic of a general conservatism on the question of the state and the constitution.

Proposals for change can be put forward but they will only be implemented if Labour ministers are prepared to devote the time and energy to achieve them, and if they are backed by a determined prime minister. As we have seen, past Labour governments and leaders do not have a good record in this respect: MacDonald, Attlee, Wilson and Callaghan all disappointed would-be Whitehall reformers. Wilson's reforming image and modernization rhetoric, in particular, raised hopes that were to be bitterly frustrated. Given the many pressing policy problems it would face, would an incoming Labour government in the 1990s be any different? It would be hazardous to make any firm predictions on this matter, but it is significant that before the 1987 election, leading Labour politicians were pointing to machinery-of-government issues, such as an FoI Act, as 'low cost, no cost' measures of great symbolic importance for a radical administration and which could have a high priority in its programme.[26] And Labour has made enough commitments on the record for its own back-benchers and activists, as well as the other opposition parties and outside groups, to cause it great embarrasment if it abandoned them in office. The party leadership's commitment to reform can, however, only really be seen when it enters government. In any case, the historical record shows that administrative reform is a slow-moving process, with ideas and pressure for change coming from many different sources and with the bureaucracy itself playing a key role in originating, modifying and implementing reform proposals.[27] Whitehall reform is a 'humdrum' rather than 'heroic' process, as noted earlier (chapter 3), though 'outsiders' are often so impatient for results that they are prone to interpret the inevitably slow and patchy progress as evidence of sabotage by bureaucratic vested interests (see chapter 4). A political party or its supporters formulating ideas for change is only one factor in the administrative reform process – frustration and disappointment for Whitehall's outside critics and reformers seems a built-in feature.

Another area where the record suggests that the contrast between promises and performance may produce disillusionment and breed cynicism is with machinery-of-government changes – tinkering with the departmental structure. The party has firm plans for new departments and ministerial posts, including a strengthened Department of Trade and Industry, a Ministry for Women, a Ministry for Environmental Protection, a Department for Consumer Affairs and a Department for Legal Administration. Many quasi-governmental bodies are also planned: new agencies, executives, councils and commissions. 'Labour's policymakers still tend to throw a new institution at every problem they identify', Patricia Hewitt has complained. These changes would be accompanied by the establishment of regional assemblies, intended to move powers and services away from Whitehall. Labour's new DTI, it is envisaged, would be both a power-house equal in status to the Treasury *and* largely decentralized, with its functions hived off to regional offices. This may not actually be inconsistent, but it will certainly be difficult to achieve. In fact the party's general approach to machinery-of-government changes can be criticized. As one commentator put it: 'the policy review nowhere considers the overall effect of the individual changes proposed, or how they might be co-ordinated. Nor does it contemplate the knock-on consequences for Labour ministers of attempting to implement their programme while rebuilding the governmental machine'.[28] Getting real and durable results to match the effort involved in turning the organization of Whitehall upside down is not easy, as the changes of the Wilson–Heath period surely demonstrated.

Of course, only in office will the tensions and possible contradictions between the different parts of a Labour reform package become apparent. The 1982 Fabian group pointed out that Whitehall reformers might want to achieve any or all of three objectives: (1) increasing the power of elected politicians to push through their party programme, (2) better, more 'rational' government, and/or (3) more democratic, open and accountable government. The difficulty is that these objectives may or may not coincide and in practice there will have to be some kind of trade-off. It may not be easy to find the right balancing-point between the idea of a strong Labour government carrying out its socialist mandate and the party's commitment to greater openness and stronger democratic checks, for example.[29] Technocratic ideas about Whitehall management; the issue of civil service power and allegations of bureaucratic sabotage and obstruction of socialist ministers; the controversy over class bias in recruitment; the concern to strengthen the mechanisms of accountability and dispel unnecessary secrecy – as noted in the Introduction and as apparent throughout this book, these different strands of Labour thinking about the nature, problems and reform of the Whitehall machine and the civil service, behind which lurk important differences in political philosophy and approach, are not easily reconcilable or brought together into a coherent whole. The tendency to consider particular issues *ad hoc*, and to evade fundamental questions about the basic constitutional framework that does so much to mould the organization and operations of the civil service, only adds to the problem. The tensions and ambiguities concerning the interrelated issues of power, elitism, efficiency and accountability were never properly worked out at the time of the Fulton Report in the 1960s; arguably the same was true in the 1930s, and there had been little change by the late 1980s and early 1990s.

Notes

CHAPTER 1: INTRODUCTION

1 C. R. Attlee, 'Civil Servants, Ministers, Parliament and the Public', *Political Quarterly*, 1954, vol. 25, pp. 308–15; Herbert Morrison, *Government and Parliament; a survey from the inside*, 3rd edn (London: Oxford University Press, 1964), p. 344.

2 Bernard Donoughue and G. W. Jones, *Herbert Morrison: Portrait of a politician*, (London: Weidenfeld & Nicolson, 1973), p. 153; Morrison, *Government and Parliament*, pp. 327, 344.

3 Barbara Castle, *The Castle Diaries 1964–70*, (London: Weidenfeld & Nicolson, 1984), p. 213; Tony Benn, 'Obstacles to Reform', in Ralph Miliband, Leo Panitch and John Saville (eds), *The Socialist Register 1989*, (London: Merlin Press, 1989), pp. 135, 138; Denis Healey, 'Foreword' to John Garrett, *The Management of Government*, (London: Heinemann, 1980); Denis Healey, *The Time of My Life*, (London: Michael Joseph, 1989), pp. 376, 405; Hilary Wainwright, *Labour: A Tale of Two Parties*, (London: Hogarth Press, 1987), pp. 12, 264; Arthur Henderson, *The Aims of Labour*, (London: Headley Bros, 1918), p. 62.

4 *The Labour Magazine*, July 1922, p. 127; *Socialist Commentary*, January 1961, p. 18; L. J. Sharpe, 'The Labour Party and the Geography of Inequality: a Puzzle', in Dennis Kavanagh (ed.), *The Politics of the Labour Party*, (London: Allen & Unwin, 1982), p. 157; Barry Jones and Michael Keating, *Labour and the British State*, (Oxford: Clarendon Press, 1985), p. 5; Peter Hennessy, *Whitehall*, (London: Secker & Warburg, 1989), p. 128.

5 Jones and Keating, *Labour and the British State*, pp. 2, 163, 193; H. M. Drucker, *Doctrine and Ethos in the Labour Party*, (London: Allen & Unwin, 1979), p. 69.

6 Harold J. Laski, *The Labour Party and the Constitution*, (London: Socialist League, 1933); Sir Stafford Cripps, 'Democracy and Dictatorship: The Issue for the Labour Party', *Political Quarterly*, 1933, vol. 4, pp. 467–81; Sir Stafford Cripps, 'Parliamentary Institutions and the Transition to Socialism', in *Where Stands Socialism Today?*, (London: Rich & Cowan, 1933), pp. 29–56.

7 J. Ramsay MacDonald, *Socialism and Government* (2 vols), (London:

ILP, 1909); Hugh Dalton, *Practical Socialism for Britain*, (London: Routledge, 1935), pp. 7, 15; C. R. Attlee, *The Labour Party in Perspective*, (London: Gollancz, 1937), pp. 169–70.

8 Harold J. Laski, *Reflections on the Constitution*, (Manchester: Manchester University Press, 1951).

9 Douglas Jay, *The Socialist Case*, (London: Faber & Faber, 1937), p. 317; Geoff Hodgson, 'Overstating the State', *Marxism Today*, June 1984, pp. 19–24; Anthony Wright, 'Decentralisation and the Socialist Tradition', in Anthony Wright, John Stewart and Nicholas Deakin, *Socialism and Decentralisation*, (London: Fabian Tract 496, 1984).

10 Margaret Cole (ed.), *Beatrice Webb's Diaries 1912–1924*, (London: Longman, 1952), pp. 9, 97; Rodney Barker, 'The Fabian State', in Ben Pimlott (ed.), *Fabian Essays in Socialist Thought*, (London, Heinemann, 1984), p. 32; John Callaghan, *Socialism in Britain Since 1884*, (Oxford: Blackwell, 1989), p. 109; J. M. Winter, *Socialism and the Challenge of War*, (London: Routledge & Kegan Paul, 1974); *Fabian News*, January 1897; Lisanne Radice, *Beatrice and Sidney Webb*, (London: Macmillan, 1984), pp. 12–13, 219–24.

11 Cole (ed.), *Beatrice Webb's Diaries*, p. 137.

12 K. O. Morgan, *Labour People: Leaders and Lieutenants from Hardie to Kinnock*, (Oxford: Oxford University Press, 1987), pp. 94, 96; Harold J. Laski, 'Choosing the Planners', in G. D. H. Cole (ed.), *Plan for Britain*, (London: Routledge, 1943), pp. 118–19.

13 Harold J. Laski, 'Choosing the Planners', p. 119; Harold J. Laski, 'The British Civil Service', *Yale Review*, 1936–7, vol. 26, p. 350.

14 G. D. H. Cole, *Self-Government in Industry*, (London: G. Bell & Sons, 1917), pp. 5, 66, 238, 265; G. D. H. Cole, *Guild Socialism Re-stated*, (London: Leonard Parsons, 1920), pp. 136, 140–1.

15 Tessa Blackstone, 'No Minister', *New Socialist*, Jan./Feb. 1983, pp. 44–5.

16 *Socialist Commentary*, December 1946, pp. 506–10; Richard A. Chapman, *Ethics in the British Civil Service*, (London: Routledge, 1988), pp.107–34.

17 G. D. H. Cole, 'Reform in the Civil Service', in *Essays in Social Theory*, (London: Macmillan, 1950), p. 224.

18. Drucker, *Doctrine and Ethos in the Labour Party*, p. 102.

CHAPTER 2: LABOUR GOVERNMENTS AND THE MANDARINS

1 Richard Crossman, *The Diaries of a Cabinet Minister, vol. 1, Minister of Housing 1964–66*, (London: Hamish Hamilton & Jonathan Cape, 1975), pp. 21–3; Tony Benn, *Against the Tide: Diaries 1973–76*, (London: Hutchinson, 1989), p. 245.

2 Dame Alix Meynell, *Public Servant, Private Woman: An Autobiography*, (London: Gollancz, 1988), p. 92.

3 Hugh Dalton, *Call Back Yesterday: Memoirs 1887–1931*, (London: Frederick Muller, 1953), p. 147; Sir Frederick Maurice, *The Life of Vt. Haldane of Clone, vol. 2, Haldane 1915–1928*, (London: Faber & Faber,

1939), p. 152; R. W. Lyman, *The First Labour Government, 1924*, (London: Chapman and Hall, 1957), p. 106; Ben Pimlott (ed.), *The Political Diaries of Hugh Dalton, 1918–40, 1945–60*, (London: Jonathan Cape and LSE, 1986), pp. 38–9; Sir Drummond Shiels, 'Sidney Webb as a Minister', in Margaret Cole (ed.), *The Webbs and their Work*, (London: Frederick Muller, 1949), pp. 216–17.

4 Brian Sedgemore, *The Secret Constitution*, (London: Hodder & Stoughton, 1980); Gerald Kaufman, *How To Be A Minister*, (London: Sidgwick & Jackson, 1980).

5 Crossman, *Diaries of a Cabinet Minister*, vol. 1, p. 90; Dalton, *Call Back Yesterday*, p. 219; Hugo Young and Anne Sloman, *No, Minister: an inquiry into the civil service*, (London: BBC, 1982), p. 23; Eleventh Report from the Expenditure Committee, *The Civil Service*, HC 535–II, 1976–77, q. 1924.

6 Edward Boyle, Anthony Crosland and Maurice Kogan, *The Politics of Education*, (Harmondsworth: Penguin, 1971), pp. 176, 182–3; Hugh Dalton, *High Tide and After: Memoirs 1945–60*, (London: Frederick Muller, 1962), pp. 15–17, 19.

7 H. M. Drucker, *Doctrine and Ethos in the Labour Party*, (London: Allen & Unwin, 1979), pp. 97–104; Bruce Headey, *British Cabinet Ministers*, (London: Allen & Unwin, 1974), pp. 61, 78; Allan Bullock, *Ernest Bevin, Foreign Secretary 1945–1951*, (London: Heinemann, 1983), p. 102.

8 Margaret Cole (ed.), *Beatrice Webb's Diaries 1924–1932*, (London: Longman, 1956), pp. 4, 202, 227–8.

9 David Marquand, *Ramsay MacDonald*, (London: Jonathan Cape, 1977), p. 315; John F. Naylor, *A Man and an Institution: Sir Maurice Hankey, the Cabinet Secretariat and the Custody of Cabinet Secrecy*, (Cambridge: Cambridge University Press, 1984), pp. 134–7; G. W. Jones, 'The Prime Ministers' Secretaries: Politicians or Administrators?', in J. A. G. Griffith (ed.), *From Policy to Administration: Essays in Honour of W. A. Robson*, (London: Allen & Unwin, 1976), pp. 29–31.

10 Cole (ed.), *Beatrice Webb's Diaries*, pp. 37–8; John P. Mackintosh, *The British Cabinet*, (3rd edn) (London: Stevens, 1977), p. 551; Robert Skidelsky, *Politicians and the Slump*, (London: Macmillan, 1967), p. 393; Lord Vansittart, *The Mist Procession*, (London: Hutchinson, 1958), p. 397; Marquand, *Ramsay MacDonald*, p. 306.

11 C. A. Cline, 'E. D. Morel and the Crusade Against the Foreign Office', *Journal of Modern History*, 1967, vol. 39, pp. 126–37; A. J. P. Taylor, *The Trouble Makers: Dissent over Foreign Policy 1792–1939*, (London: Hamish Hamilton, 1957), p. 168; Christopher Andrew, *Secret Service: The Making of the British Intelligence Community*, (London: Heinemann, 1985), pp. 298–313.

12 F. M. Leventhal, *Arthur Henderson*, (Manchester: Manchester University Press, 1989), pp. 144–51; Dalton, *Call Back Yesterday*, pp. 223–4, 237–8.

13 Edgar Lansbury, *George Lansbury, My Father*, (London: Sampson Low, Marston, n.d.), p. 197; Keith Laybourn, *Philip Snowden: A Biography 1864–1937*, (Aldershot: Temple Smith, 1988), pp. 96–105;

210   *The Labour Party and Whitehall*

Skidelsky, *Politicians and the Slump*, pp. 215–19; Marquand, *Ramsay MacDonald*, pp. 550–4, 795.

14 George Lansbury, *My England*, (London: Selwyn & Blount, 1934), pp. 129, 142–6.

15 Bernard Donoughue and G. W. Jones, *Herbert Morrison: portrait of a politician*, (London: Weidenfeld & Nicolson, 1973), pp. 153–4; Skidelsky, *Politicians and the Slump*, p. 406; Herbert Morrison, *Socialisation and Transport*, (London: Constable, 1933), pp. 106–7, 132.

16 Hugh Dalton, *Practical Socialism for Britain*, (London: Routledge, 1935), pp. 11–14, 21.

17 Harold J. Laski: 'The Education of the Civil Servant', *Public Administration*, 1943, vol. 21, p. 15; 'The British Civil Service', *Yale Review*, 1936–37, vol. 26, pp. 342–5; *Parliamentary Government in England*, (London: Allen & Unwin, 1938), pp. 84, 283–5, 311, 317–19.

18 Francis Williams, *A Prime Minister Remembers: The War and Post-war Memoirs of the Rt Hon Earl Attlee*, (London: Heinemann, 1961), p. 91.

19 Ralph Miliband, *Parliamentary Socialism*, 2nd edn, (London: Merlin Press, 1972), p. 294; Ralph Miliband, *Capitalist Democracy in Britain*, (Oxford: Oxford University Press, 1984), pp. 100–1; Bill Coxall and Lynton Robins, *Contemporary British Politics: An Introduction*, (London: Macmillan, 1989), p. 151.

20 Kenneth O. Morgan, *Labour in Power 1945–1951*, paperback edn, (Oxford: Oxford University Press, 1985), p. 85; Ben Pimlott, *Hugh Dalton*, (London: Macmillan, 1985), p. 426; Frank Honigsbaum, *Health, Happiness and Security: the Creation of the National Health Service*, (London: Routledge, 1989), pp. 216–17; Bullock, *Ernest Bevin, Foreign Secretary*, pp. 96–103.

21 Peter Hennessy, 'The Attlee Governments, 1945–1951', in Peter Hennessy and Anthony Seldon (eds), *Ruling Performance: British Governments from Attlee to Thatcher*, (Oxford: Blackwell, 1987), p. 32; Kevin Jefferys (ed.), *Labour and the Wartime Coalition: From the Diary of James Chuter Ede. 1941–1945*, (London: Historians' Press, 1987), p. 220; Paul Addison, 'The Road from 1945', in Hennessy and Seldon (eds), *Ruling Performance*, p. 7.

22 R. S. Barker, 'Civil Service Attitudes and the Economic Planning of the Attlee Government', *Journal of Contemporary History*, 1986, vol. 21, pp. 473–86; Emanuel Shinwell, *Conflict Without Malice*, (London: Odhams, 1955), p. 174; Sir Norman Chester, *The Nationalisation of British Industry*, (London: HMSO, 1975).

23 Morgan, *Labour in Power*, pp. 85–6.

24 *New Statesman*, 21 September 1946, pp. 199–200; Kingsley Martin, *Harold Laski*, (London: Gollancz, 1953), pp. 185–6; Labour Party Conference Report 1946, p. 165; Pimlott, *Hugh Dalton*, pp. 412–13; David Dilks (ed.), *The Cadogan Diaries*, (London: Cassell, 1971), p. 776; Morgan, *Labour in Power*, pp. 86–7, 235–6; Michael R. Gordon, *Conflict and Consensus in Labour's Foreign Policy 1914–1965*, (Stanford, California: Stanford University Press, 1965), pp. 134–7.

25 Peter Hennessy, *Whitehall*, (London: Secker & Warburg, 1989), p. 137; *Tribune*, 15 November 1946; PRO T273/232.

26 Philip M. Williams (ed.), *The Diary of Hugh Gaitskell 1945–1956*, (London: Jonathan Cape, 1983), p. 130; Pimlott (ed.), *Political Diaries of Hugh Dalton*, pp. 453–9; Philip M. Williams, *Hugh Gaitskell: A Political Biography*, (London: Jonathan Cape, 1979), pp. 196–203.

27 *Tribune*, 30 September 1949; Sir Richard Acland *et al.*, *Keeping Left: Labour's First Five Years and the Problems Ahead*, (New Statesman Pamphlet, January 1950), pp. 15, 16, 33, 46; PRO T273/235.

28 Alec Cairncross, *Years of Recovery: British Economic Policy 1945–51*, (London: Methuen, 1985), p. 20; Pimlott (ed.), *Political Diaries of Hugh Dalton*, p. 437.

29 Morgan, *Labour in Power*, pp. 81, 88–9.

30 Marcia Williams, *Inside Number 10*, (London: Weidenfeld & Nicolson, 1972), p. 344; *New Statesman*, 22 March 1974, pp. 383–4; Michael Meacher, 'Whitehall's Short Way with Democracy', in Ken Coates (ed.), *What Went Wrong*, (Nottingham: Spokesman Books, 1979), p. 170.

31 Keith Middlemas, *Power, Competition and the State, vol. 2, Threats to the Postwar Settlement: Britain, 1961–74*, (London: Macmillan, 1990), pp. 202–3; Roy Jenkins, 'The Reality of Political Power', *Sunday Times*, 17 January 1971; Shirley Williams, 'The Decision Makers', in *Policy and Practice: the experience of government*, (London: Royal Institute of Public Administration, 1980), pp. 81, 88–9; Simon Jenkins and Anne Sloman, *With Respect, Ambassador: an inquiry into the Foreign Office*, (London: BBC, 1985), p. 103; Joel Barnett, *Inside the Treasury*, (London: Andre Deutsch, 1982), pp. 18–20, 188.

32 Williams, *Inside Number 10*, p. 123; Douglas Jay, *Change and Fortune: A Political Record*, (London: Hutchinson, 1980), p. 128; *New Statesman*, 23 October 1987; Anthony Sampson, *Anatomy of Britain*, (London: Hodder & Stoughton, 1965), p. 251; Susan Crosland, *Tony Crosland*, (London: Jonathan Cape, 1982), p. 137.

33 Peter Kellner and Lord Crowther-Hunt, *The Civil Servants: An Inquiry into Britain's Ruling Class*, (London: Macdonald, 1980), p. 27; Alan Watkins, 'Labour in power', in Gerald Kaufman (ed.), *The Left*, (London: Anthony Blond, 1966), pp. 171–2; Bernard Donoughue, *Prime Minsiter: The Conduct of Policy under Harold Wilson and James Callaghan*, (London: Jonathan Cape, 1987), p. 10; Williams, *Inside Number 10*, pp. 122–3; Clive Ponting, *Breach of Promise: Labour in Power 1964–1970*, (London: Hamish Hamilton, 1989), pp. 173–4.

34 Memorandum no. 97, submitted by the Labour Party (December 1966), in *The Civil Service, vol. 5(2), Evidence submitted to the Committee under the Chairmanship of Lord Fulton 1966–1968*, (Cmnd 3638, London: HMSO, 1968), p. 655; *The Listener*, 9 February 1967, p. 184.

35 Richard Crossman, *Socialism and the New Despotism*, (London: Fabian Tract 298, 1956), pp. 15–16; Kellner and Crowther-Hunt, *The Civil Servants*, p. 230.

36 Crossman, *Diaries of a Cabinet Minister*, vol. 1, p. 616; W. A. Robson, 'What the Crossman Diaries Actually Contain', *Political Quarterly*, 1976, vol. 47, pp. 280–1; 'Symposium – The Crossman Diaries Reconsidered', *Contemporary Record*, 1987, vol. 1, no. 2, pp. 25–6, 29; Hugh

Dalton, *The Fateful Years: Memoirs 1931-1945*, (London: Frederick Muller, 1957), p. 407.

37 Barbara Castle: 'Mandarin Power', *Sunday Times*, 10 June 1973; *The Castle Diaries 1964-70*, (London: Weidenfeld & Nicolson, 1984), pp. 754-5; *The Castle Diaries 1974-76*, (London: Weidenfeld & Nicolson, 1980), p. 728.

38 Tony Benn: *Out of the Wilderness: Diaries 1963-67*, (London: Hutchinson, 1987), pp. 182, 220, 226-7; *Office Without Power: Diaries 1968-72*, (London: Hutchinson, 1988), p. 152; Hugo Young and Anne Sloman, *But, Chancellor: an inquiry into the Treasury*, (London: BBC, 1984), p. 113.

39 Tony Benn, 'Manifestos and Mandarins', in *Policy and Practice: the experience of government*, pp. 57-78; Young and Sloman, *No, Minister*, pp. 19-20.

40 Sedgemore, *The Secret Constitution*, p. 31; Expenditure Committee, *The Civil Service*, pp. lxxvii-lxxxiii; HC Debs 15 January 1979, cols 1400-7.

41 Labour Party Archives: RE515/March 1976, p. 2; RE904/Jan. 1977; 'Reform of the Civil Service', in *Statements to Annual Conference by the National Executive Committee* (Thursday), (London: Labour Party, 1978), pp. 35-52.

42 David Lipsey (ed.), *Making Government Work*, (London: Fabian Tract 480, 1982), p. 6; Kellner and Crowther-Hunt, *The Civil Servants*, pp. 233-5.

43 Benn, 'Manifestos and Mandarins', pp. 47-8; Young and Sloman, *No, Minister*, pp. 29-30; Labour Party Archives: RE1699/June 1978.

44 Arthur Silkin, 'The "Agreement to Differ" of 1975 and its effect on ministerial responsibility', *Political Quarterly*, 1977, vol. 48, pp. 73-4; Williams, 'The Decision Makers', pp. 92-3; Sedgemore, *The Secret Constitution*, p. 106.

45 Ponting, *Breach of Promise*, pp. 109-12; Middlemas, *Power, Competition and the State*, vol. 2, p. 206; Crosland, *Tony Crosland*, pp. 202-3.

46 David Coates, *Labour in Power?*, (London: Longman, 1980), p. 156; Joe Haines, *The Politics of Power*, paperback edn, (London: Coronet/ Hodder & Stoughton, 1977), pp. 16-39, 57-8; Donoughue, *Prime Minister*, pp. 63-6.

47 Barnett, *Inside the Treasury*, pp. 21-2, 58-9, 102, 179-80; Denis Healey, *The Time of My Life*, (London: Michael Joseph, 1989), pp. 380-1; Donoughue, *Prime Minister*, p. 94; Martin Holmes, *The Labour Government, 1974-79: Political Aims and Economic Reality*, (London: Macmillan, 1985), pp. 79-102, 178-80; Phillip Whitehead, *The Writing on the Wall: Britain in the Seventies*, (London: Michael Joseph, 1985), pp. 192-3; Hennessy, *Whitehall*, pp. 259-60.

48 Richard Crossman, *Inside View*, (London: Jonathan Cape, 1972), p. 77; Laski, *Parliamentary Government in England*, pp. 294-9; Crossman, *Diaries of a Cabinet Minister*, vol. 1, p. 39.

49 Mark Wickham-Jones, 'Financial Decision-Making and the Labour Government in Britain 1974-75', ECPR conference paper 1989 (mimeo); Crosland, *Tony Crosland*, p. 356.

50 A. J. A. Morris, *C. P. Trevelyan*, (Belfast: Blackstaff Press, 1977), p.

164; Labour Party Archives: International Advisory Committee paper 333C, March 1925.

51 Marquand, *Ramsay MacDonald*, pp. 416–18; Labour Party Archives: International Advisory Committee papers 333G, July 1925; 333H(b), March 1926.

52 Sir Charles Petrie, *The Powers Behind the Prime Ministers*, (London: MacGibbon & Kee, 1958), pp. 137–55; Vansittart, *The Mist Procession*, p. 371; Pimlott, *Hugh Dalton*, p. 189.

53 Harold J. Laski, *The Labour Party and the Constitution*, (Socialist League, London, 1933), pp. 21–2; Laski, 'The British Civil Service', pp. 343, 349.

54 Lansbury, *My England*, pp. 145–6; Labour Party Conference Report 1936, p. 234; Raymond Postgate, *The Life of George Lansbury*, (London: Longman, 1951), p. 295.

55 Dalton, *Practical Socialism for Britain*, p. 14; *The Reform of the Higher Civil Service*, (London: Fabian Society, 1947), p. 21.

56 A Temporary Civil Servant, 'Post-War Machinery of Government – Government Administration and Efficiency', *Political Quarterly*, 1944, vol. 15, pp. 104–5; Fabian Society Papers: K41/1, f.3–4, CSG (46) 11, August 1946.

57 HC Debs 25 March 1948, col. 3418; *Top Jobs in Whitehall*, (London: Royal Institute of Public Administration, 1987), pp. 17–18; Kenneth Harris, *Attlee*, (London: Weidenfeld & Nicolson, 1982), p. 593; Kevin Theakston, *Junior Ministers in British Government*, (Oxford: Blackwell, 1987).

58 Crossman, *Socialism and the New Despotism*, p. 16; Thomas Balogh, 'The Apotheosis of the Dilettante: The Establishment of Mandarins', in Hugh Thomas (ed.), *The Establishment*, (London: Anthony Blond, 1959), p. 124; *The Administrators*, (London: Fabian Tract 355, 1964), p. 41; Fabian Society papers: K65/3, f.86–7.

59 Labour Party evidence to the Fulton Committee, pp. 656, 664–6.

60 Anthony King (ed.), *The British Prime Minister*, (London: Macmillan, 1969), p. 109; Jo Grimond, Enoch Powell, Harold Wilson and Norman Hunt, *Whitehall and Beyond*, (London: BBC, 1964), pp. 17–18; Benn, *Out of the Wilderness*, pp. 65–6; Crossman, *Diaries of a Cabinet Minister*, vol. 1, p. 385; vol. 2, p. 200; Crossman, *Inside View*, pp. 68–9.

61 Grimond *et al.*, *Whitehall and Beyond*, p. 18; A. Shrimsley, *The First Hundred Days of Harold Wilson*, (London: Weidenfeld & Nicolson, 1965), p. 26; Williams, *Inside Number 10*, pp. 357–8; Crossman, *Diaries of a Cabinet Minister*, vol. 2, pp. 295–6.

62 B. Reed and G. Williams, *Denis Healey and the Policies of Power*, (London: Sidgwick & Jackson, 1971), pp. 249–50; Young and Sloman, *No, Minister*, p. 91.

63 Memorandum no. 78, submitted by the Fabian Society (February 1967), in *The Civil Service*, vol. 5(2), pp. 559–68.

64 Theakston, *Junior Ministers*.

65 Rodney Fielding, *The Making of Labour's Foreign Policy*, (London: Fabian Tract 433, 1975), pp. 8–10; John Garrett and Robert Sheldon, *Administrative Reform: the next step*, (London: Fabian Tract 426, 1973);

Williams, *Inside Number 10*, p. 359; Castle, 'Mandarin Power'; *The Times*, 11 July 1973, 21 January 1976; Benn, *Against the Tide*, p. 41.

66 Williams, *Inside Number 10*, p. 358.

67 Donoughue, *Prime Minister*, pp. 20–5; G. W. Jones, 'Harold Wilson's Policy-Makers', *Spectator*, 6 July 1974; Treasury and Civil Service Committee, *Civil Servants and Ministers: Duties and Responsibilities*, HC 92, 1985–86, qs 741–3.

68 R. Klein and J. Lewis, 'Advice and Dissent in British Government: the Case of the Special Advisers', *Policy and Politics*, 1977, vol. 6, pp. 1–25; Harold Wilson, *The Governance of Britain*, paperback edn, (London: Sphere Books, 1977), pp. 202–5; *Guardian*, 22 June 1978.

69 Donoughue, *Prime Minister*, pp. 36–7.

70 Treasury and Civil Service Committee, *Civil Servants and Ministers*, q. 609; Christopher Pollitt, *Manipulating the Machine: Changing the Pattern of Ministerial Departments 1960–83*, (London: Allen & Unwin, 1984), p. 110.

71 Young and Sloman, *No, Minister*, p. 91.

72 Expenditure Committee, *The Civil Service*, pp. lxxxi–lxxxii; Labour Party, 'Reform of the Civil Service', pp. 39–40; Labour Party Archives: RE784/Oct. 1976, RE775/Sept. 1976, RE904/Jan. 1977.

73 Crossman, *Inside View*, pp. 19, 88; Richard Rose, *The Problem of Party Government*, paperback edn, (Harmondsworth: Penguin, 1976), pp. 378–9.

74 Laski: *The Labour Party and the Constitution*, p. 21; *Parliamentary Government in England*, pp. 296–9.

75 Skidelsky, *Politicians and the Slump*, p. xii; R. H. Tawney, 'The Choice Before the Labour Party' (1934), in *The Attack and Other Papers*, (Nottingham: Spokesman, 1981 – first published 1953), pp. 57, 64; Pimlott, *Hugh Dalton*, p. 208; Elizabeth Durbin, *New Jerusalems: The Labour Party and the Economics of Democratic Socialism*, (London: Routledge & Kegan Paul, 1985), pp. 75–83; Lewis Minkin, *The Labour Party Conference*, (Manchester: Manchester University Press, 1980), p. 49.

76 Morgan, *Labour in Power*, pp. 97, 105; George Wigg, *George Wigg*, (London: Michael Joseph, 1972), p. 125; Barker, 'Civil Service Attitudes and the Economic Planning of the Attlee Government', p. 474.

77 Richard Crossman, 'The Lessons of 1945', in Perry Anderson and Robin Blackburn (eds), *Towards Socialism*, (Ithaca, N.Y.: Cornell University Press, 1966), p. 153; Crossman, *Diaries of a Cabinet Minister*, vol. 1, p. 118; Headey, *British Cabinet Ministers*, p. 176; Rose, *Problem of Party Government*, pp. 380–1; Labour Party Archives: RD57/May 1960.

78 Expenditure Committee, *The Civil Service*, q. 1944; Crossman, *Diaries of a Cabinet Minister*, vol. 1, pp. 28, 118, 126; Ponting, *Breach of Promise*, pp. 125–30, 137–9.

79 Michael Hatfield, *The House the Left Built*, (London: Gollancz, 1978), pp. 174–5; Barnett, *Inside the Treasury*, pp. 15, 189; Ann Robinson and Cedric Sandford, *Tax Policy Making in the United Kingdom*, (London: Heinemann, 1983), pp. 65–6.

80 *Guardian*, 28 December 1988; Hatfield, *The House the Left Built*, pp. 87–91, 118.

81 Lipsey (ed.), *Making Government Work*, p. 4; John Garrett: 'Making the Party Work', *New Statesman*, 9 September 1983, pp. 10–11; 'Priorities: the key to change', *New Statesman*, 1 August 1986, p. 12.

82 Letter to the *Guardian*, 10 December 1980.

83 Alan Watkins, 'Who's for Policy Making?', *New Statesman*, 24 September 1971, p. 383; Lipsey (ed.), *Making Government Work*, pp. 4–5; William Stallard, *The Labour Party in Opposition and in Government 1970–79*, (unpublished Ph.D. thesis, University of Keele, 1985); *Guardian*, 26 April 1990.

84 Castle, *The Castle Diaries 1974–76*, p. 75.

85 Drucker, *Doctrine and Ethos in the Labour Party*, pp. 92–3; Barry Hindess, *Parliamentary Democracy and Socialist Politics*, (London: Routledge & Kegan Paul, 1983), pp. 101–113; Barry Jones and Michael Keating, *Labour and the British State*, (Oxford: Clarendon Press, 1985), p. 151.

86 Rose, *Problem of Party Government*, p. 373; Harold J. Laski, *Democracy in Crisis*, (London: Allen & Unwin, 1933), p. 105; Laski, *Parliamentary Government in England*, p. 312.

87 Robinson and Sandford, *Tax Policy Making*, p. 84.

CHAPTER 3: THE ATTLEE GOVERNMENT AND THE REFORM OF THE CIVIL SERVICE

1 Harold J. Laski, 'Some Reflections on Government in Wartime', *Political Quarterly*, 1942, vol. 13, p. 65.

2 Peter Hennessy, *Whitehall*, (London: Secker & Warburg, 1989), pp. 120, 127.

3 Richard Crossman, 'The Lessons of 1945', in Perry Anderson and Robin Blackburn (eds), *Towards Socialism*, (Ithaca, New York: Cornell University Press, 1966), pp. 154–5.

4 E. P. Harries, 'The Future of the Civil Service', *The Labour Magazine*, March 1929, vol. 7, p. 500.

5 G. R. Searle, *The Quest for National Efficiency*, (Oxford: Blackwell, 1971).

6 Sidney and Beatrice Webb, *The Prevention of Destitution*, (London: Longman, 1916), pp. 330–1; Margaret Cole (ed.), *Beatrice Webb's Diaries 1912–1924*, (London: Longman, 1952), p. 98.

7 Sidney and Beatrice Webb, *A Constitution for the Socialist Commonwealth of Great Britain*, (Cambridge: London School of Economics/Cambridge University Press, 1975), (first published 1920), Introduction by Samuel H. Beer, p. xxvii; Cole (ed.), *Beatrice Webb's Diaries*, p. 98.

8 Webb and Webb, *Constitution for the Socialist Commonwealth*, pp. 174–6.

9 William Graham, 'Changes at the Treasury', *The Banker*, 1927, vol. 3, pp. 470–5; HC Debs 27 June 1927, cols 60–1; 14 April 1926, cols 300–4, 307.

10 Susan Howson and Donald Winch, *The Economic Advisory Council 1930–39*, (Cambridge: Cambridge University Press, 1977), pp. 10–11;

Eunan O'Halpin, *Head of the Civil Service: A Study of Sir Warren Fisher*, (London: Routledge, 1989), pp. 129–30.

11 David Marquand, *Ramsay MacDonald*, (London: Jonathan Cape, 1977), pp. 523, 535; Robert Skidelsky, *Politicians and the Slump*, (London: Macmillan, 1967), pp. 172–4; Howson and Winch, *The Economic Advisory Council*, p. 28.

12 Labour Party Archives: IAC paper 333H(b), March 1926; HC Debs 28 May 1930, col. 1269; 30 June 1930, col. 1591.

13 Harold J. Laski, *A Grammar of Politics*, 5th edn, (London: Allen & Unwin, 1967), (first published 1925), pp. 399–408; Harries, 'The Future of the Civil Service', pp. 499–500.

14 *New Statesman*, 13 September 1941, p. 248.

15 Hennessy, *Whitehall*, ch. 3.

16 Elizabeth Durbin, *New Jerusalems: The Labour Party and the Economics of Democratic Socialism*, (London: Routledge & Kegan Paul, 1985), p. 191.

17 C. R. Attlee, *The Labour Party in Perspective*, (London: Gollancz, 1937), p. 175; Harold J. Laski, *The Limitations of the Expert*, (London: Fabian Tract 235, 1931); Harold J. Laski, *Parliamentary Government in England*, (London: Allen & Unwin, 1938), pp. 266–78.

18 R. Eatwell and A. Wright, 'Labour and the Lessons of 1931', *The Historical Journal*, 1978, vol. 63, p. 43.

19 G. D. H. Cole, *The Machinery of Socialist Planning*, (London: Hogarth Press, 1938), pp. 42, 63–6; Durbin, *New Jerusalems*, pp. 260–1.

20 Cole, *Machinery of Socialist Planning*, pp. 73–5; W. A. Robson 'The Public Service', *Political Quarterly*, 1936, vol. 7, pp. 179–83; Harold J. Laski, 'The British Civil Service', *Yale Review*, 1936–37, vol. 26, pp. 333–50; Laski, *Parliamentary Government in England*, pp. 309–38.

21 Quoted in G. K. Fry, *Statesmen in Disguise*, (London: Macmillan, 1969), p. 207; Harold J. Laski, 'The Tomlin Report on the Civil Service', *Political Quarterly*, 1931, vol. 2, p. 517; Laski, *Parliamentary Government in England*, pp. 322–3.

22 Eatwell and Wright, 'Labour and the Lessons of 1931', p. 44; Hugh Dalton, *Practical Socialism for Britain*, (London: Routledge, 1935), pp. 12–13.

23 Attlee, *Labour Party in Perspective*, pp. 173–5; Kenneth Harris, *Attlee*, (London: Weidenfeld & Nicolson, 1982), pp. 589–95; Jerry H. Brookshire, 'Clement Attlee and Cabinet Reform, 1930–1945', *The Historical Journal*, 1981, vol. 24, pp. 175–88; Alan Bullock, *The Life and Times of Ernest Bevin, vol. 1, Trade Union Leader 1881–1940*, (London: Heinemann, 1960), p. 501, fn. 4; George Lansbury, *My England*, (London: Selwyn & Blount, 1934), p. 138.

24 Richard A. Chapman and J. R. Greenaway, *The Dynamics of Administrative Reform*, (London: Croom Helm, 1980), pp. 144–5; PEP (Political and Economic Planning), *Planning*, 1941, no. 173.

25 J. P. W. Mallalieu, *Passed To You, Please*, (London: Gollancz, 1942), (Introduction by Harold J. Laski), pp. 82, 149, 152.

26 Ibid., pp. 7, 8, 10–15.

27 John Garrett, *The Management of Government*, (Harmondsworth: Penguin, 1972), p. 30.

28 *Manchester Guardian*, 17 November 1942; Harold J. Laski, 'The Education of the Civil Servant', *Public Administration*, 1943, vol. 21, pp. 13–23; Harold J. Laski, 'Post-War Machinery of Government – Research, Intelligence and Administration', *Political Quarterly*, 1944, vol. 15, pp. 10–21.

29 G. D. H. Cole: 'Reconstruction in the Civil and Municipal Services', *Public Administration*, 1942, vol. 20, pp. 1–10; 'Reform in the Civil Service', in *Essays in Social Theory*, (London: Macmillan, 1950), pp. 224–44, (essay first published 1944); *Fabian Socialism*, (London: Frank Cass, 1971), (first published 1943), pp. 67–8.

30 C. E. Hill, *A Bibliography of the Writings of W. A. Robson*, (Greater London Paper no. 17, London School of Economics, 1986), p. 40.

31 *New Statesman*, 1 March 1941, pp. 203–4; 25 April 1942, pp. 269–70.

32 Labour Party Archives: RDR26/Nov. 1941; RDR52/Jan. 1942.

33 J. M. Lee, *Reviewing the Machinery of Government 1942–1952: An Essay on the Anderson Committee and its Successors*, (London: Birkbeck College, 1977), p. 12; Chapman and Greenaway, *Dynamics of Administrative Reform*, p. 127.

34 PRO CAB 87/74, MG (42) 6.

35 Chapman and Greenaway, *Dynamics of Administrative Reform*, p. 146; Brookshire, 'Attlee and Cabinet Reform', p. 181.

36 HC Debs, 19 April 1944, col. 310; Peter Hennessy, *Cabinet*, (Oxford: Blackwell, 1986), p. 37.

37 *Observer*, 7 October 1945.

38 *New Statesman*, 12 January 1946.

39 *Tribune*, 15 November 1946; 23 August 1946.

40 A. Skeffington, 'Reflections on the Civil Service', *Socialist Commentary*, November 1945, pp. 213–16; HC Debs 21 August 1945, cols. 525–6.

41 'A Temporary Civil Servant', 'Post-War Machinery of Government – Government Administration and Efficiency', *Political Quarterly*, 1944, vol. 15, pp. 93–112 (Durbin was identified as the author of this article by W. A. Robson, in *Political Quarterly*, 1954, vol. 25, p. 300).

42 *Let Us Face the Future*, (London: Labour Party, 1945), p. 7.

43 PRO T222/75: OM 383/1/03; PREM 8/17; Cmd 6525, 1944.

44 PRO PREM 8/1142.

45 Lee, *Reviewing the Machinery of Government*, p. 147; PRO CAB 134/506, MG (49) 4.

46 Alec Cairncross, *Years of Recovery: British Economic Policy 1945–51*, (London: Methuen, 1985), pp. 50–6; R. S. Barker, 'Civil Service Attitudes and the Economic Planning of the Attlee Government', *Journal of Contemporary History*, 1986, vol. 21; Hennessy, *Whitehall*, pp. 152–4; Harris, *Attlee*, p.409.

47 PRO T272/9.

48 Richard A. Chapman, *Ethics in the British Civil Service*, (London: Routledge, 1988), pp. 197–200; Hennessy, *Whitehall*, pp. 122–7.

49 Lee, *Reviewing the Machinery of Government*, p. 140.

50 PRO CAB 134/505. MG (48) 2.

51 Chapman, *Ethics in the British Civil Service*, p. 199.

52 Hennessy, *Whitehall*, pp. 125–6.

53 Ibid., p. 130; PRO CAB 134/505, MG (48) 2.

54 PRO T272/10.
55 Richard A. Chapman, *Leadership in the British Civil Service*, (London: Croom Helm, 1984), pp. 113–14.
56 HC Debs 4 March 1947, col. 36(w); Lee, *Reviewing the Machinery of Government*, p. 43; PRO CAB 129/14, CP (46) 431.
57 PRO CAB 129/18, CP (47) 121.
58 HC Debs 15 April 1947, col. 436; 24 June 1947, cols 197–202.
59 Lee, *Reviewing the Machinery of Government*, pp. 31, 48; HC Debs 10 July 1947, cols 246–7(w); PRO T162/931/E45491; PRO CAB 129/40, CP (50) 124.
60 Fifth Report from the Select Committee on Estimates, HC 143, 1946–7, pp. xxi–xxv.
61 Ibid., p. xxii; Chapman, *Ethics in the British Civil Service*, pp. 201–2; PRO CAB 134/505, MG (48) 1.
62 Kevin Jefferys (ed.), *Labour and the Wartime Coalition: From the Diary of James Chuter Ede*, (London: Historians' Press, 1987), p. 227; HC Debs 4 March 1948, col. 517; 21 January 1948, col. 344; Lee, *Reviewing the Machinery of Government*, p. 47.
63 HC Debs 6 May 1949, col. 1456.
64 HC Debs 4 March 1948, col. 515; 6 May 1949, col. 1451.
65 Ninth Report from the Select Committee on Estimates, HC 203, 205, 1947–8, qs 1904–8.
66 HC Debs 21 January 1948, cols 340–1; 15 February 1949, col. 957.
67 HC Debs 21 January 1948, cols 336–43.
68 HC Debs 4 March 1948, col. 516; 11 May 1948, col. 1961; 27 May 1948, cols 361–2.
69 HC Debs 6 May 1949, cols 1456–7, 1458–9.
70 Ibid., cols 1439–40.
71 PRO T162/931/E45491; PRO T162/969/E51965.
72 *The Reform of the Higher Civil Service*, (London: Fabian Society, 1947); Chapman, *Ethics in the British Civil Service*, p. 239; Fabian Society Papers: K41/1, f.3–4, CSG (46) 11.
73 Chapman, *Ethics in the British Civil Service*, p. 239; PRO T162/969/E51965.
74 PRO T162/969/E51965; (Book Review), *Political Quarterly*, 1948, vol. 19, p. 171.
75 Peter Hennessy, 'The Attlee Governments, 1945–51', in Peter Hennessy and Anthony Seldon (eds), *Ruling Performance: British Governments from Attlee to Thatcher*, (Oxford: Blackwell, 1987), p. 50.
76 Hennessy, *Whitehall*, p. 138.

CHAPTER 4: LABOUR AND THE FULTON REPORT

1 Treasury and Civil Service Select Committee, *Civil Service Management Reform: The Next Steps*, HC 494–II, 1987–88, q. 223; Cmnd. 4506, (London: HMSO, 1970); 'Symposium: Fulton 20 Years On – Dissenting Viewpoint', Geoffrey Fry, *Contemporary Record, 1988, vol. 2, no. 2, pp. 54–5.*
2 Geoffrey Fry, *The Changing Civil Service*, (London: Allen & Unwin, 1985), Preface and p. 156.

3 W. A. Robson, 'The Civil Service and its Critics', *Political Quarterly*, 1954, vol. 25, pp. 299–307; Robin Marris, *The Machinery of Economic Policy*, (London: Fabian Research Series 168, 1954).

4 Thomas Balogh, 'The Apotheosis of the Dilettante: The Establishment of Mandarins', in Hugh Thomas (ed.), *The Establishment*, (London: Anthony Blond, 1959), pp. 83–126; Thomas Balogh, *Planning for Progress: A Strategy for Labour*, (London: Fabian Tract 346, 1963), pp. 30–5; Labour Party Archives, RD195/Jan. 1962.

5 Brian Chapman, *British Government Observed*, (London: Allen & Unwin, 1963).

6 Peter Hennessy, *Whitehall*, (London: Secker & Warburg, 1989), p. 172.

7 Fabian Society Papers, K65–7; private information.

8 Robert Neild, 'New Functions: new men?', *The Listener*, 27 August 1964, pp. 302–4; Labour Party Archives, RD202/Jan. 1962.

9 *The Administrators: The Reform of the Civil Service*, (London: Fabian Tract 355, 1964).

10 Neild, 'New Functions: new men?', p. 303.

11 Labour Party Archives, RD201/Jan. 1962; Richard Crossman, *Socialism and the New Despotism*, (London: Fabian Tract 298, 1956), pp. 15–16; Richard Crossman, 'Scientists in Whitehall', in *Planning for Freedom*, (London: Hamish Hamilton, 1965), pp. 134–47 (originally a 1963 Fabian lecture).

12 Anthony Sampson, *Anatomy of Britain Today*, (London: Hodder & Stoughton, 1965), pp. 95, 265; Barry Jones and Michael Keating, *Labour and the British State*, (Oxford: Clarendon Press, 1985), p. 146.

13 Sampson, *Anatomy of Britain Today*, p. 265; Tony Benn, *Out of The Wilderness: Diaries 1963–67*, (London: Hutchinson, 1987), pp. 25–6; Jo Grimond, Enoch Powell, Harold Wilson and Norman Hunt, *Whitehall and Beyond*, (London: BBC, 1964), pp. 11–28.

14 F. W. S. Craig (ed.), *British General Election Manifestos 1918–1966*, (Chichester: Political Reference Publications, 1970), pp.234, 246.

15 John Garrett, *Managing the Civil Service*, (London: Heinemann, 1980), p. 11; Labour Party Archives, RD202/Jan. 1962; Balogh, *Planning for Progress*, p. 33; *The Administrators*, p. 43.

16 Neild, 'New Functions: new men?', p. 303; Sixth Report from the Estimates Committee, *Recruitment to the Civil Service*, HC 308, 1964–65, qs. 842, 850.

17 *Ibid.*, pp. xvi, xxxiv.

18 Clive Ponting, *Breach of Promise: Labour in Power 1964–1970*, (London: Hamish Hamilton, 1989), pp. 38–9; Craig (ed.), *British General Election Manifestos 1918–1966*, p. 281; Richard A. Chapman, 'The Fulton Committee on the Civil Service', in Richard A. Chapman (ed.), *The Role of Commissions in Policy Making*, (London: Allen & Unwin, 1973), p. 39.

19 Peter Kellner and Lord Crowther-Hunt, *The Civil Servants*, (London: Macdonald, 1980), p. 26; Estimates Committee, 1964–65, q. 846; Chapman, 'The Fulton Committee', p. 13.

20 Kellner and Crowther-Hunt, *The Civil Servants*, p. 27.

21 HC Debs 8 February 1966, cols 209–10; Kellner and Crowther-Hunt, *The Civil Servants*, pp. 27–8.

22 Hennessy, *Whitehall*, p. 191; HC Debs 21 November 1968, col. 1563.
23 'Symposium: Fulton 20 Years On', *Contemporary Record*, pp. 45–7.
24 Labour Party Archives, RE21/July 1966; Labour Party Archives, RE37/September 1966; *The Times*, 21 January 1967; *The Economist*, 7 January 1967.
25 Memorandum no. 97, submitted by the Labour Party (December 1966), in *The Civil Service, vol. 5(2), Evidence submitted to the Committee under the Chairmanship of Lord Fulton 1966–68*, Cmnd. 3638, (London: HMSO, 1968), pp. 652–73; *The Listener*, 9 February 1967, p. 184; Peter Shore, *Entitled To Know*, (London: MacGibbon & Kee, 1966), pp. 153–6; *Tribune*, 6 January 1967.
26 Jones and Keating, *Labour and the British State*, p. 147; Labour Party Archives, RE37/Sept. 1966, p. 16.
27 Memorandum no. 78, submitted by the Fabian Society (February 1967), in *The Civil Service, vol. 5(2)*, pp. 559–68.
28 'Symposium: Fulton 20 Years On', *Contemporary Record*, p. 45; Kellner and Crowther-Hunt, *The Civil Servants*, pp. 30–7; Hennessy, *Whitehall*, pp. 198–9; Sir James Dunnett, 'The Civil Service: Seven Years After Fulton', *Public Administration*, 1976, vol. 54, p. 373.
29 *The Civil Service, vol. 1, Report of the Committee 1966–68.*
30 HC Debs 26 June 1968, cols 455–6; Kellner and Crowther-Hunt, *The Civil Servants*, pp. 56–8; Barbara Castle, *The Castle Diaries 1964–70*, (London: Weidenfeld & Nicolson, 1984), pp. 464, 468; Richard Crossman, *The Diaries of a Cabinet Minister, vol. III, Secretary of State for the Social Services 1968–1970*, (London: Hamish Hamilton and Jonathan Cape, 1977), pp. 98, 101–3, 106–7; Tony Benn, *Office Without Power: Diaries 1968–72*, (London: Hutchinson, 1988), pp.83–5.
31 Lord Helsby, 'The Fulton Report', *The Listener*, 18 July 1968, pp. 65–7; F. A. Bishop, 'Fulton: the cart before the horse', *Spectator*, 28 June 1968, pp. 883–4.
32 Roger Opie, 'Implement at Once!', *New Statesman*, 28 June 1968, pp. 859–60; W. A. Robson, 'The Fulton Report on the Civil Service', *Political Quarterly*, 1969, vol. 39, pp. 397–414; Eric Hobsbawm, 'The Fulton Report: a further view', *The Listener*, 18 July 1968, pp. 67–8; J. A. G. Griffith, 'The Civil Service We Deserve', *Socialist Commentary*, August 1968, pp. 7–9; Thomas Balogh, 'End of the Amateur', *New Statesman*, 28 June 1968, pp. 860–1.
33 Bishop, 'Fulton: the cart before the horse'; Opie, 'Implement at Once!'.
34 Jones and Keating, *Labour and the British State*, p. 149.
35 Opie, 'Implement at Once!'; Kellner and Crowther-Hunt, *The Civil Servants*, ch. 4; Garrett, *Managing the Civil Service*, p. 191.
36 Harold Wilson, *The Labour Government 1964–70*, (Harmondsworth: Penguin, 1974), pp. 683–4; 'Symposium: Fulton 20 Years On', *Contemporary Record*, p. 48; Eleventh Report from the Expenditure Committee, *The Civil Service*, HC 535, 1976–77, q. 1931.
37 Thomas Balogh, *Labour and Inflation*, (London: Fabian Tract 403, 1970), pp. 53, 57; Michael Hatfield, *The House the Left Built*, (London: Gollancz, 1978), pp. 160–2.
38 John Garrett, *The Management of Government*, (Harmondsworth: Penguin, 1972), p. 275; Fabian Society Papers, K80/1, f. 184.

39 Garrett, *The Management of Government*, pp. 52–4.
40 John Garrett and Robert Sheldon, *Administrative Reform: the Next Step*, (London: Fabian Tract 426, 1973).
41 Garrett, *Managing the Civil Service*, p. 25.
42 A. Gray and W. Jenkins, 'Policy Analysis in British Central Government: the Experience of PAR', *Public Administration*, 1982, vol. 60, p. 447.
43 Garrett, *Managing the Civil Service*, pp. 29, 48; 'Freedom of Information Bill' and 'Reform of the Civil Service', in *Statements to Annual Conference by the National Executive Committee* (Thursday), (London: Labour Party, 1978), pp. 11–52; Central Policy Review Staff, *Review of Overseas Representation*, (London: HMSO, 1977).
44 Christopher Pollitt, *Manipulating the Machine: Changing the Pattern of Ministerial Departments, 1960–83*, (London: Allen & Unwin, 1984), pp. 107–19.
45 Labour Party Archives, RE721/July 1976; Expenditure Committee, *The Civil Service*, vol. III, pp. 841–8, 1090–123.
46 Hennessy, *Whitehall*, pp. 265–6.
47 'Reform of the Civil Service', Labour Party, pp. 40–3; *Government Observations on the Eleventh Report from the Expenditure Committee 1976–77*, Cmnd. 7117, (London: HMSO, 1978).
48 George Brown, *In My Way*, (Harmondsworth: Penguin, 1972), p. 157; G. K. Fry, *The Administrative 'Revolution' in Whitehall*, (London: Croom Helm, 1981), pp. 131–4.
49 Rodney Fielding, *The Making of Labour's Foreign Policy*, (London: Fabian Tract 433, 1975), pp. 5–13.
50 Hennessy, *Whitehall*, pp. 266–73; Tessa Blackstone and William Plowden, *Inside the Think Tank: Advising the Cabinet 1971–1983*, (London: Heinemann, 1988), ch. 8; Fry, *The Administrative 'Revolution' in Whitehall*, pp. 134–9.
51 HC Debs 15 January 1979, col. 1425; Garrett, *Managing the Civil Service*, p. 3.

CHAPTER 5: EFFICIENCY OR DEMOCRACY? LABOUR AND CIVIL SERVICE RECRUITMENT

1 *The Independent*, 3 August 1988; Lord Crowther-Hunt, giving evidence to the House of Commons Expenditure Committee, October 1976; Gavin Drewry and Tony Butcher, *The Civil Service Today* (Oxford: Blackwell, 1988), pp. 108–9; Harold J. Laski, *Parliamentary Government in England*, (London: Allen & Unwin, 1938), pp. 316, 324–8, 335–7; Harold J. Laski, 'Introduction', in J. P. W. Mallalieu, *'Passed To You, Please'*, (London: Gollancz, 1942), p. 7; Herman Finer, *The British Civil Service*, (London: Fabian Society and Allen & Unwin, 1937), p. 94.
2 J. Donald Kingsley, *Representative Bureaucracy*, (Yellow Spring, Ohio: Antioch Press, 1944), pp. 112–13, 279–80, 282.
3 Laski, *Parliamentary Government in England*, p. 321; Robert T. Nightingale, *The Personnel of the British Foreign Office and Diplomatic*

Service 1851-1929, (London: Fabian Tract 232, 1930); A. F. Grewar Roy, 'Labour and the Foreign Office', *Socialist Commentary*, August 1946, pp. 423-6; *Tribune*, 21 March 1947, pp. 7-9.

4 Labour Party Conference Report 1946, pp. 152-3, 164; 1947, p. 165.

5 Samuel Krislov, *Representative Bureaucracy*, (Englewood Cliffs, N.J.: Prentice-Hall, 1974), p. 13.

6 Marcia Williams, *Inside Number 10*, (London: Weidenfeld & Nicolson, 1972), pp. 346, 349, 353.

7 Eleventh Report from the Expenditure Committee, *The Civil Service*, HC 535-I, 1976-7, pp. lxxix-lxxxiv; Rodney Fielding, *The Making of Labour's Foreign Policy*, (London: Fabian Tract 433, 1975), pp. 11-12.

8 Geoffrey Fry, *The Changing Civil Service*, (London: Allen & Unwin, 1985), pp. 18-19; H. E. Dale, *The Higher Civil Service of Great Britain*, (London: Oxford University Press, 1941), p. 107; R. A. Chapman, 'Profile of a Profession: The Administrative Class of the Civil Service', in *The Civil Service, vol. 3(2), Surveys and Investigations*, (London: HMSO, 1968), p. 9; Richard A. Chapman, *The Higher Civil Service in Britain*, (London: Constable, 1970), p. 116; Sir Geoffrey Jackson, *Concorde Diplomacy*, (London: Hamish Hamilton, 1981), p. 80.

9 Kevin Theakston and Geoffrey K. Fry, 'Britain's Administrative Elite: Permanent Secretaries 1900-1986', *Public Administration*, 1989, vol. 67, p. 134; Kenneth Robinson, 'Selection and the Social Background of the Administrative Class', *Public Administration*, 1955, vol. 33, p. 388; H. R. G. Greaves, *The Civil Service in the Changing State*, (London: Harrap, 1947), pp. 65-6; Thomas Balogh, 'The Apotheosis of the Dilettante: The Establishment of Mandarins', in Hugh Thomas (ed.), *The Establishment*, (London: Anthony Blond, 1959), p. 88, fn. 1.

10 Candace Hetzner, 'Social Democracy and Bureaucracy: The Labour Party and Higher Civil Service Recruitment', *Administration and Society*, 1985, vol. 17, pp. 97-128.

11 Ibid., p. 110; Arthur Henderson, *The Aims of Labour*, (London: Headley, 1918), pp. 62-3; Ernest Bevin, *The Job to be Done*, (London: Heinemann, 1942), pp. 68-9; Alan Bullock, *The Life and Times of Ernest Bevin, vol. II, Minister of Labour*, (London: Heinemann, 1967), pp. 199-201; Alan Bullock, *Ernest Bevin, Foreign Secretary 1945-1951*, (London: Heinemann, 1983), pp. 72-4.

12 Lisanne Radice, *Beatrice and Sidney Webb*, (London: Macmillan, 1984), p. 8; Francis Lee, *Fabianism and Colonialism: The Life and Political Thought of Lord Sydney Olivier*, (London: Defiant Books, 1988), p. 45.

13 Labour Party Archives: IAC paper 333H(b), March 1926.

14 Harold J. Laski, *A Grammar of Politics*, 5th edn (London: Allen & Unwin, 1967), pp. 406-8; Harold J. Laski, 'The Tomlin Report on the Civil Service', *Political Quarterly*, 1931, vol. 2, p. 509; Laski, *Parliamentary Government in England*, pp. 332-3, 335; Kingsley, *Representative Bureaucracy*, p. 143.

15 G. D. H. Cole: 'Reconstruction in the Civil and Municipal Services', *Public Administration*, 1942, vol. 20, pp. 7, 9-10; 'Reform in the Civil Service', in *Essays in Social Theory*, (London: Macmillan, 1950), p. 232.

16 Harold J. Laski, 'The Reform of the Civil Service', *New Statesman*, 6 March 1943, p. 154; Laski, 'Introduction', in Mallalieu, *'Passed To You, Please'*, pp. 14–15; W. A. Robson, 'The Public Service', *Political Quarterly*, 1936, vol. 7, p. 184.

17 G. R. Searle, *The Quest for National Efficiency*, (Oxford: Blackwell, 1971), pp. 79–80; Rodney Barker, *Education and Politics 1900–1951: A Study of the Labour Party*, (Oxford: Clarendon Press, 1972), pp. 15–16, 106; O. R. McGregor, 'Civil Servants and the Civil Service 1850–1950', *Political Quarterly*, 1951, vol. 22, p. 162.

18 *The Reform of the Higher Civil Service*, (London: Fabian Society, 1947), pp. 20–1; *The Administrators*, (London: Fabian Tract 355, 1964), p. 25; G .K. Fry, *Statesmen in Disguise*, (London: Macmillan, 1969), pp. 99–100.

19 *Report of the Committee on the Civil Service, 1966–68*, Cmnd 3638, (London: HMSO, 1968), p. 12.

20 Laski, 'The Tomlin Report on the Civil Service', p. 508; Robson, 'The Public Service', p. 184; R. K. Kelsall, *Higher Civil Servants in Britain*, (London: Routledge & Kegan Paul, 1955), pp. 70–1; Richard A. Chapman, *Leadership in the British Civil Service*, (London: Croom Helm, 1984), pp. 113, 118; Fabian Society, *Reform of the Higher Civil Service* p. 18; Balogh, 'Apotheosis of the Dilettante', pp. 91–2, 110.

21 *The Civil Service, vol. 3(1), Social Survey of the Civil Service*, pp. 401–7; *Report of the Committee on the Civil Service 1966–68*, p. 31.

22 *The Method II System of Selection: Report of the Committee of Inquiry*, Cmnd 4156, (London: HMSO, 1969); Expenditure Committee, *The Civil Service*, q.1091; Thomas Balogh, *Labour and Inflation*, (London: Fabian Tract 403, 1970), p. 58.

23 Expenditure Committee, *The Civil Service*, vol. III, pp. 1090–4; Labour Party, 'The Reform of the Civil Service', in *Statements to Annual Conference by the National Executive Committee* (Thursday), (London: Labour Party, 1978), pp. 49–52.

24 Barry Jones and Michael Keating, *Labour and the British State*, (Oxford: Clarendon Press, 1985), p. 144; Labour Party Archives: RE904/Jan. 1977; RE1664/May 1978; RE1699/June 1978.

25 Labour Party, 'Reform of the Civil Service', (1978), p. 41; John Garrett, *Managing the Civil Service*, (London: Heinemann, 1980), pp. 29–36.

26 *Labour's Programme 1982*, (London: Labour Party, 1982), p. 206; David Lipsey (ed.), *Making Government Work*, (London: Fabian Tract 480, 1982), p. 10.

27 Hetzner, 'Social Democracy and Bureaucracy', pp. 120–1, 125.

CHAPTER 6: LABOUR, PARLIAMENTARY ACCOUNTABILITY AND OPEN GOVERNMENT

1 Richard Crossman, *Socialism and the New Despotism*, (London: Fabian Tract 298, 1956), p. 20.

2 *Departmental Committee on Section 2 of the Official Secrets Act*, (Franks Committee), Cmnd 5104, (London: HMSO, 1972), vol. 4, p. 190.

3 William Gwyn, 'The Labour Party and the Threat of Bureaucracy',

Political Studies, 1971, vol. 19, p. 385; Sidney and Beatrice Webb, *A Constitution for the Socialist Commonwealth of Great Britain*, (Cambridge: London School of Economics and Political Science/Cambridge University Press, 1975), (first published 1920), pp. 129, 140, 172.

4 W. H. Morris Jones, *Socialism and Bureaucracy*, (London: Fabian Tract 277, 1949); Gwyn, 'The Labour Party and the Threat of Bureaucracy'; Crossman, *Socialism and the New Despotism*, pp. 6, 18, 20, 24.

5 Herbert Morrison, *Government and Parliament*, 3rd edn, (London: Oxford University Press, 1964), p. 181; David Marquand, *Ramsay MacDonald*, (London: Jonathan Cape, 1977), p. 97; A. H. Hanson, 'The Labour Party and House of Commons Reform', in *Planning and the Politicians*, (London: Routledge & Kegan Paul, 1969), p. 46.

6 Hanson, 'The Labour Party and House of Commons Reform', pp. 49–58; F. W. Jowett, *What is the Use of Parliament?*, (Pass On Pamphlets, no. 11, (London: Clarion Press, 1909); F. W. Jowett, *Parliament or Palaver?*, (London: ILP, 1926); Independent Labour Party, *The Reform of Parliament*, (Report to the National Administrative Council of the ILP from the Committee on the Machinery of Parliamentary Government, 1925).

7 J. R. MacDonald, *Socialism and Government*, (London: ILP, 1909), vol. 2, pp. 37–8; Harold J. Laski, *Reflections on the Constitution*, (Manchester: Manchester University Press, 1951), pp. 50–2; Morrison, *Government and Parliament*, pp. 168–71; ILP, *The Reform of Parliament*.

8 Harold J. Laski, *A Grammar of Politics*, 5th edn, (London: Allen & Unwin, 1967), pp. 335–40; W. I. Jennings, *Parliamentary Reform*, (London: Gollancz, 1934), pp. 50–5; Select Committee on Procedure, HC 161, 1930–31, q. 2; Hanson, 'The Labour Party and House of Commons Reform', pp. 53–4.

9 Harold J. Laski, 'The Civil Service and Parliament', in *The Development of the Civil Service*, (London: P. S. King, 1922), pp. 20–36; ILP, *The Reform of Parliament*, pp. 27–31.

10 Labour Party Archives: IAC Paper 333H(b), March 1926; MacDonald, *Socialism and Government*, vol. 1, p. 115; Select Committee on Procedure 1930–31, qs 12, 35.

11 Reginald Bassett, *The Essentials of Parliamentary Democracy*, 2nd edn, (London: Frank Cass, 1964), p. 152; Jennings, *Parliamentary Reform*, p. 112; Labour Party Conference Report 1934, pp. 261–3.

12 Harold J. Laski, *The Labour Party and the Constitution*, (London: Socialist League, 1933), p. 16; Harold J. Laski, *Parliamentary Government in England*, (London: Allen & Unwin, 1938), pp. 211–12; Jennings, *Parliamentary Reform*, pp. 142–3; Hugh Dalton, *Practical Socialism for Britain*, (London: Routledge, 1935), p. 85; Labour Party Archives: RDR26/Nov. 1941; Sir Stafford Cripps, *Democracy Up-To-Date*, 2nd edn, (London: Allen & Unwin, 1944), pp. 78–9.

13 Morrison, *Government and Parliament*, pp. 148, 231; James MacGregor Burns, 'The Parliamentary Labour Party in Great Britain', *American Political Science Review*, 1950, vol. 44, p. 859; R. T. McKenzie, 'Laski and the Social Bases of the Constitution', *British Journal of Sociology*, 1952, vol. 3, pp. 260–3.

14 Bernard Crick, *The Reform of Parliament*, 2nd edn, (London: Weiden-feld & Nicolson, 1970), pp. 195–7; Nevil Johnson, 'Select Committees and Administration', in S. A. Walkland (ed.), *The House of Commons in the Twentieth Century*, (Oxford: Clarendon Press, 1979), pp. 460, 464.
15 Alf Morris (ed.), *The Growth of Parliamentary Scrutiny by Committee*, (Oxford: Pergamon, 1970), p. 2; John Mackintosh, 'Failure of a Reform: MPs' Special Committees', *New Society*, 28 November 1968, pp. 791–2; H. V. Wiseman, 'The New Specialised Committees', in A. H. Hanson and Bernard Crick (eds), *The Commons in Transition*, (Glasgow: Fontana, 1970), pp. 198–223; S. A. Walkland, 'Parliamentary Reform, Party Realignment and Electoral Reform', in David Judge (ed.), *The Politics of Parliamentary Reform*, (London: Heinemann, 1983), pp. 43–4.
16 Mackintosh, 'Failure of a Reform'; *The Times*, 13 March 1969; Richard Crossman, *The Diaries of a Cabinet Minister, vol. 2, Lord President of the Council and Leader of the House of Commons 1966–68*, (London: Hamish Hamilton and Jonathan Cape, 1976), vol. 2, p. 308.
17 Morris (ed.), *The Growth of Parliamentary Scrutiny by Committee*, pp.9, 109–23; Select Committee on Procedure, HC 303, 1964–5, pp. xiii–xiv.
18 *The Times*, 13 March 1969; Barry Jones and Michael Keating, *Labour and the British State*, (Oxford: Clarendon Press, 1985), pp. 154–5.
19 Jones and Keating, *Labour and the British State*, p. 155; Gwyn, 'The Labour Party and the Threat of Bureaucracy'.
20 Labour Party Archives: RD774/May 1964.
21 R. Gregory and D. Hutchesson, *The Parliamentary Ombudsman*, (London: Allen & Unwin, 1975); G.K. Fry, *The Administrative 'Revolution' in Whitehall*, (London: Croom Helm, 1981), p. 166; Labour Party Archives: RD782/May 1964.
22 Crossman, *Diaries of a Cabinet Minister*, vol. 2, p. 150; George Brown, *In My Way*, (Harmondsworth: Penguin, 1972), p. 144; Fry, *The Administrative 'Revolution' in Whitehall*, pp. 165, 171–2.
23 John Garrett, *Managing the Civil Service*, (London: Heinemann, 1980), pp. 168–9; Peter Kellner and Lord Crowther-Hunt, *The Civil Servants*, (London: Macdonald, 1980), pp. 246–7; Harold Wilson, *Final Term: The Labour Government 1974–1976*, (London: Weidenfeld & Nicolson and Michael Joseph, 1979), p. 223.
24 'Reform of the House of Commons', in *Statements to Annual Conference by the National Executive Committee* (Thursday), (Labour Party, London, 1978), pp. 5–10; John Garrett and Robert Sheldon, *Administrative Reform: the Next Step*, (London: Fabian Tract 426, 1973), pp. 11–12; Jones and Keating, *Labour and the British State*, p. 156.
25 Labour Party Archives: RE1695/June 1978; RE1697/June 1978; Jones and Keating, *Labour and the British State*, p. 157.
26 MacDonald, *Socialism and Government*, vol. 2, p. 36; John F. Naylor, *A Man and an Institution: Sir Maurice Hankey, the Cabinet Secretariat and the Custody of Cabinet Secrecy*, (Cambridge: Cambridge University Press, 1984), pp. 137, 178; Laski, 'The Civil Service and Parliament', pp. 25–8.

27 Webb and Webb, *Constitution for the Socialist Commonwealth*, pp. 172–3, 193, 195; George Lansbury, *My England*, (London: Selwyn & Blount, 1934), pp. 128, 130; Compton Mackenzie, *My Life and Times: Octave Seven 1931–1938*, (London: Chatto & Windus, 1968), p. 85.
28 PRO CAB 21/1624; PRO CAB 129/4; Sir Richard Acland *et al.*, *Keeping Left*, p. 42; HC Debs 3 July 1950, cols 25–6.
29 *The Administrators*, (London: Fabian Tract 355, 1964), p. 22; *Report of the Committee on the Civil Service 1966–68*, Cmnd 3638, (London: HMSO, 1968), paras 277–80.
30 Cmnd 4089, (London: HMSO, 1969); Jonathan Aitken, *Officially Secret*, (London: Weidenfeld & Nicolson, 1971).
31 HC Debs 29 June 1973, cols 1906, 1912; Anthony Wedgwood Benn, *The New Politics: A Socialist Reconnaissance*, (London: Fabian Tract 402, 1970), pp. 19–21; Tony Benn, *Office Without Power: Diaries 1968–72*, (London: Hutchinson, 1988), p. 67; *The Times*, 11 July 1973.
32 James Michael, *The Politics of Secrecy*, (Harmondsworth: Penguin, 1982), p. 197.
33 Tony Benn, *The Right to Know*, (Nottingham: IWC Pamphlet no. 62, 1978); Labour Party, 'Freedom of Information Bill', in *Statements to Annual Conference by the National Executive Committee* (Thursday), (London: Labour Party, 1978), p. 12; HC Debs 15 June 1978, col. 1271.
34 Bernard Donoughue, *Prime Minister: The Conduct of Policy under Harold Wilson and James Callaghan*, (London: Jonathan Cape, 1987), p. 122; Tony Benn, *Against the Tide: Diaries 1973–76*, (London: Hutchinson, 1989), p. 648; Denis Healey, *The Time of My Life*, (London: Michael Joseph, 1989), p. 449.
35 Kellner and Crowther-Hunt, *The Civil Servants*, p. 267; HC Debs 19 November 1975, col. 8; Franks Committee, vol. 4, pp. 189–90; HC Debs 1 July 1976, col. 653.
36 HC Debs 22 November 1976, cols 1878–81; *Reform of section 2 of the Official Secrets Act 1911*, Cmnd 7285, (London: HMSO, 1978); Labour Party, 'Freedom of Information Bill', (1978), p. 12; Benn, *The Right to Know*, p. 5; HC Debs 19 July 1978, cols 546–7.
37 HC Debs 24 November 1976, cols 26–7; 26 January 1978, cols 691–4(w).
38 *New Statesman*, 10 November 1978.
39 HC Debs 19 January 1979, cols 2169–71.
40 *Open Government*, Cmnd 7520 (London: HMSO, 1979).
41 Trevor Barnes, *Open Up! Britain and Freedom of Information in the 1980s*, (London: Fabian Tract 467, 1980), p. 4.
42 Labour Party Conference Report 1979, p. 235; Merlyn Rees, 'The parameters of politics', in Richard A. Chapman and Michael Hunt (eds), *Open Government*, (London: Croom Helm, 1987), pp. 31–8.

CHAPTER 7: LABOUR, THATCHER AND THE FUTURE OF THE CIVIL SERVICE

1 *New Statesman*, 31 December 1982, p. 7; Eleventh Report from the Expenditure Committee, *The Civil Service*, HC 535, 1976–77, pp.

lxxx–lxxxi; Tony Benn, 'Manifestos and Mandarins', in *Policy and Practice; the experience of government*, (London: Royal Institute of Public Administration, 1980), p. 64; Marcia Falkender, *Downing Street in Perspective*, (London: Weidenfeld & Nicolson, 1983), p. 260.

2 Sir John Hoskyns: 'Whitehall and Westminster: an outsider's view', *Parliamentary Affairs*, 1983, vol. 36, pp. 137–47; 'Conservatism is not Enough', *Political Quarterly*, 1984, vol. 55, pp. 3–16; Geoffrey Fry, *The Changing Civil Service*, (London: Allen & Unwin, 1985), pp. 26–7.

3 Michael Meacher, 'Whitehall's Short Way with Democracy', in Ken Coates (ed.), *What Went Wrong*, (Nottingham: Spokesman Books, 1979), p. 186.

4 *The Times*, 4 November 1982; Treasury and Civil Service Committee, *Civil Servants and Ministers: Duties and Responsibilities*, HC 92, 1985–86, qs. 730–3; Richard Norton-Taylor, *The Ponting Affair*, (London: Cecil Woolf, 1985), p. 132; 'A Week in Politics', Channel 4, 24 May 1985;*Tribune*, 10 May 1985; Sir Robert Armstrong, speech to CIPFA conference, June 1985 (mimeo).

5 Hugo Young and Anne Sloman, *No, Minister: An Inquiry into the Civil Service*, (London: BBC, 1982), pp. 94–5; *FDA News*, February 1983; Treasury and Civil Service Committee, *Civil Servants and Ministers*, pp. 135–6 and qs 505–9; *Independent* 9 January 1989; Michael Meacher speech to *Tribune* conference, 25 November 1989 (mimeo).

6 David Lipsey, 'Coming in: Labour and the civil service', in Ben Pimlott (ed.), *Labour's First Hundred Days*, (London: Fabian Tract 519, 1987), pp.24–5; *Guardian*, 24 May 1990.

7 Treasury and Civil Service Committee, *Civil Servants and Ministers*, qs 727–8; 'Reform of the Civil Service', in *Statements to Annual Conference by the National Executive Committee* (Thursday), (London: Labour Party, 1978), p. 40; David Lipsey (ed.), *Making Government Work*, (London: Fabian Tract 480, 1982), pp. 9–10.

8 *Independent*, 9 January 1989; Clive Ponting, *Whitehall: Changing the Old Guard*, (London: Unwin Hyman, 1989), pp. 47–8; *Guardian*, 21 July 1986; Lipsey (ed.), *Making Government Work*, pp. 15–16; Tessa Blackstone, 'Advice at the Centre', in Pimlott (ed.), *Labour's First Hundred Days*, pp. 27–30.

9 *Independent*, 9 January 1989; *Guardian*, 21 July 1986; Tessa Blackstone, 'No Minister', *New Socialist*, January/February 1983, p.44.

10 Labour Party Archives RE775/September 1976; Young and Sloman, *No, Minister*, p. 97; *FDA News*, February 1983; Treasury and Civil Service Committee, *Civil Servants and Ministers*,. p. 516.

11 Memorandum no. 97, submitted by the Labour Party (December 1966), in *The Civil Service, vol. 5(2), Evidence submitted to the Committee under the Chairmanship of Lord Fulton 1966–1968*, Cmnd 3638, (London: HMSO, 1968), p. 663; Thomas Balogh, 'The Apotheosis of the Dilettante', in Hugh Thomas (ed.), *The Establishment*, (London: Anthony Blond, 1959), pp. 121–2; Labour Party Archives RE1664/May 1978; *Guardian*, 26 November 1980.

12 Lipsey (ed.), *Making Government Work*, pp.21–2; Labour Party Conference Report 1984, p. 117.

13 *Meet the Challenge, Make the Change: Final Report of Labour's Policy*

Review for the 1990s, (London: Labour Party, 1989), p. 59; HC Debs 2 February 1989, col. 444.

14 HC Debs 29 June 1973, col. 1909; *Guardian*, 28 February 1985; Treasury and Civil Service Committee, *Civil Servants and Ministers*, qs 758 and 602; Brian Sedgemore, *The Secret Constitution*, (London: Hodder & Stoughton, 1980), pp. 163–4; *Guardian*, 21 September 1984.

15 Labour Party Conference Report 1985, p. 24; HC Debs 14 April 1986, col. 576; *Social Justice and Economic Efficiency: First Report of Labour's Policy Review for the 1990s*, (London: Labour Party, 1988), p. 34; HC Debs 2 February 1989, col. 442.

16 Roy Hattersley, *Choose Freedom: the Future for Democratic Socialism*, (Harmondsworth: Penguin, 1987), p. 137; Sedgemore, *The Secret Constitution*, p. 180; *Guardian*, 22 December 1980; Treasury and Civil Service Committee, *Civil Servants and Ministers*, q. 517; Labour Party, *Meet the Challenge, Make the Change*, p. 56.

17 Treasury and Civil Service Committee, *Civil Service Management Reform: The Next Steps*, HC 494, 1987–88, q. 219; John Garrett, *Managing the Civil Service*, (London: Heinemann, 1980), p. 191; Memorandum by John Garrett to Treasury and Civil Service Committee, *Efficiency and Effectiveness in the Civil Service*, HC 236–III, 1981–82, pp. 45–8.

18 Peter Hennessy, *Whitehall*, (London: Secker & Warburg, 1989), pp. 593, 619; HC Debs 24 November 1986, col. 17; John Garrett, 'Clips and jabots', *New Statesman*, 8 October 1982, pp. 11–12; John Garrett, 'Priorities: the key to change', *New Statesman*, 1 August 1986, pp. 12–14.

19 HC Debs 18 February 1988, col. 1150; *Independent*, 21 November 1988.

20 Treasury and Civil Service Committee, *Civil Service Management Reform: the Next Steps*, pp. 48–55; Ponting, *Whitehall: Changing the Old Guard*, pp. 27–32, 69–74.

21 *Independent*, 21 November 1988, 11 June 1990; *New Socialist*, June/July 1990, p. 7.

22 Labour Party, *Meet the Challenge, Make the Change*, pp. 44–5; *Guardian*, 17 February 1989.

23 HC Debs 21 February 1990, cols 1009–10, 1025–7.

24 *The Times*, 19 May 1983; *Looking to the Future*, (London: Labour Party, 1990), p. 10; HC Debs 21 February 1990, cols 996–1000.

25 *Financial Times*, 9 June 1989.

26 Bryan Gould, 'Low cost: high benefit', in Pimlott (ed.), *Labour's First Hundred Days*, pp. 21–3.

27 Richard A. Chapman and J. R. Greenaway, *The Dynamics of Administrative Reform*, (London: Croom Helm, 1980); John R. Greenaway, 'Historical Perspectives Upon the Thatcher Government's Whitehall Reforms', *Public Administration Bulletin*, 1985, vol. 47, pp. 5–17.

28 *New Socialist*, June/July 1990, p. 7; *Independent*, 2 October 1989.

29 Lipsey (ed.), *Making Government Work*, pp.1–2.

Index

Abel-Smith, Brian 53, 57
Admiralty 20
Allen, Sir Douglas 184
Allen, Sir Philip 128
Anderson, Sir John 91
Armstrong, Sir Robert 189, 195
Armstrong, Sir William 131
Assheton Committee 98, 102

Balogh, Thomas 35, 51, 52–3,
  114–15, 116, 120, 121, 126, 130,
  132, 140, 147, 154, 155–6, 193
Bank of England 22, 29, 30, 78
Banks, Tony 60, 192
Barnett, Joel 33, 43, 44, 66
Benn, Tony 2, 4, 12, 15, 16, 19,
  36–7, 40–1, 42, 55, 59, 60, 129,
  133, 139, 169, 180, 181, 183, 184,
  187, 189–90, 193, 195, 197
Bevan, Aneurin 4, 26
Beveridge, William 9, 78
Bevin, Ernest 19, 26, 27–8, 79, 143,
  144, 147–8, 149, 166, 168
Bishop, F.A. 129
Blackstone, Tessa 10, 139, 192
Bondfield, Margaret 20
Boyle, Sir Edward 123
Bray, Jeremy 122, 198
Bridges, Sir Edward 11, 28, 29, 30,
  91, 97–8, 99–101, 102, 103, 104,
  106, 110–11
Brook, Sir Norman 111
Brown, George 33, 120, 138–9, 173
Burns, Sir Terence 189

Cabinet Office 34, 53

Cabinet Secretariat 17, 20, 83, 120
Cairncross, Sir Alec 31
Callaghan, James 13, 33, 36, 43–4,
  55, 57, 61, 68, 120, 136–7, 138,
  159, 182–4, 186, 189, 191, 195,
  204
Castle, Barbara 19, 35–6, 54, 55, 59,
  69
Cecil, Lord Robert 47
Central Economic Planning Staff 99
Central Policy Review Staff (CPRS)
  134, 136, 139–40, 192
Churchill, Winston 91
civil service: code of ethics 195–6;
  efficiency 7, 8, 11, 75–6, 197–9;
  elitism 8, 9, 12, 39, 79, 127, 139,
  141–57; generalist administrators
  9, 76–7, 84–5, 87–8, 109, 116–17,
  119, 126, 128, 139, 140, 197–8;
  management reform 11, 73–112,
  113–40, 197–203; recruitment 11,
  12, 88, 96, 100, 102, 107, 109,
  115, 116, 126, 132, 134, 139,
  141–57; relations with Labour
  ministers 1–2, 11, 13, 15–45;
  senior appointments 23–4, 47–8,
  49–50, 51, 54, 59–61, 138,
  189–91; size 103–6, 107; training
  2, 7, 8, 11, 75, 76, 86, 88, 89, 92,
  96, 98, 100, 102, 110, 115, 116,
  117, 127, 201; workers' control in
  9–10, 202
Civil Service Clerical Association 10
Civil Service College 129
Civil Service Commission 117, 126

Civil Service Department 129, 134, 138
Civil Service Selection Board (CSSB) 102, 103, 107, 109, 115, 154–5
Clarke, 'Otto' (Sir Richard) 146
Cohen, Sir Andrew 146
Cole, G.D.H. 9–10, 11, 22, 82, 83, 84, 88–9, 150–1, 159, 166
Colonial Office 16
Cooper, Geoffrey 99, 101, 106–8, 111, 178
Cripps, Sir Stafford 4, 26, 29, 30, 91, 97, 98, 99, 101, 166, 167
Crosland, Tony 17, 45, 116, 169
Crossman, Richard 2, 15, 17, 19, 34–5, 38, 39, 44, 51, 52, 61–2, 64–5, 73–4, 119, 158, 160–1, 168, 169, 171, 172, 173
Crowther-Hunt, Lord (Norman Hunt) 16, 40, 123, 124, 125, 128, 131, 133, 136, 137–8, 141, 154–5
Cunningham, Dr Jack 190, 191, 192

Dale, H.E. 146
Dalton, Hugh 4, 17, 18, 22, 24, 26, 28, 29, 31, 35, 47, 48, 63, 85, 97, 103, 167, 168
Dalyell, Tam 194, 196
Davidson, Arthur 180
Defence, Ministry of 53, 190
devolution 40
Diplomatic Service 21, 45, 79, 87, 124, 136, 138–40, 143–4, 145, 146, 147–9; *see also* Foreign Office
Donoughmore Committee on Ministers' Powers 8
Donoughue, Bernard 34, 56, 58, 182, 195
Duncan Committee 138–9
Dunnett, Sir James 128
Durbin, Evan 49, 82, 95, 96, 101–3, 217 fn 41

École National d'Administration (ENA) 2, 115, 117, 127
Economic Advisory Council 78, 82
Economic Affairs, Department of (DEA) 42, 53, 65, 121

economic planning 27, 63–4, 65–6, 82–3, 89, 98–9, 116
Ede, Chuter 26, 98, 104
Energy, Department of 39, 41–2, 184
English, Michael 137
Expenditure Committee Report on the Civil Service 38, 137–8, 145, 155, 174

Fabian Society 4, 7–8, 11, 12, 54, 63, 68, 113, 127–8, 133, 143, 145, 146, 148, 151, 157, 159; 1947 report on *The Reform of the Higher Civil Service* 11, 48, 49–50, 108–11, 152, 154; 1964 report *The Administrators* 11, 51, 115–18, 123, 124, 126, 152, 179; 1982 report *Making Government Work* 40, 156, 188, 191, 193, 194, 203, 205
Financial Management Initiative 198
Finer, Herman 142
Fisher, Sir Warren 77, 90
Foot, Michael 4, 170, 174, 176
Foreign Office 9, 21–2, 25, 26, 27–8, 38, 45–7, 48, 79, 87, 98, 124, 136, 138–40, 141, 143–4, 145, 146, 147–9, 190; *see also* Diplomatic Service
Foster, Christopher 53.
Franks Committee 159, 180, 183
freedom of information 12, 161, 181, 182, 183, 184, 185, 186, 194–5; *see also* Official Secrets Act; open government; secrecy
Fuel and Power, Ministry of 27
Fulton Committee (and Report) 11, 13, 34, 36, 52, 113–40, 146, 153, 154, 179, 188, 197, 198, 199, 206
Fulton, Lord 123, 125

Gaitskell, Hugh 29, 30, 48, 53, 82, 95
Gardiner, Lord 171
Garrett, John 55, 113, 125, 131–2, 133–5, 136, 137–8, 140, 174, 197–8, 199
Graham, Willie 77

Griffith, John 130
Griffiths, James 63
Guild Socialism 9–10, 159

Haines, Joe 42
Haldane Committee 7, 8, 75–6, 77
Haldane, Lord 20, 77–8
Hall, Glenvil 103, 107
Hall, Robert 146
Halls, Michael 132
Hankey, Sir Maurice 20
Hardie, Keir 147, 148, 177
Harries, E.P. 75, 79–80
Harris, John 53
Hattersley, Roy 196–7, 199
Healey, Denis 2, 17, 43, 53, 182, 189
Health, Ministry of 26
Health and Social Security, Department of 36, 41, 53, 57
Heath, Edward 38, 131, 132, 136, 187
Heffer, Eric 136
Heiser, Sir Terence 190
Helsby, Sir Lawrence (Lord) 121, 123, 129
Henderson, Arthur 3, 17, 21–2, 47, 79, 147, 148, 177, 178
Hennessy, Peter 26, 28, 33, 73, 93, 101, 111, 184, 200
Heseltine, Michael 198
Hewitt, Patricia 200, 205
Hobsbawm, Eric 130
Holland, Stuart 55
Home Office 38, 41
Hoskyns, Sir John 188
Houghton, Douglas 172
Hunt, Norman *see* Lord Crowther-Hunt

ILP 22, 147, 162, 163, 164, 165
IMF 37, 43
Industry, Department of 38, 39, 40
Institute for Public Policy Research 68, 200

Jay, Douglas 6, 29, 33, 48, 119
Jenkins, Roy 32, 42, 53, 68, 129, 182
Jennings, Ivor 160, 164, 166

Jones, Elwyn 171, 173
Jowett, Fred 162–4, 165, 193
junior ministers 50, 54, 59, 170

Kaldor, Nicholas 53
Kaufman, Gerald 16
'Keep Left' Group 30, 178
Kingsley, J. Donald 142–3, 144, 145–6
Kinnock, Neil 69, 189, 191–2

Labour Governments: (1924) 6–7, 10, 19–21, 77–8, 162, 177; (1929–31) 19–24, 47, 78–9, 166, 177–8; (1945–51) 1, 5, 6, 9, 10–11, 25–31, 48, 50, 73–4, 93–112, 143–4, 154, 157, 160, 167–8, 178; (1964–70) 1–2, 5, 32–45, 52–4, 121–32, 144, 161, 168–73, 179; (1974–9) 1–2, 5–6, 10, 32–45, 56–61, 135–40, 156, 161, 173–6, 181–6, 187–8
Labour Party: Advisory Committee on Education 151–2; conference 13, 27–8, 39, 60, 66, 69, 70, 138, 143–4, 175, 185; evidence to Fulton Committee 34, 52, 125–7, 128, 153, 193; Finance and Economic Policy Committee 116; Home Policy Committee 125, 136; International Advisory Committee 45–7, 55, 79, 148–9, 165–6; Machinery of Government Study Group 13, 39, 41, 60, 136, 137, 138, 155–6, 174–5, 181–2, 183, 185, 188, 191, 192; National Executive Committee (NEC) 13, 39, 55, 58, 60, 65, 66–7, 68, 69, 70, 83, 86, 90, 125, 156, 166, 172, 175, 183, 185, 194, 203; policy-making in opposition 44–5, 47, 61–72, 83, 132–3; Policy Review 69, 194, 196, 197, 201; Research Department 39, 60, 63, 64, 67–8, 125, 126
Land Commission 65
Lansbury, George 22–3, 48, 177–8
Laski, Harold J. 4, 5, 8–9, 11, 12, 24–5, 27, 31, 44, 47–8, 62, 70–1, 73, 79, 80–5, 86–8, 90, 91, 111,

113, 126, 141–2, 144, 145–7, 149–50, 151, 153, 163, 164, 165, 166, 167, 168, 174, 177, 193
Lever, Harold 173–4
Lipsey, David 190

McDonald, Dr Oonagh 195, 196, 198
MacDonald, Ramsay 4, 20–1, 45–6, 77, 78, 79, 145, 159, 162, 165, 166, 176–7, 204
Mackenzie, Compton 178
Mackintosh, John 169–70
Machinery of Government Committee 91, 92, 97, 98, 101, 106, 108, 112
Mallalieu, J.P.W. 28–9, 86–7, 94–5
Marek, Dr John 201–2
Marris, Robin 114
Masterman Committee 11
Meacher, Michael 16, 32, 188, 190
Mendelson, John 170
Middleton, Sir Peter 189
Miliband, Ralph 25–6
ministerial cabinets 9, 11, 47, 52, 53, 54, 59, 126, 133, 134, 137, 138, 192–4, 204
Monck, Bosworth 108, 110, 152
Morel, E.D. 21
Morrel, Frances 41, 156
Morrison, Herbert 1, 2, 5, 21, 33, 48, 63, 83, 90, 91, 97, 98, 159, 162, 167–8
Mosley, Oswald 22, 78–9

nationalization 27, 63, 65, 79–80, 84, 89
Neild, Robert 53, 115–16, 118–19, 121, 123
New Statesman 32, 80, 86, 89–90, 91, 94
Next Steps Initiative 198–202
Noel-Baker, Philip 47
Number 10 Policy Unit 56–7

Official Secrets Act 5, 161, 176–86, 194, 195, 196; *see also* freedom of information; open government; secrecy
ombudsman 168, 171–3

open government 7, 12, 134, 135, 158, 179, 180, 182, 184, 185, 186, 194–5; *see also* freedom of information; Official Secrets Act; secrecy
Opie, Roger 129–30, 131
Owen, Sir David 32–3, 139–40

Pliatzky, Sir Leo 43, 146
Ponting, Clive 191, 195–6, 199–200, 203

Radice, Giles 199
Rees, Merlyn 183, 186
Robson, W.A. 6, 82, 83–4, 89, 110–11, 114, 130, 151, 153, 160, 217 fn 41
Rosenberg, Rose 47

secrecy 3, 158, 159, 176–86; *see also* freedom of information; Official Secrets Act; open government
Sedgemore, Brian 16, 38–9, 41–2, 59–60, 155, 187, 195, 197
select committees 8, 12, 135, 158, 161, 165–6, 167, 168–71, 173–6, 196–7
Sharp, Dame Evelyn 15, 35, 99
Sheldon, Robert 55, 123, 133, 134–5, 136
Shinwell, Emanuel 26, 27, 63
Shore, Peter 126, 129, 171, 182
Silkin, John 189
Simey, Lord 123, 128
Skeffington, Arthur 95
Snowden, Philip 21, 22, 78, 79, 177
special advisers 47, 48, 52–3, 54, 57–60, 117, 139, 192
Stewart, Michael 53, 170, 175
Struass, George 175
Staw, Jack 58

Tawney, R.H. 63
Thatcher, Margaret 57, 60, 61, 135, 140, 174, 187, 189, 190
Thomas, J.H. 16, 20, 78
Trade, Department of 38
Trade and Industry, Department of 137, 205
Transport, Ministry of 23, 53, 54, 65, 137

Treasury 1, 2, 9, 22, 24, 25, 26, 27, 28–30, 35, 36–7, 38, 42–4, 53, 77, 78, 83, 87, 92, 96, 97–8, 102, 105, 106, 110, 115, 117, 120, 126, 138, 174, 182, 205
Trend, Sir Burke 34, 53
Tribune 28, 30, 94–5, 126, 143

Union of Democratic Control (UDC) 21, 45
Union of Post Office Workers 10

Vansittart, Robert 47

Wainwright, Hilary 2–3
Walsh, Stephen 16
War Office 16
Webb, Beatrice 7–8, 11, 12, 19–20, 75–7, 148, 160, 164–5, 177, 203
Webb, Sidney 7–8, 11, 12, 16, 19, 20, 75–7, 148, 160, 164–5, 177, 203
Wells, H.G. 159
Wheatley, John 21
Williams, Francis 25
Williams, Marcia 32, 33, 34, 52, 55, 56, 144–5, 187
Williams, Shirley 32, 41, 68, 116, 123, 195
Wilson, Harold 13, 17, 33–4, 43, 45, 52–3, 54, 56, 64, 68, 114, 119–20, 121, 122, 124–5, 129, 131, 132, 136–7, 139, 168, 172, 173–4, 182, 204
Wilson, Sir Horace 146–7
Women, proposed Ministry for 198, 205

Zinoviev Letter 21, 45, 79
Zuckerman, Sir Solly 53

For Product Safety Concerns and Information please contact our EU
representative GPSR@taylorandfrancis.com
Taylor & Francis Verlag GmbH, Kaufingerstraße 24, 80331 München, Germany

9 781138 325852